THE WOMAN'S BOOK OF RESILIENCE

THE WOMAN'S BOOK OF

resilience

12 QUALITIES TO CULTIVATE

BETH MILLER, Ph.D.

INTERDEPENDENCE

CONNECTION

PARTS

MEANING

NEEDS

VULNERABILITY

GIFTS AND TALENTS

SUFFERING

PERSISTENCE

HUMOR

FORGIVENESS

LIMITS AND BOUNDARIES

CONARI PRESS

First published in 2005 by Conari Press,
an imprint of Red Wheel/Weiser, LLC
York Beach, ME
With offices at:
368 Congress Street
Boston, MA 02210
www.redwheelweiser.com
Copyright © 2005 Beth Miller

Library of Congress Cataloging-in-Publication Data

Miller, Beth
  The woman's book of resilience : 12 qualities to cultivate / Beth Miller.
       p. cm.
  Includes bibliographical references and index.
  ISBN 1-57324-964-5 (alk. paper)
  1. Women--Psychology. 2. Resilience (Personality trait) 3. Self-realization
in women. 4. Self-actualization (Psychology)—Problems, exercises, etc.
5. Self-management (Psychology)—Problems, exercises, etc. I. Title.
  HQ1206.M498 2005
  155.6'33—dc22

                                                    2004018757

Typeset in Dante by Gopa & Ted2, Inc.
Printed in Canada
TCP

12 11 10 09 08 07 06 05

 8 7 6 5 4 3 2 1

contents

foreword

IN MY YEARS OF EXPERIENCE as a psychotherapist and Jungian psychoanalyst, I have listened to untold numbers of people speak of sexual and emotional abuse, devastating loss, physical trauma, and life-threatening illness. I have often wondered why, given similar circumstances, some people are laid waste by these events while others find ways to survive them and even thrive as a result. And, there are many in between who suffer but still carry on reasonably satisfactory lives. Is there something special that some people are born with and others not? Or is it that mysterious quality like a tender plant that needs to be nourished and strengthened in order to reach its inborn potential?

Psychotherapist Dr. Beth Miller defines *resilience* as the quality that enables people to bounce back when life knocks them off balance. Resilience is for the soul like a good mattress for the body; it gives support and helps to resist a tendency to slide down into depression.

We were born resilient. The very act of getting born entails working our way out of a space that has become too tight, fighting our way to freedom down a dark narrow passage, accepting help when we need it, and sometimes, when it is too tough, to allow someone to intervene with a knife because that is the only way. And then we face light and gasp for air for the first time without knowing what either light or air is. Something powerful in us wants to live, and so we come howling into the world.

It has been theorized that the way we traverse the birth canal affects our start on our lifelong path. We can't be sure of how much that influences our future course; we can only be sure that we are here, and that we are on our way. Some people strongly believe that they can succeed, that they can overcome every obstacle. Some think that life is filled with impossible tasks. Both are right. Attitude is a major factor in determining how we deal with the obstacles on the road. But what about the vast majority of people in between? What of people who think they might be able to succeed but have some doubts, and people who would like to change their ways but lack the courage?

Beth Miller has not been afraid to put her head in the lion's mouth. At midlife she left a comfortable marriage to return to graduate school, earned a doctorate in psychology, worked with groups of male sex offenders in a treatment center, taught psychology at the California Institute of Integral Studies, and established a private practice in individual and group psychotherapy in San Francisco. Over the past ten years, she developed and tested a program for developing resilience in women. This book contains a distillation of her program. It will appeal to those who believe that their lives can be more fulfilling and that they can deal better with problems and relationships than they now do. Dr. Miller describes a series of qualities that lead from embracing your vulnerabilities through analyzing your problems, getting your needs met, setting limits, giving up resentments, using humor, and practicing forgiveness to improving your ability to communicate. She provides exercises to help you practice the steps in everyday life. The book is a valuable personal guide; it can be used with a friend or partner, and it can serve as a model for support groups.

June Singer, Ph.D.

introduction

A pearl is a beautiful thing that is produced by an injured life.
It is the tear [that results] from the injury of the oyster.
The treasure of our being in this world is also produced by an injured life.
If we have not been wounded, if we have not been injured,
then we will not produce the pearl.
—S. HOELLER

MOST OF US want to see ourselves as survivors, as having that deep sense of confidence that allows us to conquer our personal demons and catastrophes. We want that exhilarating feeling of accomplishment and achievement. We want not just to survive but to thrive.

We want to think we'll be able to overcome unrequited love, have the confidence to look for another job, learn how to live with loss and disappointments creatively and constructively, whether it is not being able to have a child or being passed over for a promotion. We want to believe that we'll have courage when we fail and know how to keep trying, especially when the addiction, pain, loss, or fury appears to be getting the best of us.

We want to be resilient. We want to bounce back from misfortune and thrive from difficulties.

Sensing its importance to people's ability to cope with adversity is how I came to study the quality of resilience a little over a decade ago. At first I just loved the sound of the word. It seemed to embody a certain lightness and buoyancy. As a psychotherapist working with people stung and damaged by all sorts of life events, I had a sense that resilience might be the single most important capacity people need to develop in order to cope with their demons, with life's inevitable misfortunes, *and* with a vastly changing world.

As I delved into the subject, I immediately thought of the many children who survive horrific backgrounds relatively intact and began to wonder why they are able to do so when others are crushed by similar circumstances. I wondered the same thing about adults who managed to bounce back from profound losses, personal addictions, and serial disappointments. How is it that some of us are able to stand back up from tragedy able to love while others are permanently scarred? Why are some people resilient and others not?

The further into that question I got, the more I became entangled in a debate similar to the nature-nurture one. My research led me to believe that we are born with a temperament that determines, to a large degree, how we relate to the world and each other and how much stress and tragedy we can withstand without breaking. But if that's the case, I then went on to wonder, if resilience is inborn, what happens to those of us who do bend too far under hardships? Is that it for us, or can we actually develop bounce-ability and *become* resilient *again?* If temperament plays such an important role in our ability to be resilient, can those of us who are more tender *increase* our resilience? Can those areas in all of us that leave us quivering become stronger?

I discovered many things:

Resilience is natural. Bones heal, hearts mend, and the human spirit's destination is enlargement. Change or misfortune is part of the human journey through life. In fact, without troubles we would not have the need to be resilient. There are changes throughout our natural development, like birth, adolescence, midlife, and death. There are changes in our societal initiations, like marriage and career choices or shifts. There are cataclysmic events like earthquakes and hurricanes. We torture each other with rape, holocausts, wars, slavery, and oppression.

But our culture teaches us to pick ourselves up again, brush ourselves off, and start all over again. Our myths regale us with triumphant phoenixes rising out of the ash heaps. We swell with pride when ordinary people champion over horrendous odds.

We know that resiliency reigns because we survive to tell our tales of misfortune, trauma, abuse. Indeed, we are built to be able to go to the edge of life and come back with heart and soul elevated, with the ability to evaluate and reevaluate what is important in light of whatever adversity is going on in our lives, with the ability to deepen our understanding of ourselves and the environment we live in. We are built to be resilient, to be able to take sure and steady steps over rocky terrain.

No one is resilient all the time. Even for those of us who appear naturally resilient and take life in stride, there will be pockets of our lives that are more difficult to navigate. One aspect of our life can be flexible; for example, being a crackerjack on the job is easy but relationship breakups do us in; major crises are manageable but not so the everyday disappointments. Many bright, capable people can feel overwhelmed by a calamity or an unexpected turn in the road.

Also, what is easy for one person is hard for another. It is irrelevant and even destructive to compare ourselves to others, because pockets of resilience and pockets of vulnerability differ from person to person. Some people are so disciplined that losing control to an addiction is anathema. Others make friends so easily they cannot imagine being lonely. It is important to locate the areas in our own lives where we find ourselves down for the count and not look to others as a benchmark.

We may be designed to be resilient and flourish, yet life and *how we perceive and receive hard times* can crush this natural ability. Poverty, abuse, unrelenting difficulties, overwhelming loss all can and do take their tolls on our ability to thrive. And, yet, even with all these difficulties, what most often determines our resiliency is *how we perceive the event* and what it means to us. The literature on resilience speaks of working well, playing well, and *expecting well*. Not too much *or* too little. From growing up in a profoundly neglectful environment without enough to eat to parenting an autistic child, being resilient means not denying the reality of the situation, not wishing for it to be different, and not succumbing to a victim mentality. Instead, expecting well, seeing clearly, knowing that what is, is, and then finding what you can do about it—these are the keys to resilience. The child who finds a kindly neighbor who invites her in for dinner, the parents who give their child all the love and support they have without waiting for their child to do what a child without autism would be able to do—expecting well frees us up to creative responses.

Resilience can be crushed out. We need to be resilient to be human and we are born with that quality—but what happens when life crushes us over and over or trauma, disappointments, and loss are too horrific to bear, what about when we break in certain places? The astonishing number of depressions, the varying degrees of anxiety lived with on a daily basis, mental illness, the loss of work hours as a result of not being able to face the day, suicides and violence in the home, work, and world reveal the crushing blow that life can deliver. Sometimes we have to relearn to be resilient. We feel wrung out or walked on. How do we rekindle the ability to bounce back and not merely survive, but thrive?

We can learn to be resilient. The work that I have been doing for the past ten years is based on the reality that resilience can be cultivated, relearned, developed. While I began my study with the question, "Who is naturally resilient and who is not, and why?" I soon moved away from those artificial poles, and through years of research and interviews developed an understanding of the way the most resilient people think, process, and behave. It is out of that work that I designed the Art of Resilience Process.

For the past ten years, as I have worked with people in my individual practice, in groups on resilience, in classrooms, conferences, and seminars, I have continued to marvel at the elasticity of the human spirit and how, given the proper ingredients, people show up in more and more resilient fashion. I have borne witness as people who heretofore saw themselves as weak and victimized discover their innate strengths and talents enough to bring a new bounce to their step. I have helped hundreds of people find meaning within the black holes and noticed that, as a result, they have developed (or found within themselves) more creative responses to their difficult times. I have walked along the hopeful journey of cultivating resilience and developing the mental and emotional acumen of producing pearls from injured lives.

● the art of resilience process

As I see it, resilience has twelve qualities that interrelate like spokes on a wheel. The Art of Resilience Process is designed to teach you how to strengthen each spoke of this wheel and thereby increase your resilience quotient. The process is designed as a *preventative tool*. Each quality can and will definitely help when you find yourself in the middle of or in the aftermath of a crisis or difficulty, but a more fundamental use of cultivating resilience is using this process to strengthen your muscles of flexibility during calmer times.

The center of the resilience wheel, I have found, is making friends with your vulnerability. As counterintuitive as this might sound, think about the difference between an oak tree and a reed during a violent windstorm. As Aesop illustrated in his fable, "The Oak and the Reed," the reed responds to the oak, "I secure myself by a conduct that is the reverse of yours: instead of being stiff and stubborn, and being proud of my strength, I yield and bend to the winds. I let the storm pass over me, knowing how fruitless it would be to resist."

The moral of this fable: A person of a quiet, still temper—whether it be given him by nature or acquired by art—calmly composes himself in the midst of a storm, so as to elude the shock, or receive it with the least detriment. He is like a prudent, experienced sailor who, in swimming to the shore from a wrecked vessel in a swelling sea, does not oppose the fury of the waves, but stoops and gives way that they may roll over his head.

The doctrine of absolute submission in all cases is an absurd dogmatical precept . . . but, upon particular occasions, and where it is impossible for us to overcome, to submit patiently is one of the most reasonable maxims of life.

The process works in a spiral, beginning and ending with embracing our vulnerability. We begin by recognizing our more tender spots and move to strengthening the qualities listed on the wheel. So, in order to flex the vulnerability muscle, to learn that our strength truly does lie in our flexibility, we must build connections and interdependence, own our talents and gifts, take

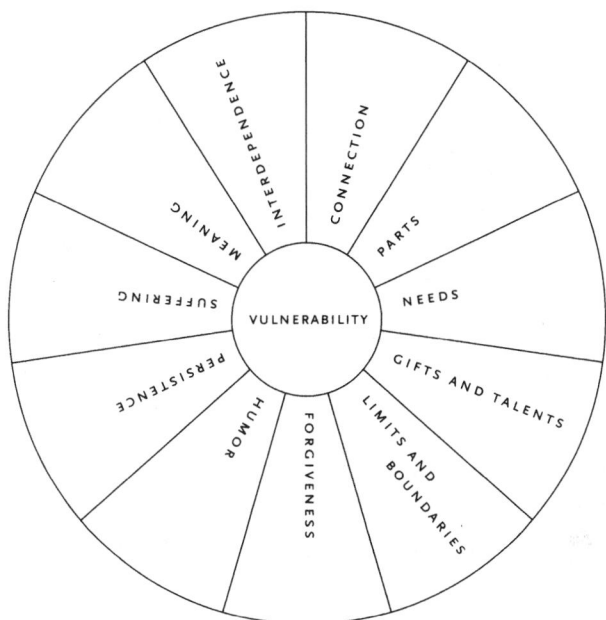

THE WHEEL OF RESILIENCE

good care of ourselves, strengthen the core of our being, learn what we can manage for life's overwhelming times, and increase our repertoire of responses to hard and challenging times. In order to enlarge our sense of self, we must learn to sit with suffering, staying long enough to discover the pearls in minor and major irritations, and not running away prematurely. We must learn to how to laugh at life, even during the dark times, and also know how to say, *"Enough already!"* These are the twelve spokes of the wheel, each one designed to brace and support our deepest self. By bracing and supporting our deepest self, we can be more and more comfortable with our vulnerability—and back to further strengthening the other qualities. That's what cultivating resilience is all about. The chapters that follow are designed to help you develop each of these qualities of resilience. They can be read straight through or used as reference when you feel the need to cultivate a particular strength or be reminded of how to take a particular approach. The qualities do not need to be worked in any particular order. You will find exercises at the end of each chapter to help guide you in this journey. These, too, can be revisited over and over with the intent of going deeper and deeper into the psyche. If only one of the exercises feels right for you, do only one. If they all work, go for it. *I encourage you to make them work for you—rather than make yourself work for them.*

In each chapter I use mythology, interviews, and/or personal stories to bring life and dimension to the approaches of this resiliency process. Throughout these pages you will meet many courageous and impressive women. Though their paths are varied, their stories unique, their talents and abilities particular, their resilient attitudes can be beacons of light for you as you find the courage and strength to master your own demons or overcome life's hardships. I tell their stories to show you that you *can* deal with sorrow and tragedy, you *can* find your power and your voice, you *can* squarely face life's hard times, inequities, and diabolical schemes—and even thrive.

(Out of respect for confidentiality, I use composites and pseudonyms to detail the lives and behaviors of these quiet heroines.)

Becoming resilient is not an easy process, and it has no definitive ending. It takes hard work, perseverance, willingness, and desire. You have to be willing to take yourself on. *But it can be done.* May you find through the teachings in this book that you do possess the strength of a reed, the composure to ride out even the mightiest of storms, the willingness and ability to give way so that the waves may roll over your head.

undressing: i am open 1

The world's mine oyster,
Which I with sword will open.
—WILLIAM SHAKESPEARE

LIFE IS UNFAIR. Some of us will never be rich; some of us will never be beautiful; some of us will never have parents who love us. Some of us carry more burdens than others. Some of us were abused and some of us were tortured. Tragedy is everywhere, and death is certain. We all have to learn to live with these realities.

That is why we need resilience. The ability to be resilient is what helps us bounce back from the edge, helps us find our strength in adverse circumstances, helps us thrive in this life—and it most often begins with opening the inner doorway to our own vulnerability. No matter how tiny a crack we may feel ready to open. Because becoming resilient requires a willingness to fall apart for a time—and getting to know ourselves at our rawest—so that we may open ourselves up to those deepest of inner resources that can enable us to bend and flex with whatever life brings our way.

●we are all vulnerable

All of us, out of necessity, have built up defenses to protect ourselves from others, to avoid being or feeling hurt, feeling out of control or helpless. We shy away from people who appear needy and often blame others to avoid the truth of our own vulnerabilities. We cling to the familiar, the known, even if it's not in our best interests to do so: a relationship that is not constructive, a job that bores us to death, an outmoded identity or pattern or behavior. We fear change, so we look for ways to keep the status quo. But in order to put our lives back together, we need to acknowledge that we are tender, that we don't know everything, that we cannot control everything, that we need each other. In other words, we need to be vulnerable.

We may fear our vulnerability, but the truth is we are *all* vulnerable. We are physically vulnerable for many months and for the first many years could not survive on our own. We are wholly dependent on human kindness and suffer greatly when others fail us.

We are mentally vulnerable in that we have the consciousness to know that we and those we love will die. We not only experience abandonment, we know ahead of time that we are susceptible to being left alone. As a psychologist, I see this existential anxiety in almost every person who walks into my office. We know we are alone; we are on a journey only we can navigate, even when we have help from others.

We are vulnerable to our environment through our dependency and conditioning. We learn early on how our parents, families, and neighbors think and feel. We learn from them the "right" way of behaving, what is considered good, what is bad, what we want to be, who we don't want to be.

We are emotionally vulnerable to loving, hating, and indifference; to a wide range of feelings: sadness, anger, joy, devastation, ecstasy. We can't be open to joy without also being open to pain.

We are vulnerable to each other. The neighbor's loud music or barking dog that keeps us awake. We know the dangers of toxic wastes, nature's furies, and the economic ups and downs around the world. We are aware of the precipice we live within and on.

As women we know additional vulnerabilities—and we know that our vulnerability is seen as a weakness. We are vulnerable because our history of second-class citizenship and our lack of access to education or the circumstances to be self-sufficient and equal made us even more dependent on others than men are.

We have also had our vulnerability reinforced by the dominant culture, which sees us as unfocused, fickle, and too emotional to get the job done well. We know that we are often (yes, still!) perceived as weak, inferior, and dependent, and in many cases we have internalized this view of ourselves. It's no wonder we view our vulnerability as a detriment; it's no wonder we feel we must never show it.

◉ it's our strength

I'd like to suggest that our history of being second-class, our struggles and our innate access to emotions and feelings position us to see our vulnerability as strength and to model that for the world. Instead of defending against the sore spots and tender mercies, we can model how to use them to produce rich and appropriate responses to whatever situation we may find ourselves in, to be far more flexible and versatile in all things.

I am convinced that an underlying reason behind judgments, blaming, threats, alienation, and even violence is the desire to hide our vulnerability—our failures, intimidations, weakness, helplessness. I am convinced that a means of increased psychological and spiritual growth begins with recognizing the insecurities that cause us to lash out in a reaction. As women we can model how being relatively unguarded allows us to *respond* rather than react, to be open and receptive students of life.

I am not advocating indiscriminate openness or a permanent wearing of your heart on your sleeve. There is a time and place for guardedness and lack of trust; there are times for skepticism and for protecting yourself from some people and circumstances. But it is powerful to know and be comfortable with your own vulnerability and exercise the choice of when to be open or not.

Knowing and admitting that we are insecure, afraid, out of our league, or lost in the woods puts us more in charge of our emotions and our situations. We are much less likely to be blind-sided by our "weaker" emotions. And since much of being resilient is about prevention—taking precautions before being run over by a truck or preparing the home before the earth quakes—it is smart and prudent to become more and more familiar with our vulnerability.

I had been working with my client Carolyn for two years when she began to plan her wedding day, which was fast approaching. As so many women do, she wanted this day to be picture perfect. The man she was marrying was funny and playful, a wonderful complement to her serious approach to life. The setting they chose, a bucolic, open grassy expanse overlooking acres and acres of grapes in the wine country, reflected her sophisticated and cultivated taste. She helped the caterer design an elegant vegetarian meal and chose wild and varied flowers, further adding her personal signature.

When she had first come to see me, Carolyn was just twenty-four years old. Her mother had recently been diagnosed with cancer, and Carolyn was struggling to balance her caretaking role with a busy career as a trial attorney. She felt tremendous pressure to perform well on every front.

A strong, direct, and very capable young lady, Carolyn had always been cast in the adult role in her household, which left her with the double-edged sword of being extremely competent and having many unmet needs. Her mother had been a harsh critic—pushing her to try harder when she felt tired, criticizing her when an A was not an A+, expecting her to hold herself together when the family went through difficult times—and Carolyn had internalized this well. She was more apt to beat herself up for what she did *not* do for her mother or for when she was *not* there for her than to cut herself slack because she did so much. She did not truck with weakness or softness. Not surprisingly, then, during her mother's illness Carolyn's stamina was impressive. But her soul was burning out.

She would come into my office absolutely exhausted and having no idea how to relax or let go of some of the responsibilities without feeling guilty or worrying that she was not doing enough to keep her mother alive longer.

One summer evening, she came into my office looking put together, as usual, plunked herself down in the oversized chair, and said, "It's over. Mom died last night."

Neither of us was expecting it this soon; her mother had rallied so many times before, inspiring hope and optimism in all who cared for her. With my own sadness and surprise showing, I leaned toward her and took her hands in mine as she cried in relief, shock, sorrow, and pain. She could easily cry because she had lost her mother and missed her terribly, but she could not possibly have admitted needing something herself or allowed herself to be taken care of.

As her wedding day approached, Carolyn missed her mother more and more. She would talk about how much her mother would have loved this time, about how she wished she could ask her mother to help her choose a dress and to help her decide which earrings were the perfect match. When she had fights with her fiancé or felt prewedding jitters about her choice of a mate, she longed to have her mother there for a heart-to-heart.

The week before the wedding, Carolyn came to see me, inconsolable. She spoke through tears. "I just know if my mother were alive she would do something very special for me the day of the wedding. It would be something I had not thought of, something that would tell me she was thinking of me on this big day."

We both knew that there was no one who would or could fill this role for her. Her mother had many friends who loved Carolyn, but she had no desire to turn to them. Only her mother would do, and her mother was not here.

Near the end of the session I said to Carolyn, "I don't mean to be presumptuous, but I am wondering if there is anything I can do?"

Without missing a beat, Carolyn cried harder and asked, "Would you come and see me right before I walk down the aisle?"

I was deeply touched, and my eyes filled as we cried together. It takes profound strength to admit that you need someone when you have been taught that you do not have needs or that the needs you have are wrong or irrelevant in the face of others' needs. By letting down her guard, she could begin to trust that I would be there to "see" her at that archetypal moment before she wed.

I once read about a nun who worked in a rough area of New York. Each evening, before leaving the church for the day, she checked herself for her level of vulnerability. On the days she felt particularly soft, she took a taxi home. Even on the days she was in a stronger frame of mind, she took precautions as she walked the dangerous streets to her bus stop. She did not turn a fool's eye to her circumstances or condition.

On the other hand, I have watched people pull out their stiff upper lip and muscle strength *without* admitting their vulnerability. This gritting the teeth does not bring resiliency; instead the stiff and muscled "heroine" is brittle and vulnerable to the next thing or person who is stronger and louder.

If we do not allow the vulnerability, the softness, or the tenderness, we are more apt to end up with sharp edges and holes in our heart. For example, a woman I worked with insisted that the barbs and slights from her husband didn't bother her. She could easily grin and bear it, especially understanding his warped "sense of humor." Her avoidance of the pain his remarks instilled in her left her open to being treated the same way by her children.

During my own childhood I perfected the defense of denial. It took me years and years of concentrated effort and analysis to free the pain and thaw the icicles that kept me frozen within myself and unable to love or be loved. It took devotion to rediscover my vulnerability, and it takes faith and trust to remain in touch with it on an everyday basis.

A woman I worked with had, in childhood, developed a habit of using garbled talk so her father would not hit her for back-talking. This was a creative response to a threatening environment, possibly the only way she could find to maintain herself in the face of worrying she would lose her father's love and incite his anger. As an adult, however, this garbled talk kept her from being understood and seen, kept her at a distance from others when she desired to be close. What ultimately helped this woman was not just changing the behavior, but understanding it as a creative response to an outdated situation. She now has a better chance of becoming free to relate intimately *because* she allowed herself to be vulnerable to the old feeling of needing her father's love, of wanting to be seen and not hurt. She allowed herself to fall apart a little in order to emerge stronger.

● taking the inner journey

Like so many of you I grew up with the myth of the hero and was told that conquering ourselves and the world was our most important challenge. That holds for some times in life, but once you experience loss, sorrow, or significant change, you recognize that there is another journey to make: a descent into the soul to understand the flow of feeling, emotion, and lost parts of ourselves. A journey to discover the threads that bind us to each other and to all aspects of the living world.

Myths of descent usually begin with an unexpected twist of fate or a deliberate dive into the underworld—the unknown path that lies ahead when we experience loss, tragedy, or serious disappointment—and the road not taken that calls to us when we enter a new passage. These myths give us a framework for overcoming adversity and enlightening the process of redemption, showing the heroes and heroines figuring out their own way and righting their course as a result of a great fall.

One such legend comes to us from ancient Sumeria: the tale of Inanna. In his book *From the Poetry of Sumer,* Samuel Noah Kramer tells of the power and influence Inanna's journey held for the people of that time: "The goddess who outweighed, overshadowed, and outlasted them all was a deity known to the Sumerians by the name of Inanna, 'Queen of Heaven.'" Inanna is the tale of a woman's journey from her early days of being courted, admired, and enriched to her descent to the underworld in her middle years. It is about sacrifices she must make to achieve wisdom and affirm her purpose of life.

Inanna was much loved and revered, yet she voluntarily abandoned her office of holy princess of heaven and earth to descend into the underworld. This was a descent of uncertainty and danger, a descent to journey within the depths of the psyche. Before her departure she spoke to her faithful friend, Ninshubur, leaving elaborate instructions. If Inanna did not return, her friend must go to the gods and ask them all to save her, not leaving to chance that she might not be able to recover.

Inanna departs to the underworld to see her older sister, Ereshkigal, raw, bitter, and entangled, the Queen of the Underworld. But this place of grief and sorrow is not one we enter lightly. Inanna passes through seven gates, and at each one she is required to surrender a talisman or article of clothing, leaving her bowed and naked upon her entrance to the throne room. Her journey is stark and perhaps surprising, given that she has volunteered to go deep within herself. She is willing to unburden herself from all she has held dear, and yet when at each surrender she asks for the meaning of this stripping she is told that the ways of the underworld are perfect and may not be questioned.

> *Then Ereshkigal fastened on Inanna the eye of death.*
> *She spoke against her the word of wrath.*
> *She uttered against her the cry of guilt.*
>
> *She struck her.*

Inanna was turned into a corpse,
A piece of rotting meat,
And was hung from a hook on the wall.

This is what a transformation—or the conscious reflection on a lifetime loss or change—can feel like. We descend to the underworld, leave behind all earthly attachments and accomplishments, and don't know what will happen next. It is a time of facing ourselves, looking squarely at the demons and feeling like we are a piece of flesh hanging from a hook on the wall, being seasoned and matured! This is a chilling image of vulnerability, a raw look at surrender. Why would Inanna leave her secure world and walk into the void voluntarily?

Because we cannot live a conscious life without facing the terrors of uncertainty and the unknown. Always staying within the safe zone simply doesn't work. No, our task is to open ourselves to the darkness—the realm of emotion, feeling, the unknown—and experience the anguish of sorrow, uncertainty, confusion, and powerlessness. We must be willing, mentally and emotionally, to be confused, to be wrong, to take a risk, fall down, skin our knees, be wrong again, be confused again, feel the pain and sorrow. Because until we are ready to let go—of what is no longer working, of people who stand in our way, of our familiar defenses—we will never grow.

In a society that believes we must be strong and positive, where we shun our negative and vulnerable feelings, carrying our burden of self-doubt with dignity is a socially significant statement. In our world, where we find it hard to experience pain or to realize that we feel small in certain ways, we can set a rare example by continuing to walk erect and by carrying our woundedness with consciousness and dignity.

Collectively it is time to validate, honor, respect, and make room for falling apart, admitting vulnerability. It is time to bring reasonable and appropriate falling apart into fashion. It is a long process, and we can find and learn our own rhythms, our own ebbs and flows as we have patience and compassion with ourselves. To be a student of life is to be vulnerable—open to life, to learning, to experiences, to you, to emotions—and willing to accept things as they are.

Everyday life is full of struggles, and we have daily opportunities for descent: experiencing arguments and conflicts, admitting discomforts, anger, and fear. Sometimes we are faced with major problems and challenges, and many times we are just faced with bad traffic, holes in our pantyhose, and not being able to get adequate attention at the bank, store, gas station, fill-in-the-blank. In fact, as we often hear, it can be easier to deal with the really big stuff; it is the everyday annoyances and irritants that begin to wear and can cause an emotional meltdown.

We often thirst for intimacy and spend much of our time running at top speed. We go on a job interview; we need to learn a new job, task, or challenge. We lose money on bad investments. We meet and lose friends and partners. We desire to start our own company and risk failure. We have more than enough chance to feel vulnerable and out of sorts on an everyday basis. Here, too, it is important to recognize and admit our vulnerability so that we might deal with it in a straightforward manner.

Being successful at facing our vulnerabilities—our failures, our missteps, our lack of control over events and other people—is an art form. It is an art form to apologize, to let go of what is not working, and to face change with an open heart and mind. It takes courage and dedication to face ourselves and seek out deeper truths about ourselves.

What do you imagine when you hear the word *vulnerability?* The soft spot on a newborn's head, the fuzz on a peach, the sensitive and tender skin of the genitals, the underbelly of a newborn kitten or puppy? The scariness of being unguarded? The unpleasant feeling of weakness? How often have you had a dream of being naked in a public place? Of being ashamed of the most delicate parts of your personality?

When you hear yourself bitterly referring to the unfair difference between your lot in life and your friends' or that of other members of society, try to hear the deeper truth of jealousy or sadness or disillusionment. When you find yourself stamping your feet in frustration because you are not getting the kind of help you want from a loved one, sit a moment and recognize your desire to be rescued or taken care of. Without judgment, try to experience the softer, tenderer underbelly of your psyche.

The frontier is visible. The stories abound. The stage is set for acknowledging, welcoming, and inviting our vulnerability to the dinner table.

exercise

REFLECTION

As you consider the following questions, there are a few effective tools you can use to help you connect with your answers. You can write in a journal to free associate and explore your thoughts, feelings, and experiences; create pieces of artwork to investigate the ideas through images, colors, and correlations; and/or simply use your imagination to access associations, pictures, feelings, dreams, hopes, and fears.

Remember the last time you were criticized (by someone well intended):

- ▶ How did you react? (What were your defenses?)
- ▶ What were the underlying vulnerabilities? (You felt hurt, insulted, humiliated . . . ?)
- ▶ How can you befriend this part of yourself?

Remember the last time you did not get what you wanted:

- ▶ How did you react?
- ▶ What were the underlying vulnerabilities?
- ▶ How can you befriend this part of yourself?

Remember the last time you, metaphorically, were naked out in public:

- ▶ How did you react?
- ▶ What were the underlying vulnerabilities?
- ▶ How can you befriend this part of yourself?

who do you call at 3 a.m.? 2

I WILL PRACTICE AND INCREASE MY ABILITY TO CONNECT

A friend is one to whom one may pour out all
the contents of one's heart, knowing that the gentlest
of hands will take and sift it, keep what is worth keeping
and with the breath of kindness blow the rest away.
—ARABIAN PROVERB

CYNTHIA AND SUSAN were best friends, but recently Cynthia had begun noticing how often Susan spoke harshly and sometimes cruelly to her husband. This made Cynthia uncomfortable. She decided to bring it up with Susan. She approached the subject gently, suggesting that Susan's behavior was probably unconscious. After all, she knew Susan to be a sensitive and caring person.

Being confronted like this gave Susan the opportunity to soul search and look for a deeper feeling that might have been causing her to act out in this way. Was there something in her marriage that was troubling her? Was she carrying over something from some other relationship and taking it out on a safer person? Was this a residue from childhood? Whatever the source and reason, Cynthia's willingness to speak the truth about something unpleasant gave Susan the opportunity to deepen herself and her marriage.

We all need people in our lives with whom we can tell our truths and wrestle with our demons—and to be available to them for the same.

You are inconsolable over losing someone you love, and the darkness of the hour is hounding you. You need a confidante, a best friend who has been around as long as well-worn bedroom slippers. You need the partner, lover, spouse sleeping next to you to wake up.

You have been fired unexpectedly, and you're ganging up on yourself, your self-worth plummeting southward. You need someone to talk to and express your feelings and experience as well as receive support, understanding, and help. Someone to walk along with you during the crisis or struggle so the trauma is not compounded by unnecessary loneliness. Someone who can help you sort out the real from the self-destructive.

Who do you go to for truth telling? Who can you count on to tell you the way it is, even risk upsetting you? Who do you trust enough to tell you the hidden truth that you would benefit from knowing and doing something about? Who do you call at 3 A.M.?

You just received a raise and new title. You are going to have a new baby or grandbaby. You just made a financial killing or your company went public. You are in love (and with the right person).

Who do you call in the afternoon when you are feeling so much excitement and joy you are sure you are going to burst? Who do you call to share your pleasure and accomplishments?

Who are your friends? Who is your support? Do you have a very best friend, an important confidante? Do you have a circle of friends, a web of acquaintances?

Strengthening these connections and opening ourselves to honest communication—these are the subjects of this chapter.

Some women—Oprah Winfrey and Anna Quindlen are a notable two—have best friends they speak with at least once a day. They keep an exchange going—keep the channels wide open for check in, banter, intimacy, and comfort. Some days it might be a quick hello, "I'm here, how are you?" Other days there might be time and need for a long chat or an intimate soul talk. But these women value each other deeply, know each other fundamentally, and can be there for each other in a split second's request—and at a level that can leave each shaking with the recognition of sacred meeting. They can say *anything* to each other and ultimately feel better for it. They can listen deeply and communicate love without saying a word.

We cannot become resilient in isolation. Not even introverts, recluses, and the deeply pained and shamed. We are social creatures, and we need to know where to go to connect and refuel. We need to have a community of at least a few people, animals, or nature who will always be there for us, no matter what.

Children who have recovered from severe trauma will often tell poignant and heartwarming stories of finding a receptive teacher, neighbor, or adult friend who, with a look, glance, respectful touch, or open arms, kept them alive, kept their spirits alive. One young woman, severely wounded from years and years of unrelenting torture at the hands of her parents, told me the story of making contact with a kind elderly neighbor who looked into the child's eyes and told her it would not always be that bad. The young woman said that this single gesture not only offered hope but assured her that she was not crazy or overreacting.

"Someone else was aware that there was something seriously wrong." The young woman felt validated and strengthened. She credits this warmth of human contact with keeping her this side of insanity.

Other at-risk children, showing an instinct for connection, find creative ways to find support from kind adults. Shy, introverted children look to characters in books, images in mythology, or the quiet den of an introverted adult. The more outgoing spread their wings to meet generous souls in their extended world. However they manage it, these naturally resilient young people make sure to find a connection—a positive connection—because they know that they *need* other people who can mirror something positive back to them.

If we are lucky, there are several people who fill this role in our lives, and we choose to whom to go for support based on the kinds of issues we're dealing with. One client told me:

> If I need a really good cry, I'll go to a friend who understands and is comfortable with emotions. She won't try to fix me and she is not afraid of strong feelings. If it's about relationships or finances or some catastrophe, I'll choose my friend who is best at those issues. Someone who has been there and knows the terrain and/or who knows me well enough to tell me the truth. Overall, though, I go to someone who will be honest with me.

Not only does this give us the best chance of receiving the kind of support we need, but it also preserves the quality of our relationships. No one person can be there for us all the time. That's too heavy a burden to place on any relationship. Too much energy coursing through a circuit will finally blow. Instead, the idea here is to spread the wealth, to have a circle of partners, friends, family members, mentors, people who've known you the longest and aren't afraid of your "shadow" material, colleagues for work-related issues, perhaps a therapist or spiritual advisor.

● choosing who to turn to—and who not to

San Francisco Chronicle columnist Joan Ryan wrote a wonderful column about who to call when we're in need, in which she talked about a woman named Janie who reached out to a needed friend during an excruciating and dark time:

the night she fully understood her son would not recover from his severe illness. She was crying into the phone . . . when [her] friend asked if she could call her back. Janie, taken aback, said fine, and waited and waited for the phone to ring. Suddenly, headlights appeared in her driveway, and her friend emerged from the car in her nightgown. "I'll remember that for as long as I live," Janie says now.

Friends have an inside track and often know just what we need: a young woman with whom I worked, going through an agonizing breakup with the man she had intended to marry, knew she had to talk and cry with her best friend. But she was bowled over with appreciation when this best friend, living on the opposite coast, flew out for the weekend, and regaled her with stories of hilarious revenge. "Let's collect mosquitoes and let them loose in his house!" "Let's order twenty-five pizzas to be delivered COD to his house." They spent the weekend together going for long walks, crying and laughing together. When her friend left, the young woman knew she was loved and carried that with her as she felt the awful pangs of grieving.

On the other side of the coin are the grievous disappointments, the times we expect someone to come through for us and they don't. I remember working with a young woman whose husband had struck her across the face and, desperately needing comfort, she had called her mother, who lived 4,000 miles away. She was devastated when her mother said, "Oh, Tina, what did you do to get him so mad?"

Tina had been savagely beaten by both parents as a child and had lain shivering as she watched her father beat her mother dozens of times. She herself had gone through years of abusive relationships before marrying her husband, a passionate man who was devoted to Tina and their children. The marriage had lasted many years, but it was always tumultuous, fighting and making up, arguing and settling things. That particular night, however, her husband had lost control and hit her across the cheek. Tina was beside herself and without much thought reached out for her mother.

In a more calm and rational time, Tina would have known not to call her mother, but in an unguarded moment, and quite desperate for support, she forgot what she knew. Now feeling doubly humiliated, she showed tremendous courage by picking up the phone again and calling the friend who could and did help.

As you think about who you would want in your support circle, it's important to consider people's various strengths and limitations. Often we can intuit who will really be there for us and under what circumstances, but sometimes we find out the hard way. I think of Lydia. She is someone who sees the world through her emotions, and each time she turns to her friend Kathy for support she feels worse than before. Kathy sees the world through her intellect and believes Lydia is too sensitive to her emotions, a belief that is often revealed in the way she responds to Lydia's many crises. Understand, there is nothing wrong with either style, but if Lydia needs a "warm fit," Kathy is probably not her best choice!

We need to find people who can really understand where we're coming from. If we've experienced something extremely painful, say we've lost a child or a parent or we've been battered, it can be lonely and disorienting to talk with someone whose only real experience with pain is rude drivers or loud-mouthed bosses. Helpful and healthy communication requires a "good fit."

● connections and vulnerability

There is something about allowing ourselves to open up and be vulnerable to people when we're in need that often results in a deepening of the relationship. And these deeper, more intimate relationships, in turn, satisfy something within us that enables us to deal with the unbearable and discover larger and larger perspectives on our own lives.

I'm reminded of a piece I read, again in the *San Francisco Chronicle,* by Susan Parker, who writes a column about life since her husband, Ralph, was paralyzed in a bike accident. This particular column was about a trip she and Ralph had taken to see some old biking buddies who had moved to another state. It had been four years since they'd seen each other, but these were the people they had called right after the accident, the kind of people you want to have around when the chips are down.

Aimee and Patrick welcomed Susan and Ralph with open arms and hammers in hand. Patrick insisted on nailing the handicap ramp into their carpet. When Susan protested, Patrick responded, "We're going to replace this carpeting someday anyway." The four proceeded to talk about what they would all do on this much-treasured visit. Among the many possibilities, Aimee mentioned giving Ralph a bath. "It will be fun," she insisted. Aimee was a nurse and knew the difficulties Ralph faced in the hygiene department. Susan and Ralph did not have a large enough bathroom or the right equipment, and Ralph had not had a proper bath in a very long time.

Aimee knew the possible repercussions: skin breakdown and sores that can lead to serious health problems, so she arranged to use a wheelchair-accessible bathroom at a local hospital. After putting Ralph into a specialized, waterproof wheelchair, Aimee and Susan soaped him, scrubbed him, rinsed him, dried him, dressed him, and brushed his teeth. "Ralph treated the excursion as if he had won the lottery," Parker wrote. "'This is great,' he shouted as we rolled him out of the hospital. 'Wow, do I feel good.'"

Without much ado these wonderful friends had given of themselves practically, as well as nonchalantly, offering tons of love and attention, giving Ralph a special treat that would have been very difficult to do elsewhere or otherwise. Giving (and receiving) under circumstances so tender and prone to embarrassment or misunderstandings requires everyone to stand tall in the face of vulnerability and allow the interchange of intimacy and connection. It requires us to become sensitive and aware of our tender spots—it requires us to accept our humble humanity and allow our trusted circle to know us well.

It is in our closest friendships that we can fully realize who we are. Anna Quindlen, novelist, relays it thusly: "I only really understand myself, what I'm really thinking and feeling, when I've talked it over with my circle of female friends. When days go by without that connection, I feel like a radio playing in an empty room."

As our friendships deepen, we often reveal parts of ourselves that have been tucked away or hidden, even from ourselves . . . and when somebody reaches out to us, we often discover that we are truly seen. In Chinese Zen, the concept of intimacy is synonymous with enlightenment or realization. Through vulnerability and intimacy, we come to know ourselves and the world. I know this from my own experience:

One day I was at a party with some women friends. I was in a playful mood and began teasing two of them about knowing something they did not know. From my peripheral vision I could see Sandy reaching across to me. Her hand was up, face level. Without any thought and in the flash of a second I reacted. Sensing danger, I pulled back, ducked, and cringed; and because I had no time to hide my vulnerability, I was suddenly exposed. Over the years I had become masterful in covering up my childhood terrors, and I am not surprised when close friends tell me they cannot see the effects of my early life. But when I saw Sandy's hand come toward me, my instinct was to recoil and protect myself.

As it turns out, of course, Sandy was only reaching out to pat my face affectionately; she was totally dismayed by my reaction. And what a shock it was for me to see my terror reflected on the other women's faces. The look of their faces remained burnt into my awareness for a long time. Suddenly my friends got a glimpse of the intimidated, frightened part of me that I had always kept so hidden.

The unexpected benefit was that I now had witnesses for my experience. People I cared for saw what had happened to me. I was no longer alone in that realm—and I was safe. Mixed in with the embarrassment was a tremendous sense of relief. By showing my vulnerability, I was unwittingly exercising my resilience muscle.

● the power of support groups

We are social animals. We need each other for our very survival. Nowhere is this more evident than in concentration camps, in military compounds, in dens of slavery, in repressed regimes, where prisoners will use every ounce of their human ingenuity to get messages to each other to ease their loneliness and despair and share their suffering. Communication, their only possible form of connection, gave them the strength to survive. Stories have been told and studies generated that show our pure genius for making contact, even in the most extreme of situations. The creating of Morse codes, the banging of objects on the ground, the singing of spirituals, the call of whistles—whatever it takes to remind us that we are not alone.

Often what we need most in upsetting or threatening situations is a way to compare our emotional experiences with others. We need to hear that other people share our feelings, that our emotional reactions to terrible times and our feelings of having reached our limit are normal, not a sign that we are pathologically weak.

Of course we don't have to be political prisoners to understand this need for validation and support. A woman I work with lived with debilitating anxiety because she felt ambivalent about having children. Living in a culture that places such a high value on motherhood and maternal sacrifices, she felt sure she was a freak for not being sure if she wanted children. We were both delighted when she found a workshop for women who wanted to discuss this issue in safety and confidentiality. After attending the workshop, Roberta returned to my office visibly lighter, relaxed and smiling. The weekend was a success; she met several other women she respected and learned from, and she felt fully engaged in all the exercises. She loved the free time to talk between sessions and over lunch. She had time to think and reflect, time to tell others how she felt, and time to hear other stories. She left feeling a great relief, not because she had made up her mind about having children but because she felt peaceful about being ambivalent. She was not alone in her distress, and she could now trust herself and the process of working it out over time.

Finding group support doesn't necessarily come through organized workshops. In the middle of winter I was invited to celebrate my friend Cindy

Walker's sixtieth birthday. The invitation announced that the "queens" would be arriving: dress would be evening wear (tiaras acceptable), and we were to come prepared to spend the whole evening; there would be no early leave-taking.

And so, seventy-five women from all over the United States descended on a sparkling, snow-covered Salt Lake City, Utah, ready to celebrate our friend Cindy. Here we were: friends of hers from kindergarten, her bridesmaids from umpteen years ago, a friend she had met as an exchange student in Poland, her daughters and daughters-in-law, her women doctors, her neighbors, friends from her book clubs and church groups, every woman friend with whom she has stayed in contact through countless moves around the states.

Cindy is a no-nonsense woman; one could even say she's a force to be reckoned with. She is passionate and outspoken and accomplished and considers it frivolous to be concerned with appearance. So imagine our surprise when we discovered that she had hired a woman to come to her home the day before her party to offer manicures and pedicures to her family and friends. She not only was the first to have her nails done, but she had her makeup done as well! She was turning sixty, and she decided was going to do something for herself she had never done before.

Cindy had planned a sumptuous feast and a singing revival of her favorite songs. After she presented a carnation and story about each woman in the room, she had me say a few words about resilience. For obvious reasons, I chose to emphasize friends and support and helping each other through rough times. I talked about this group and how we were an embodiment of a spontaneous support group, how every one of us was connected to this amazing woman, every one of us called her a friend and meant it from the heart.

I then asked the women in the room to share their thoughts about why Cindy was their friend. (This was not on Cindy's agenda; she told me later how stunned she was—and how much she surprised herself by *not* putting a stop to it!)

One of the first people to get up was Cindy's daughter Kathy, who told a story about standing in the receiving line at her wedding, when her new husband leaned over and whispered, "Everyone your mother introduces me to says they are her very best friend!" Kathy then looked around the room and said the same thing to us that she had said to her new husband that day. "They are!"

Jeannine, Cindy's daughter-in-law, stood and said, "Cindy, I will never forget one of our first heart-to-heart talks when I joined your family. You told me that if Aaron and I had an argument and he came to you with his complaints you would not automatically take his side. You would give me the respect to include my point of view as well. That has meant the world to me because I knew then that I could trust you."

The stories went on, leaving us all crying, laughing, ooohing and aaahing. Eight hours later, the police called looking for an elderly woman who was attending the party. "She is never out this late," her husband had told the police when he called, worried that something had happened to her. We all went home with tremendous smiles on our faces and warmth in our hearts.

Cindy still talks about how the evening was the single most important healing experience of her life:

> Ever since that night I feel okay in a way I have not felt before. I don't have to measure up; I am okay as I am. I sincerely believe I could not have accepted the teacher of the year award with such dignity and confidence if I did not have the reminder of my dear friends' love and respect.
>
> I have always been quick to turn the attention and care to others; if I had not been forced to do otherwise that night I would not have heard and felt how much people cared for me. Seventy-five people cannot be wrong. I know how deeply I feel for everyone who was in my home that night; hearing and believing how much they care for me was profoundly and lastingly healing.

The power of that connection for Cindy allowed her to stand tall and resilient when she next had to face, for her, the awkward and difficult situation of accepting the teacher of the year award. Rather than convincing herself she did not deserve such recognition, she could rely on the genuine response she had received from her "closest" friends.

● our health depends on it

It turns out that having the support of a group doesn't just *feel* good; it is, empirically, good for us, especially during stressful times. As we learn more and more about the connection between mind and body, we are also becoming aware of the link between illness and social isolation. When people in stressful situations do not have someone in whom to confide, their immune response apparently weakens. In James Pennebaker's study of 2,000 people who had suffered trauma, including physical abuse, rape, or the death of a loved one, those who managed to confide in someone about the event were found to be healthier. Those who hadn't discussed their experiences developed more illness of various sorts—from headaches to lung disease.

We have discovered that when stress is high, people without psychological support suffer as much as ten times the incidence of physical and emotional illness as do those who are able to get such support. As I was preparing this chapter, in fact, a new study from Yale came to the public's attention. Lisa Berkman, a public health specialist from Yale, monitored 200 older men and women who had suffered heart attacks. She found that those with the most support from others lived the longest after the attack. Dr. Berkman explains that emotional support contributes to healing for physical reasons, "If you feel like you have emotional support, you may be less stressed. Your blood pressure doesn't shoot up, and your heart doesn't race." The comfort and solace of connection makes a difference.

Whether our connection is to lots of people, to family members, to a very special person, to nature and all her gifts, to the deepest part of ourselves through meditation and prayer, or to the divine on a mountaintop as we exclude ourselves from the rest of humanity, there is no doubt that we need to be in contact.

Whether we are introverted and savor those few meaningful meetings of like kind, or extroverted and thrive from the stimulating interactions of lots and lots of people in a small room; whether we like to be around other people all the time or whether we need time alone with infrequent, but comfortable and intimate, shared time with someone else; we all share the essential need of healthy connection and contact.

● a skill worth mastering

Being connected, of course, is a two-way street. We need not only to be willing to be seen and known in deeper and deeper ways but to know and see the other person and be as open to them as we can, too.

Since most of us are conditioned, from an early age, to protect and guard ourselves, this requires taking risks, being flexible (resilient!), trying on different beliefs, and not giving up when communication gets messy, painful, and possibly raw. This kind of sophisticated communication is a *skill*, an art; it can (and must) be learned, practiced, and mastered. The rest of this chapter is devoted to the *skills* of communication.

Overall, *practice observing and listening with keen attention*. As you interact with others, try to watch and listen to what they respond to and what makes them defensive. Observe when you become defensive. Watch for those instances of masterful timing where an exchange between people approaches a well-choreographed ballet. What communication skills do you observe? What can you take away and practice as you cultivate your own connections?

●befriending your imagination

One of the keys to this kind of sophisticated communication is imagination, the ability to construct internal images of situations and see through various possible outcomes in "our mind's eye." It has been found that people who show natural resilience in difficult situations use precisely this imaginative function in order to structure and sequence the event and adapt accordingly.

Sports psychologists confirm this further in their reporting of the effectiveness of imagining the perfect golf swing or foul shot. We know that with practice, imagined practice, athletes show marked improvement because mental practice turns on most of the brain circuits that would be used in swinging or shooting for real.

Now, let's put this together with neurobiology's reports of the differences between a peak performance and a mental collapse. Whether we respond to a situation or failure by panicking and saying "I don't know if I can do this" or by embracing the challenge with "I've been preparing for this all my life" determines which chemical will course through our systems. In the challenge response, the body is flushed with adrenaline and sugar, creating a heightened awareness and the flow people mention about a peak performance. The fearful response produces hormones laced with cortisol, which not only impairs performance but also does damage to the arteries and liver and can lead to depression.

Imagination allows us to see all the views of the situation, the varying pieces of the puzzle, and gives us the opportunity to arrange and rearrange to our heart's content. We can imagine the possible consequences of "If you say this or do that" as we include the potential responses you will receive. We can imagine how we might feel if the deal goes one way or another, gauging the levels of comfort we have with the different scenarios. If Tina had been able to use her imagination regarding a possible conversation with her mother, it is likely she would not have called her. She would have called her helpful friend first.

Within the context of imagination we can be as creative as we have the capacity for—finding absurd, humorous, outlandish, conservative, ridiculous, and traditional solutions. We can try out how these responses will or will not help, and we can even imagine letting go of any attachments to outcome, giving ourselves the inner freedom to show up at the dialogue table with tremendous inner conviction and ability to listen to other parties.

Use your imagination and see the process through. Become aware of the pitfalls and strong emotions and see yourself ordering and mastering the sequences of the interaction.

- Are you up against a stressful talk with your husband or partner and worried sick about how it might go?
- Are you planning a big event for work or a wedding for a family member?
- Do you want to ask for a promotion and a raise?
- Is it time for a serious talk about drugs or sex with your teenager?
- Do you need to fight for a cause, personal or civic?
- Are you faced with a medical issue and need to be assertive with the doctors or insurance?

You *can* have a say in how you *respond* to life's challenges, and your imagination can be one of your best allies. Imagine healthy communication, imagine intimate conversations, imagine navigating angry disagreements, imagine a series of hard compromises, imagine staying calm during stormy fights, imagine a loved one misunderstanding you and being able to try again, imagine being open and vulnerable when it is hard and frightening. And when it doesn't work out and there is a real mess, imagine learning after the fact and imagine how differently you would respond the next time the same thing or something similar presented itself.

● choosing wisely

As you work on strengthening your connections with others and developing your communication skills, I ask you to consider the following pointers:

- ▶ Choose people you can trust.
- ▶ Choose people who want and bring out the best in you.
- ▶ Choose people who accept you for who you are, including your faults and foibles.
- ▶ Avoid people who raise themselves by lowering you.
- ▶ Know what you are asking for, and practice asking in a straightforward manner, free of manipulation, undue aggressiveness, or attempts to make the other person feel guilty.
- ▶ Check out what might be going on instead of making assumptions: "I think you are upset. Are you? Is it something I have done?"
- ▶ Practice letting go when you cannot get what you want.

I imagine this type of straightforward, nonreactive communication as a martial art. In the arts when someone comes at you, the form is to let the energy be absorbed or moved aside. The other person is then left with their own energy source, not able to get caught up in your reaction or fight, and assuming it is because of you that they are behaving in such and such a manner.

As your connections deepen, keeping the following points in mind will further facilitate the martial arts of communication.

- *Know how others perceive you.* A psychologist expert in group therapy once trained me to lead groups. He is very tall, large, with a full head of white hair and a full white beard. He had long ago figured out what projections he received whenever he walked into a room, especially when he was doing the training. He knew he would be seen as the all-knowing father figure, or the authority who dictated all things, or the omnipotent and all-caring protector. He knew he would be seen this way even if he didn't carry any of these attitudes or traits within or didn't agree with these perceptions, and this knowing gave him the chance to voice these projections and deflate many unconscious assumptions. On the other hand, I worked with a woman who did not know how others saw her and continually misinterpreted their behavior toward her. She is a strong and very efficient woman who walks down the street in a bold fashion. She manages to hold down a prestigious position in a law firm while raising three children. She had often found other women to be unfriendly and had her feelings hurt when she assumed they did not like her. A good friend took her aside and informed her that others saw her as unavailable because she was so busy and conceited because she accomplished so much. She knew she was friendly and accessible; now she needed to understand the misperception so she could reach out.
- *Listen well.* Good listening is an art form and cannot be underestimated. Listen without interruption, listen with intended focus, and listen without forming a response in your mind. Listen to the sounds and meaning being offered. Listen to your own inner being, listen very carefully to those people near and dear to you, and especially listen well to those who are not on your side. Listen to the world you inhabit, keep open to nature and the rhythms of the universe.
- *Hear what is being said and hear what is being implied.* Be open to what is being said, sung, screamed, smiled, moaned, and cried.
- If you are not being listened to, *demonstrate an inner conviction* by sustaining your point of view in a heartfelt and nondefensive manner; be secure enough in your position to *be open and sensitive to the other's needs and concerns.*

- *Know when to retreat and replenish.* In the Buddhist traditions of Southeast Asia there are twenty-one different words for silence: the silence between thoughts, the silence of a concentrated mind, and the silence of awareness. In this fast-paced world of ours, give yourself time for contemplating, a quiet time, an inner time. Communicate with silence, with your inner world. Take time to listen to the sounds of nature; have time go slowly and involve you with mundane tasks and empty space to allow the deeper heart to come to light.
- *Know when to hide away,* when you are feeling overly sensitive or vulnerable and any comment or interchange will sting.
- *Learn, practice, and master genuine interest in others and the world around you.* Ask people about their dreams, their successes, and their families. Be open to another point of view; find what you can learn from it. Listen carefully when someone is unhappy with you or your behavior; distinguish if the person is for you and allow yourself to be communicated with.

And remember this: In the final analysis, no matter how well you communicate, there are no guarantees. No matter how well you do, others will still disappoint, disagree, refuse, and possibly get angry. That's why it's so important to practice letting go, detaching from the outcome without blaming yourself or the other person. Remember you did your best, and with genuine detachment you can begin to imagine alternatives. And with alternatives you are practicing resiliency.

Communication:
- ▶ The ability and willingness to clearly express what is on your mind and in your heart and to actively hear the response
- ▶ The ability and willingness to hear what is being expressed to you and take it in before reacting
- ▶ The ability and willingness to make a connection

---

exercise

REFLECTION

Use a journal, artwork, and/or imagination to help you connect with your answers to the questions below (see the exercise in chapter 1 for more explanation).

Remember a time when you felt criticized, disappointed, or embarrassed, and ask yourself these questions:

▶ What am I feeling? What do I need? How is this experience affecting me?

▶ Is this a time to reach out to another person? Is this a time to listen to my inner knowing? Can I be still and hear myself?

▶ Where was the breakdown in communication? What was being said to me? How are my feelings clouding the issue?

Remember a time when you had difficulties in a relationship or discussion, and ask yourself these questions:

▶ What do I do with the information that this conversation or relationship is not going well? What are my expectations? Overestimating myself and the environment? Underestimating myself and the environment? Reasonable? What would make them reasonable?

▶ When it is not going well, do I know how to resteer the car between the white lines and get back in the lane?

▶ Do I get the exact same response or reaction from my spouse, my friend, my boss, or my partner whenever I mention a topic, a subject, a feeling? What can I figure out about the exchange? What do I know about myself?

▶ What can I learn from listening carefully and deeply? What can I learn from not criticizing or judging myself or the other person? What can I learn from wanting the communication to lead to compromise?

▶ How can I learn to be clear and straightforward in my communication and be a respectful, effective listener?

hands on, hands off 3

The truth must
dazzle gradually
or everyone
be blind
—EMILY DICKINSON

CONTROL has gotten a bad reputation. To say, "She is a control freak" or "What a terrible, controlling person she is" is to suggest that such a person should really loosen up! And yet, do you remember the Bop-Bag toy—the blow up toy that was painted like a man or a clown? He had big weighted feet so you could hit him again and again; each time, he would right himself. No matter how hard or from what angle you punched him, kicked him, hit him, or knocked him down, he would bounce back up and face you with his permanent grin. This toy is designed to give a child a sense of control. What an image of resilience. He bounces back no matter which position or how hard you punch him. It might be hard to imagine. But that bounce-ability is what successfully navigating the waters of adversity requires us to have. This step is about control. Real control *and* perceived control. A reasonable and discoverable degree of control. Because we need a degree of control in order to bounce back from hard times and to flourish as a result of being knocked down. Implicit in the very idea of resilience is that life is full of hardship, struggle, or tragedy. Resilience is, in large part, about taking control after such difficulties.

You break off a relationship and watch all the pieces of your life take a different turn. More time for laundry and videos, yes, but what about the social events and vacations you will now attend alone? What about the sad look in friends' and family members' eyes, and what about the possible downward turn your esteem might take? What about the feelings of sadness, sorrow, anger, and grief? How intense and long-lasting might they be?

Someone close to you dies, and you know the experience of finality. You feel the daunting chasm of never being with that person again and all that

that means—every holiday and meaningful event without this person and a chronic feeling of missing him or her. Your child starts taking street drugs, and neither of your lives is ever the same again. To be able to weather these storms and possibly grow from them requires a portion of control, the ability to see a problem or crisis or trauma as something that can be worked on, overcome, changed, endured, or resolved in some way. *This is about knowing what is within your command so you can let go of what is not.*

The control we need in order to be resilient is not about omnipotence or dictatorship; it is about a reasonable assessment of the environment. What has happened, and how much positive impact can I have for a positive outcome? How much of this task can I truly do something about? How can I manage my emotional reaction to keep things constructive?

The inner control needed is not about non-feeling or non-caring, it is not about repression or suppression; it is about having the ability to manage negative and troublesome emotions associated with the task or relationship at hand.

I am the steward of my own ship:
I can choose my own emotions and behaviors.

● the perception of control

Recently I have come across research indicating that people who come into therapy believing that the outcomes of their life events were contingent on their behavior were three times more likely to experience successful outcomes in therapy than were clients who viewed events as being outside of their personal control. What intrigues me even further is that this reality includes people *perceiving* a semblance of control, even if they do not really have that much say in the matter. The very matter of perception can affect a positive outcome.

A woman I know went through months and months of agonizing fertilization treatments. The doctors and experts had given her and her husband very little reason to hope, but she persisted with every treatment feasible. She said she had always seen herself having a baby and she wasn't going to be discouraged by the experts. A short time after the medical teams had said there was nothing else they could do, this woman, with utter inner conviction, started drinking coffee again. She had remembered the caffeine positively interacting with her hormonal cycle, giving her the sense that she had more chance of ovulating and conceiving when she drank coffee.

She became pregnant the next month. Was it the coffee? Was it her unwavering conviction that she would become pregnant? Was it a matter of time? Impossible to answer, but it seems reasonable to at least consider that, given the mind-body connection, her perceived control had some effect on the outcome.

How do people wrest an amount of control to help them cope and resolve hard issues? The rest of this chapter illustrates idea after idea showing people finding parts of the problem they could manage and handle. People controlling pieces of the whole picture:

Patricia is weary from supporting herself for forty years. She is looking forward to retirement in two years with great zeal, and she is finding it very difficult to show up at work effectively. She dreads Sunday evenings and drags herself to work each day until she realizes she is four dental appointments away from retirement and relaxes. Four dental appointments sound easier to wait for and muster through than two years of working 10-hour days.

Karen Duffy, cover girl and MTV actress, had a serious illness and a year of chemotherapy. She dealt with her condition a bit at a time. She told herself she would not be ill until the expiration date on the milk carton. She worked at staying well for that length of time—and then she bought a new bottle of milk with a new expiration date.

A San Francisco bartender, Fred Skau, was overwhelmed by the staggering amount of money needed to help his friends diagnosed with HIV. He put a glass jar on his bar, called Pennies from Heaven, and collected 60 million pennies over eight years.

And to deal with his emotions? "I have my times when I go out to the beach, kick the sand, yell at the waves, throw rocks, and get it all out. Then I go back and do what needs to be done."

A colleague's grandfather was a farmer during the Depression. He owned land in the dustbowl of the Midwest and went through very rugged hard times trying to keep his family intact and fed during the country's devastating losses. And yet he says times are much harder now.

Why? Because at least he owned his own land back then. No one on the fifty-fourth floor of some building in some far-away city could take it away from him. He might not be able to bring in a decent wage from farming, but he could always grow enough food to feed his family. He believed that, as bad as things are, the wolf at the door or the landowner on the fifty-fourth floor does not have to have complete power or control over you or your life. You have to find what you can control, guide, direct, orchestrate, or negotiate for yourself.

Marcy graduated from college and looked forward to her blossoming career in public relations. Her dream was to own her own company. She was venturing out on her own, giving up being financially supported by her parents. She experienced sheer terror when she looked into the future and saw the need to support herself for the next twenty or thirty years. She began to feel overwhelmed having to work all that time, with only minor vacations for relief, and worried about being sick, being in a car accident, or not being able to support herself financially. By breaking things down, instead, she concentrated on creating a budget, using each day to network and build her support system, and put away a small amount each week for a "rainy day."

Vladimir Horowitz, renowned pianist, said when he did not practice one day, he knew it; when he did not practice three days, his audience knew it.

Ellen Langer, Ph.D., a psychologist at Harvard University, found that the people in nursing homes who were required to dress themselves or choose which foods to eat had lower mortality rates than those people with comparable health who had all their needs taken care of by the attendants. She argues that nursing home life should be made more complex, not easier. "It's important for people to be in control of their lives, and the way to be in control is to be in the active process of mastering something." Langer goes on to say, "If all you think about is how you're likely to fail at a challenge, you probably will. But if you ask yourself, 'What are ten ways I could succeed at this?' your chances of success are much greater."

In *Women Who Run with the Wolves*, Clarissa Pinkola Estés writes:

> We all hope that if we work hard and have a high holy quest, we will come up with something, a substance, a material, something or other that will—flash!—make everything orderly forever. But that is not the way it works. . . . We can have all the knowledge in the universe and it comes down to one thing: practice. It comes down to going home and step-by-step implementing what we know. As often as necessary, and for as long as possible, or forever, whichever comes first.

Calvin and Hobbes was a popular cartoon in many newspapers. Calvin, an adorable, devilish child, had an imaginary tiger friend, Hobbes, with whom he talked over all his problems. One time he told Hobbes:

> Problems often look overwhelming at first. The secret is to break problems into small manageable chunks. If you deal with those you're done before you know it. For example, I'm supposed to read this entire history chapter. It looks impossible, so I break the problem down.

Hobbes responds, "You focus on reading the first section?"
"No," responds Calvin, "I ask myself, 'Do I even care?'"

Elizabeth told me about her experience in therapy and the appreciation she has for the time it takes to heal—realizing that "as it goes slowly so it goes genuinely" and she can count on it being solid and lasting. She says, "Something wicked happened when I was a child" and it planted a tiny seed deep within her. She forgot about the seed and the wicked deed and then, lo and behold, as an adult she finds a full-grown redwood tree within her, blocking out the sun, taking up way too much room, deeply rooted and using energy and resources for its survival, denying her the needed energy and space. She went on to describe the process required for cutting down a full grown redwood tree: "You cannot simply axe it—you need to begin by topping it, cutting back the branches, gathering the fallings and burning them, all in preparation for the final cutting away of the solid trunk. This takes time, patience, and hard work." If you were given, all at once, all the food you will eat until the day you die, it would be overwhelming. Eating three times a day is manageable. A task at a time.

● breaking it down

Many of life's events can be broken down into manageable pieces. Here are some examples.

- ▶ When a project is very complex, break it down. Anyone writing a dissertation or a book, starting his or her own company, or raising a child can attest to this wisdom. Parcel out the problem into sections and figure in a reward and/or ritual after significant junctures are completed. Each little piece achieved will give you impetus to go on to the next.
- ▶ If you are experiencing fear—a tight knot in the gut—imagine it

parceled out into many little packages, each piece contained in itself. Disseminate the fear into manageable chunks and handle them one at a time. Do the same with any emotion.

If you are beginning an exercise program, remember to start slowly and build up. Beginning runners start out by stretching and limbering. They say it is best to begin with a short distance, add a bit longer run to each day. Once they get a rhythm established they can begin doing a little more each day. This is based on the principle of optimum performance: not wearing something or someone out but steadily building and becoming stronger each day.

▶ When learning something new, start on a small scale and work your way up. A friend of mine bought a home with a full yard to landscape and maintain. She had never done any gardening before and didn't have a particular bent or talent. She believed that she should just know how to do this and should be able to manage it as well as anyone else. In truth, the project was overwhelming and daunting and stayed that way the entire fifteen years she lived there. She maintained the perspective of seeing the landscaping as the entire front and back yard, and she continued her belief that she should know how to garden (how hard could it possibly be?). As a result the yard did not look as she would have liked and she got minimal pleasure out of it.

When she moved into a city she had a tiny little planter box outside her living room window and a few large plants on the deck. She loves working these two places and cares for them both as if they were her flesh and blood children. She feels on top of their care. This small area was more manageable for her and allowed her the proper rhythm to learn how to garden.

▶ Christmas clubs work on the premise of breaking things down into manageable pieces. By putting away a certain amount of money each month you have a sizeable chunk of cash in December to shop for the holidays without bankrupting yourself in one month's overspending. In that vein, a group of my women friends put away $120 every month for two years. We used the money to vacation in a villa in Italy for two weeks. The trip was extra delicious because it was all paid for before we even left our homes.

▶ The model of recovery for addictions is based on one day at a time and distinguishing what you can control and what you cannot. The idea of never drinking a glass of wine again can lead to defiance and rebellion—too big a picture. Managing one day at a time quiets the restless mind and allows for minor successes leading to more success.

▶ If you are trying to manifest a dream, remember that it can take time and lots of small steps to realize larger visions. I believe in dreams. Nighttime dreams that come to us with bits and pieces of information about ourselves and how we are in the world and daytime dreams that can forecast what we would like for ourselves. In either case it takes time to assimilate and absorb the unconscious into our everyday conscious life. It was fifteen years ago that I had a dream of one day practicing psychotherapy in a Victorian building. That was before any schooling—any paper written, any exam taken—and long before the arduous journey of years of internships and licensing exams. In fact, the process took so long I forgot I had imagined myself in a Victorian. I forgot until the sunny day recently when I looked up at my building in San Francisco and consciously realized I had my dream office.

▶ A talk show host was interviewing a vegetarian restaurateur, and he was curious how to help people convert from cooking with meat to cooking satisfying vegetarian dishes. "Cook one new recipe at a time—cook a new meal once a month," was the response from the expert. The talk show host laughed and said he understood the concept because "nobody lives in Manhattan—it's too damn big. Everybody lives in a neighborhood. I'm from the east side."

▶ It is extremely difficult to get our heads around horrific events or evil acts like war, slavery, and holocausts. Often they are too big and abstract to get hold of with any depth of meaning. And yet when we hear an individual story or detail the whole picture can become vivid and accessible.

▶ Gary Paulson writes about his experience of running the famous dog-pulled race in *Winterdance: The Fine Madness of Running the Iditarod:*

It is almost impossible to articulate the race as a whole. It can be broken down into sections, days, hours, horrors, joys, checkpoints, winds, nights, colds, waters, ices, deaths, tragedies, small and large courages. But as a whole, to say generally what the race is like, there are no exact words.

No exact words for the race as a whole. As most of these examples show, there are many, many times we cannot grasp the whole, especially when it entails something difficult. To be resilient, to stay in the game, and hopefully to see it through to a satisfying end, we need to see the pieces of the problem. These examples highlight how different people, in different circumstances, found a semblance of control over a problem, which in turn gave them a flexibility of resilience. An important theme throughout the examples is the *attitude* of "I can do this—I will find a way through the difficulty. I want to do this and I want to do what I need to do." In fact, I purposely use the words *I will* to begin each spoke of the resilience process. Thinking about and applying the spokes this way indicates this attitude of self-determination and will power, implying a sense of control and beginning with an attitude of intention.

The sense of control discussed in this chapter is completely in the service of resilience.

The grandfather's pleasure at not being indebted to the anonymous man on the fifty-fourth floor did not mean he was immediately wealthy or not suffering the consequences of a collective depression. People still died from AIDS, Patricia needed to show up at work for the next two years, and Marcy had to learn to support herself. Control in the service of resilience is to make the situation and/or emotions manageable so you can, as the Bop-Bag toy, right yourself as many times as necessary while riding out the hard time, or righting yourself after the blow. It is not intended to control any outcomes; in fact, resiliency is not about outcomes. By its nature, resilience is pliable—not rigid. The bamboo, the willow, and the reed bend during a storm, and therefore the winds and rains will not buffet them; they bend and survive the storm. Control in the service of resilience implies we can choose to find the appropriate times to bend and we, too, can survive the storm.

exercise

MAP YOUR MIND

There is a process called mind mapping that helps break large and cumbersome issues into bite-sized pieces.

Begin by writing a subject—a project, relationship, job, emotion, issue, or goal—in the middle of a large piece of paper. What is it you are working on, what is the current challenge in your life? For example, you have just suffered a loss. Begin by writing this loss in the center of the paper. Draw a circle around the words, and then draw a line out from the circle. On this line, write your first thought. Draw out another line from the circle for your second thought, and so on.

Look at these thoughts. When you see these thoughts on paper, in front of you, you might think of more minute parts of the ideas. Draw additional lines out from the first ones, and write the details on these. Think of the middle circle (the problem or issue) as the tree, the lines leading out from it (your thoughts) are the branches, and the next lines (the details) are the twigs coming off the branches.

You are getting more and more detail. Now imagine yourself above this problem or issue, looking down at it. You will see the entire issue at once and what relates to what. (You can even use different colors for the trunk, branches, and twigs.)

You can do a complete second mind map devoted entirely to emotions and feelings if needed or desired.

Put your mind map in a place you will see it each day, and add to it as it seems appropriate. Reflect on how to use the information on the map to help you through the difficult time. This can be a way to break many things down and see the concerns, tasks, or emotion in easier-to-handle bits.

not that one, *this* one 4

These days, though, I'm letting my real taste, or lack of it,
whatever, show through. These days I look at the sample that
the painter who knows so much about color is saying looks
wonderful and I think, "Well, no, not wonderful, not to me."
—ADAIR LARA

ONE DAY RECENTLY I saw a woman fall. I was walking with a friend on a busy city street, when, as if in slow motion, the woman walking just ahead of us missed her step on a curb and fell flat on her face. The fall must have taken her by complete surprise. She didn't shield it with her hands; instead she fell forcefully. I watched her head bounce on the sidewalk.

I hurried over to her, bent down, and asked if I might help. Without even looking at me, she said no, she was fine, thank you. And then she simply got up and walked away. My heart was still beating fast; I couldn't imagine how she was okay.

My friend and I continued our walking down the street. A block away we met the woman returning from her quick errand. She had a huge "egg" on her head, visibly throbbing and already every shade of black and purple, as well as serious abrasions on both her arms. It was obvious she was far from okay.

The experience led me to reflect on my own experiences of falling (in all senses of the word), as well as the experiences of so many other women I have known. I particularly remember lamenting the common feeling of humiliation, especially if the "fall" happened in public. Not focused on whether we were physically hurt, needed medical attention or just love and support, or even a moment or two to simply recollect ourselves before getting up, we worried about being humiliated and embarrassed.

And another story of like kind: I was walking, semi-hurriedly, to the bathroom in a crowded movie theatre, knowing I'd have to face a line. As I neared the bathroom, a couple in front of me, walking oddly and slowly, blocked my way. I could not get around them. The woman of the couple was also headed to the bathroom, and indeed there was a line, so I queued up behind her.

Now, for the first time, I could see her face, which was contorted in agony.

She was obviously not just experiencing mild discomfort but real physical pain. When she noticed me looking at her, she explained that she had had to go to the bathroom for a half-hour but hadn't wanted to miss any of the movie. Sensing her real distress, I suggested that she go to the head of the line.

She didn't respond—just continued to stand there in her private pain. Then she looked at me pleadingly and said, not exactly *to* me but as if she was speaking out loud to herself, "I can't stand this."

"My God," I said, "please, go plead your case to the woman in front or try the men's room," which was right across the hallway. Again she appeared not even to register my words. By this time she was standing with her legs pressed together tightly and her face crunched in pure agony.

Just as I was beginning to feel truly unnerved, she blurted out, "I cannot do this! I have to find another bathroom," and turned and walked away in a very slow, clumsy, pigeon-toed way, her inner thighs pressed together. She briefly stopped to look into the men's room for her male friend and then walked on.

For reasons I will never know, this woman simply could not or would not ask for help, could not or would not make her needs and situation known, even to take care of a very real biological need. As I reflect back on the scene, I imagine the private horror of not being able to say, or better yet, assert herself in such a time of genuine need. I see her vulnerable to a humiliating or painful experience because she could not say, out loud and publicly, "Look at me, please, I need some help and I need it now."

Just what *was* her risk? The risk of being scorned, not listened to, not believed? The risk of having too much attention paid to a humiliating moment? Why did this seem greater than the risk that she would be able to get to the toilet before her bladder burst?

What these stories reveal is the raw face of shame—the shame that can squelch the hurt and the desperate. Shame powerful enough to have people wish or believe they were invisible, not really there, not connected to anyone else, not mattering. Shame that impedes our willingness and ability to take ourselves seriously. In this chapter we look at what gets in the way of taking care of ourselves, of getting our needs met; how to move through those obstacles and know where else to turn when our needs cannot be met.

● the raw face of shame

The Greek root of the word *shame* is *scham,* the skin used to cover the exposed, vulnerable parts of a person. I have watched shame work "miracles" as it turns attractive women into believing they are ugly, bewitching confidence into self-loathing, talent drowned in addiction, and beauty of the soul torn apart by eating disorders and other self-destructive behaviors. So while the stories I've just recounted might seem unusual or extreme, most of us know full well the feelings of shame in one form or another.

We are living in a world that looks askance at vulnerability and fragility. As women, we have learned to feel ashamed of our tender sensitivities and often feel humiliated when they are revealed. However unnatural it may be to be ashamed of our needs—and it certainly is—we have been handed a legacy of being subordinated, powerless, manipulated to believe we are inferior citizens; in fact, we have, often, through history, been scapegoated—scapegoated to carry the *extra* burden of shame for the rest of the society.

Let's look at one way we inherited this legacy of shame for having needs. Throughout time, the human being has been all too aware of the dangers and threats to life and limb. Whether it is natural forces, human enemies, or the awareness of the inevitability of death, our lineage shows the human attempting to appease and avoid these forces. It is not a good idea to be overly susceptible or vulnerable to these threats, and so, in biblical times our ancestors employed the use of a scapegoat—a literal goat, symbolically dressed in all the sins and vulnerabilities of the citizens of the society—and then deliberately exiled from the community that was attempting to find security. And, if our ancestors did not use an exiled goat, they would slay a beast or victim in order to appease the gods with a sacrifice. Over time, the concepts of victimization and scapegoating became intimately connected; the word *victim* originally meant a beast selected for sacrifice. Our relatives, in a ritualistic fashion, commonly practiced either sacrificing a beast/victim or excluding a scapegoat—two ways of symbolically making the rest of the community feel safe from harm. The finding and labeling of a scapegoat would "ensure" that the rest of the community would be safe from unpleasant and overwhelming feelings of vulnerability and helplessness. If the victim or scapegoat could be seen by the gods as carrying all the community's wrongdoings, then the average, model citizen would be seen as strong and sinless.

In order for this ritual to work effectively, it was important for the community to genuinely see the scapegoat as bad, evil, sinful, dirty, wrong. When you believe that there is something wrong with the victim or scapegoat, and therefore it is deserving of punishment, then you don't have to be susceptible to the senseless and irrational terrors of the world. It is best, of course, if the scapegoat embodies those qualities the dominant group considers absolutely *other,* such that society is willing to sacrifice, for only in isolation (not connected to the dominant clan) can this *other* absorb the great variety of the community's hostile and contradictory accusations. That's why scape-

goats are most often sought among the weak and powerless; they cannot strike back in revenge, and therefore cannot plunge society back into reciprocal violence. Any bully on the schoolyard knows this instinctively.

We live in the wake of three patriarchal religions that posit the view that women are dangerous, unequal to men, and have the ability to distract men from important work. Women's sexuality, emotions, and natural work of nurturing and caretaking are seen as troublesome, weak, and inferior. To the degree that any individual woman buys into this scapegoating as the weaker and inferior sex is the degree to which the woman will render herself invisible, not wanting to take up any space and certainly not needing anything.

To need is to be present, alive, and deserving. To be a scapegoat means your role is to sacrifice your needs for the good of the dominant society. To "go against" the role given can induce a feeling of being wrong, standing out too much, and experiencing shame. Women still collectively carry the shame of needing something for themselves. And not just women who identify themselves as victims, either. It is a rare woman who does not hold, in some fashion, the scapegoat complex. It's as if we are all following an eleventh commandment: *Thou shalt not need!*

● needs? who me?

I would be a wealthy woman if I had a nickel for every woman who told me it was selfish or unnecessary to think of herself before others or to go out of her way to get her needs met. The baby needs me, the dog needs me, the Third World needs me, the environment is dying, and my husband's work is more serious and therefore more important. If not selfish then not deserving; if not deserving then invisible; if not invisible then overreacting; if not overreacting then too unimportant to be taken seriously.

A woman I work with is very strong and powerful in the work world. In fact, she is the president of a firm made up mostly of men. She manages to deal effectively with her work world as well as raise her family. One day she found herself with a splitting headache. She was at work and did not have any Excedrin in the office. She would not buy herself another bottle because she had one at home. She didn't "need" another bottle, so she suffered the headache until she got home four hours later. Why? Because on some level she didn't believe she should *have* needs; and certainly she couldn't justify buying another bottle of aspirin *for herself* when she could surely survive the headache until she got home.

Another woman I work with is nothing short of a warrior for every family member, client, and cause that requires her attention. She is truly strong,

stable, and impressively capable. It took two years of concentrated effort before she could say, "I need your help" to her daughter.

Women do have needs—naturally and genuinely. Simply because we don't recognize, vocalize, and activate them does not mean we aren't attempting to meet them, however. Just like any other oppressed energy, needs go underground and come out in another fashion—often indirectly, covertly, slyly. Sometimes we might not even be conscious that we are managing to get our needs met, and sometimes such subterfuge results in us settling for secondary gains—in other words, when we cannot say *directly* that we want and need to be taken care of or given attention, we will, as one example, sometimes magnify, massage, or fabricate ailments to get the attention or care or to avoid being abandoned. It doesn't matter that we do not need to be sick; in fact, it is often a big price to pay simply to get attention.

Not only do we, at times, settle for secondary gains, but we also build a reservoir of resentment. Resentment toward the people who are getting all of our attention at the expense of us taking care of ourselves, resentment that we are not able or willing to take ourselves seriously, and resentment at the gargantuan price we pay for not getting our own needs met. Gillian wanted to keep two old flowerpots that had never been used but would make a designer-quality end table. Her husband Stan said absolutely not. "I am not lugging them in the car for 200 miles and having them take up extra space in our home. We do not need any more furniture." End of discussion. For the umpteenth time, Gillian gave in. She was used to it. Her wants and needs had always been given little airspace or consideration in this marriage. She gave the flowerpots away. She gave them away to a woman she didn't even care for, which, in some ways upped the martyrdom quotient. A possible secondary gain—she found a way to express her irritation and see herself as such a "good" person!

Around the same time Stan began to have some physical ailments and exhibited a great deal of stress and anxiety about his well-being. He was feeling too weak to assist himself, but Gillian promised to call and inquire about getting him some help in the local hospital. Somehow she just couldn't seem to remember to make that call. This passive-aggressive behavior was her way, however unconsciously, of getting her needs met—the need to be heard, the built-up anger at not being taken into consideration, the need to be taken seriously, to believe she has equal weight in a discussion. Because these needs did not get brought to consciousness and acted on in a direct fashion, they came out in less-than-helpful and constructive ways. And because she was not able or willing to make enough waves to get her needs met directly, her resentment kept her from being available when Stan genuinely needed her.

● taking ourselves seriously

We are trained to think it selfish to consider ourselves, but needs are natural *and necessary* to being resilient. To be resilient requires overcoming the resistance and collective tide of not being deserving or taking yourself seriously. A sentence in the research on resilience marked itself indelibly into my psyche: "The resilient have an uncanny ability to get their needs met"—no false modesty or blind eye to real needs and the importance of taking care of themselves. They did what they needed to stay strong and upright.

In their work on children, psychologists Michael Murphy and Michael Moriarty found that resilient children had a pattern of reaching out and finding "another mother" in the neighborhood. My friend Suzanne, who suffered untold physical abuse by her stepmother, tells me how she picked her boyfriends in high school. "I checked out their mothers. If the mothers were cool and available I would go out with the guy. That way I could spend time in the kitchen with the mom." (The secondary gain was getting a substitute mom out of the deal—which was worth it even if she did not like the guy all that much!)

In addition to finding that kids would seek substitute parents, Murphy and Moriarty found that resilient children would work to excel in an area that would increase their resourcefulness—instinctively knowing that this would enable them to feel good about themselves and allow them to carry on with their lives and purposes.

For example, look at two little girls who lived in similar circumstances of abject poverty and neglect. They literally did not have enough to eat and were left to their own devices for hours at a stretch. One of the little girls, feeling ashamed and helpless, sat in the dark, twirling her hair and thinking of all the food she would eat if she had the money to go to the store. The other little girl, recognizing her physical and emotional hunger and using her observation skills, remembered what she knew about her neighborhood. There was a family down the street that was not much better off financially but somehow that mother managed to feed her family every evening at 6 P.M. The little girl knew that if she showed up right before suppertime she would be invited to join them. She not only found a way to fill her empty tummy, she fueled her self-respect with her resourcefulness *and* got to be around other people for a meal. Getting her needs met increased her sense of confidence, esteem, and security. It gave her a sense of her own power to know that she was capable of taking care of herself when the occasion required.

In order to bounce back, we need to take care of ourselves. We hear the message every time we fly: In case of an emergency, put on your oxygen mask or life vest first before attempting to help others. You cannot be helpful to others if you are not breathing! The same principle applies here: Being depleted, martyred, bruised, or otherwise occupied steals the very thunder needed to survive and triumph. In order to be available for life's ups and downs, to be resilient, we must discover what soothes, comforts, aids, supports, and enables us to take care of ourselves. An African proverb says the same thing poetically: "Be wary of a naked woman offering you a dress."

● oh my, i *do* have needs!

When my mother was diagnosed with adrenal cortex cancer, she went through a debilitating several months digesting the information and making decisions about treatment and possible end-of-life options. When she came through the radiation treatment after the trauma of the surgery, the cancer (which had metastasized) had abated long enough for both of us to catch our breath. I found myself so depleted from the previous months that I wondered whether I could hold up for the duration of her illness and likely subsequent death. My circuits were near overload.

A quiet voice of wisdom kept murmuring to me that I needed to rest and soak up warmth. When I stopped resisting (and stopped listing the dozens of reasons I could not afford to take care of myself at this time), I took several days off and checked into the Miyako Hotel in San Francisco. The Miyako Hotel has Japanese baths in every room; just what the Great Doctor was ordering. I followed the Japanese ritual of washing and rinsing outside the bath and then settling into a deep bathtub filled with hot, scented water, and spent three days taking so many baths and soaks that I lost count.

I left the room long enough to get a couple of Shiatsu massages and explore a new restaurant for each meal. I had a new novel by Robertson Davies in my room and a special handpicked pound of See's chocolate candies. I spent luxuriating time watching the clouds form and reform, wondering at the beauty of the sunrays bursting from the seams and partitions of the clouds. I deeply listened as the rain fell, bringing such welcome refreshment for a thirsty and dry Earth. I could identify with the earth and feel its gratitude at being nourished and brought back to a moist life through the washing sprinkle of the clouds.

In just three days I was returned to health and contentment, as I remembered all the parts of me back into one whole. This was not a matter of escape or a dalliance. This was essential for synthesis and for recovering the resources sorely needed to continue to face, endure, and resolve the ongoing issues of my mother's illness and our two roles in her life and death.

When I do groups for women who want to increase their resilience quotient, we do a powerful exercise for needs. I ask them to pair up and face each other, each holding a blank piece of paper. Each woman is given fifteen minutes to answer the question, "What do you need?" Her exercise partner acts as a recorder, writing down each need the woman verbalizes and asking the question again. "What do you need?" You would be amazed how long fifteen minutes is when faced with looking deeper and deeper into an area that has been unused and undervalued.

The answers get richer as the women delve into the parts of their psyche holding this information in reserve. "I need help." "I need some rest." "I need to know I am loved." "I need reassurance." "I need to exercise my authentic voice." "I need proper medical care, with dignity." "I need to know my place in the world." "I need to have compassion." "I need to forgive." "I need the laundry to disappear." "I need my kids to stop fighting." "I need to be accepted for being gay." "I need to exercise more." And so on and so on.

We also spend a great deal of time committing to getting some of these needs met. An assignment might be to spend the week looking for unmet needs and declaring to yourself that you will find ways to fill the need. Here are a few stories that have come out of this group process:

Megan, a young, energetic woman, owned a printing company with her husband. Week after week, she came to the workshop overworked and stressed about work. As the company's owners, she and her husband faced enormous responsibilities and overwhelming decisions on a regular basis, and she was wearing out. Through the time spent focusing on her needs, Megan was able to hear her inner voice, and even more significantly, was able to tell her husband how she was feeling and how taking care of themselves could make a big difference.

At the end of a very frantic week, Megan's husband, having listened to her newfound awareness of her needs, planned ahead and took her out to Fort Point, the dreamlike place under the Golden Gate Bridge that was immortalized in Alfred Hitchcock's *Vertigo* with Jimmy Stewart and Kim Novak. He brought two wine glasses, a bottle of wine, some cheese and bread, and a transistor radio. He found some romantic music on the radio and invited his wife to dance with him in the moonlight next to the sound and smell of the Pacific Ocean.

For two people who are stretched to the wire with deadlines, finances, and racing-against-the-clock lifestyles, this time out at the ocean was manna from heaven. They forgot their troubles for a few hours, experienced the redemption of nature and romance, and rekindled their connection.

Carly, a free-spirited woman with an incredibly soft-spoken manner, was well liked in the group for both her natural wisdom about life's ups and downs (she is a recovering heroin addict) as well as her consistent interest in each woman's story and plight. She listened avidly to everyone when they spoke and added spirited insight when needed. She remembered when she was eight months pregnant with her son and was deathly afraid she would be just like her own mother. She felt immobilized by terror.

She sought out a kindly older psychologist whom she saw only once. She told him her concerns and fears; leaning forward in his chair and taking both of her hands in his large hands, he looked straight in her eyes and told her, "You are nothing like your mother. You can go home and have your baby and love it. You and your baby will both be fine." His sincerity, reassurance, and grandfatherly wisdom was all Carly needed at that time. She relaxed and found the love she had stored in anticipation of her baby's birth.

A woman I read about, Elizabeth, received a diagnosis of breast cancer, and her life turned upside down for seven months. She faced surgery, radiation, and the tremendous pressure of having to make medical decisions that would have profound effects on her health and life / survival. She is someone who had always found her juice for life and her sense of personal worth in ambition, in professional success, and in keeping up a high-powered pace so she could provide for the three sons she was raising on her own. Busy, productive, active, able to hold her own—that was the way it was "supposed to be" for her.

The cancer diagnosis pulled her up short and forced her to slow down. Her sister, who lives in Oklahoma and had battled breast cancer ten years earlier, called to invite her down for a visit. "I found a really good deal on Southwest Airlines and I would like you to come stay with me for two weeks. I am going to be at the lake; we can sit quietly, watch the water and sunsets, and let anyone who would like to see you come to visit you at the lake so you do not have to move."

Elizabeth went for two weeks and stayed for a month. Her time at the lake was quiet and poignant, time for healing and time for making family connections without rush and without agenda. During the second two weeks she helped her brother, who had just stepped down from a political position and was facing an end to a long marriage, move into his new apartment. She was able to adjust the right warm touch so that his new place wouldn't feel like a barrack. "Take this extra chair; our sister has plenty of other furniture and your place will be so much more comfortable with two chairs. Take this bookcase; there are others in the house. Books will add warmth to your apartment." Elizabeth and her brother found a meeting of the hearts that helped them both through hard times.

She also spent some time with her other brother and his wife. She had known his wife since elementary school, but they had not spent much time together as adults. On this visit they found just how much they had in common as adults and enjoyed both quilting and talking about it together. Again, it was soothing, quiet time that helped Elizabeth heal, not only in body but also in spirit.

When Elizabeth returned to the Bay Area she was met by the old voices that told her to get busy, that she would only be of value if she was *doing* something. But she did not have the energy.

Now she could respond to her new needs by remembering the time and experience she had had in Oklahoma. Even the memories and the retelling brought her to the inner place of peace and comfort, the place she knew she both needed and wanted to live from. She had already done the "busy, productive" life; now she desired a quieter life. While her head still argued that she "should" be busier, her soul and heart knew something different. She had learned to listen to her own rhythm and recognize her needs; she devoted her energy to finding and living from this newly balanced life, hearing and listening to her need for quietude and deeper connections, as well as being busy when called for.

● what do *you* need?

For many of us, simply taking ourselves and our place in the world seriously enough even to include our needs in the equation is the hardest part. If asked, we wouldn't know what our needs were. In order to hear our own answers, we have to be able to get quiet inside. And to be able to get quiet inside sometimes requires us to be willing—willing to act as if we take ourselves seriously, willing to sit quietly and hear the inner wisdom of needs, and willing to put into action what we find out.

Most times, if we can do that—if we can get quiet inside and clear the air—we can hear the voice of our needs. And other times it takes experience and seasoning. When I was younger I collected things. I had very little idea of who I was or what I liked or what I had a knack for, so I collected it all. I only cooked because I was a mother, but I collected every kitchen utensil and gadget imaginable, sometimes two of the same thing so if one were dirty I would use the second. Of course, none of this made me a better cook or made me like to cook. I just had a lot of stuff.

Much later, when I started all over, I gratefully simplified my life. By this time I had come to love cooking and was often amazed that I could whip up scrumptious meals with archaic, simple tools. When I received a state-of-the-art marble cutting board I felt euphoric. I had learned the preciousness of what's needed and what's fitting. I had learned the meaning of everything in its right time. Philosopher and psychologist Abraham Maslow made a career of studying human development as a progression of satisfied needs. He believed that we can only "self-actualize," or become our true selves, when our more primary needs of survival, safety, and belonging have been fulfilled. Here is a brief recap of Maslow's hierarchy of needs.

1. Physiological needs: air, water, food, elimination, sex, activity
2. Safety needs: escape fear and pain, physical security, order, physical safety
3. Belonging and love needs: to love and be loved, have friends, be part of a family
4. Self-esteem needs: to feel competent, independent, successful, respected, and worthwhile
5. Self-actualization needs: being one's true self, achieving one's highest potential, wanting knowledge and wisdom, being able to understand and accept oneself and others, being creative and appreciative of beauty in the world. A self-actualized person is happy, realistic, accepting, problem oriented, creative, democratic, independent, and fulfilling a mission or purpose in life.

To a great extent, I think Maslow was correct. I know many, many midlife women who, after applying themselves for many years, have reached a place of considerable comfort. They are married, financially solvent, have grown children and grandchildren with whom they spend varying amounts of satisfying time; they have warm circles of supportive friends, feel substantially respected by their peers, and have time to read, travel, and participate in the finer culture and arts of their worlds. One would say they have reached level 5 on Maslow's hierarchy.

Now many of these women are devoting themselves, with great courage and steadfastness, to knowing themselves at a deeper level, healing places that still have them partially hobbled, spending considerable time looking for solutions to society's ills, and taking time to appreciate the beauty around them, whether it be the richness of a bird's plumage, the talent of a renowned or new artist, or the sound and rhythm of the ocean. They have the time to ask the fundamental questions for self-actualization now that their basic needs are deeply fulfilled.

My sense, however, is that Maslow's hierarchy of needs is often experienced in a spiraling fashion. The starving artist or philosopher comes to my mind. Or a need that burns so intensely it takes precedent over basics. Some folks have a love of freedom that surpasses safety, or feel an I-must-make-my-dream-come-true urge that takes center stage until it is seen to the end. For others, a particular environmental cause is so important that it doesn't matter if the world sees you as successful or popular. So while we can become familiar with our needs in a developmental fashion, we are, instead, called upon to meditate on our personalities, our desires, and our place in life to find the evolving nature of our deepening needs.

⬤ when needs *can't* be filled

At another end of the spectrum, it is certain that there are times we, no matter our intentions and capacity, simply cannot get our needs met. The need for nothing to change, the need for enough sex, the need to never feel alone, the need for the exact right companionship, the need to have all needs met, the need for the right person to be there at the right time. It is unrealistic for us to assume that some or all of our needs will always be met. What do we do then? I work with many women whose mothers died when they themselves were children or teenagers. They grew up without their biological mothers and have an emptiness or hole that cannot be filled. As Carolyn in chapter 1 discovered, every time another special or difficult occasion arises, the motherless daughter feels the loss or vacuum all over again. But the fact remains: Their mothers are not here, and they need to discover alternate ways to fill the need for mother. (And let's face it. Sometimes, even when a mother is alive, the need cannot be filled.)

Jane, who is getting married to her woman lover, feels the depth of disappointment when her mother will not accept that she is gay and getting married. Jane needs to turn elsewhere to get the support and attention she needs for this wonderful occasion. She turns to her rabbi, who blesses her and welcomes her and her partner into the family.

The child growing up in abject poverty who is neither fed nor nourished turns to her kindly neighbor.

When a need cannot be filled, we must *learn* how to delay gratification; we must learn to practice waiting, to find substitute means and/or to look in other places for satisfaction. In fact, for most of us there will likely never be enough security, love and friends, attention, food, respect, support, understanding, knowledge, purpose, and so on; when all else fails, we need to learn how to let go. How to be alright with missing something or someone. How to let go of what we cannot or will not have. *It is the marriage of knowing when and how to get your needs met and knowing when and how to seek alternatives and let go that results in a resilient response.*

Judy is unhappy with her house because it is not her dream home and she does not have the means to buy what she wants. She is better off letting go of her unrealistic longing.

Patricia's forty-fifth birthday arrived without her having birthed any children; she was forced to say good-bye to a long-held desire. She concentrated on loving her extended family and found a satisfying-enough alternative.

When Edith's husband's cancer could no longer be held at bay, she had to find the courage to let him go and tell him she would be okay by herself. She would increase her self-sufficiency.

When Margaret moved 3,000 miles from her lifetime friends, she had to let go long and deep enough to make new friends. We need to practice letting go and give ourselves the reward that comes from not holding on too tightly or inappropriately.

Psychologically, however, we rarely let go without having something else to reach for. As the trapeze artist keeps the next swing in sight before letting go of the old, it behooves us to have Plans B and C in place as we traverse the land of letting go. Traversing the land of letting go further refines our deepest and most important needs and gives us more understanding, as we take ourselves seriously, of what we want out of life. Listen to the Lady Ragnell story to help illustrate this wisdom.

● who are you and what do you need?

There is a legend out of the Arthurian times about Lady Ragnell. King Arthur is threatened by a neighboring king and is given a reprieve as long as he can answer the enemy king's riddle: "What do women want?" He is given a year to roam the lands and find the correct answer. Arthur returns to his castle and laments his situation with his knights, including his nephew Gawain. Gawain was by reputation the bravest in battle, wisest, most courteous, most compassionate, and most loyal to his king.

Gawain, along with Arthur and the other knights, heads out to solve the riddle. Many return with possible answers, only to be told they are not correct. Arthur, on his travels, meets a "grotesque" woman, who is almost as wide as she is high, with skin mottled green, open sores on her face, spikes of weedlike hair covering her head. She tells Arthur she is the enemy king's stepsister and knows the answer to the riddle.

King Arthur offers her gold and jewels, but she will have none of that. Her condition in return for the answer is a marriage proposal from Sir Gawain. A marriage proposal that Gawain is to freely give.

Arthur is incensed and remiss to even discuss this with his nephew. Gawain, however, when hearing the conditions readily agrees and disregards Arthur's distress. "The Lady Ragnell is the king's stepsister? Yes, I think she would know the right answer. How fortunate that I will be able to save your life." Gawain finds Lady Ragnell, and on the condition she offer the riddle's answer, regally proposes to her and sets the wedding date.

King Arthur rides off to face his enemy with several answers to the riddle. After trying several and hearing they are wrong, he offers Lady Ragnell's. "What a woman desires above all else is the power of sovereignty—the right to exercise her own will." The enemy king is furious but abides by his promised word and spares Arthur's life.

Sir Gawain and Lady Ragnell are to be married. There is stupefaction throughout the land, but Gawain remains steadfast and loyal. The couple goes through the nuptials and partying after. Finally the time has come for the newlyweds to begin their intimate lives together. "You have kept your promise well and faithfully," Lady Ragnell observes. "You have shown neither revulsion nor pity. Come now, we are wedded! I am waiting to be kissed."

Gawain goes to her and kisses her. When he steps back there stands a slender young woman with gray eyes and a serene, smiling face.

Ragnell tells him that her stepbrother always hated her and had knowledge of sorcery. He had cast a spell on her that could only be broken if the greatest knight in Britain would willingly choose her for his wife. She adds that she can be this shape at night and her former grotesque shape at day, or he can have her be grotesque in their private chambers and her own shape out in the world for others to see. Lady Ragnell cautions Gawain to choose carefully and wisely.

"It is a choice I cannot make, my dear Ragnell. It concerns you. Whatever you choose to be—fair by day or fair by night—I will willingly abide by it."

With that Lady Ragnell beams a smile and tells Gawain that his answer has broken the evil spell completely. The last condition has been met. "If, after marriage to the greatest knight in Britain, my husband freely gives me the power of choice, the power to exercise my own free will, the wicked enchantment will be broken forever."

● power of choice

Lady Ragnell was held captive by an evil spell that disallowed her from doing for herself—not so very different from women of today who are subtly or overtly bound to the collective scapegoating of doing for others and sacrificing themselves. In her imprisoned self she was grotesque (as defined in the dictionary: "odd or unnatural in shape, appearance, and manner"), not attractive or appealing. When she was released to her original self (normal shape, appearance, and manner), she reclaimed freedom and the responsibility of choice, independent thinking, and conscientious action.

Ask yourself:

▶ How seriously do I take the freedom to exercise free will?
▶ What choices do I make?
▶ How well do I know myself and what I need?
▶ How willing am I to stand up for my choices?
▶ What does *sovereignty* mean to me—in real life and not the abstract?

I told this story of Lady Ragnell to Samantha, a young client with a great deal of talent and ambition. She wept when it ended. It hit her so pointedly and visibly that it brought tears to my eyes as well.

When Samantha first came to see me she had taken the courageous step of going into business for herself, doing freelance work and choosing only jobs she wanted to do. She is rich in confidence about her abilities to create and sustain her career. She has a strong mind and is equally comfortable in the creative and practical realm. She instinctively knew when to raise her rates, did so without much ado, and manages her money well enough to save each month for retirement. Her field is the creative arts, and when a well-known firm called her to hire her for a project, she did not blink an eye at the prospect of working with the famous in her field.

But when it comes to relationships Samantha's experience is very different. "I met this guy and things seem pretty good between us. He's really cool and much more accomplished than anyone I have dated before. I don't think he is someone I will be with forever but I sure like being with him for now." As time went by Samantha talked more and more about this man's story. In a subtle but definite way, the time we spent together became about him. This was not a new thing for Samantha.

When she first came to see me she had been in a steady relationship for more than eighteen months. Most of the time we spent together she talked about this steady boyfriend and what made him tick. The stories, the examples, and all the analysis were "related" to Samantha and her personal concerns or her feelings, but, she was pretty much wrapped up in *his* woes, challenges, and needs.

After she broke up with the first boyfriend, she vowed to herself that she would concentrate on her story and her own needs. One day she arrived and told me that there was something she wanted to talk about that meant the world to her, but she was too embarrassed to talk about it because it might seem petty. She had been to the movie theatre with a good friend, and upon leaving the darkened theatre she realized she had left behind her umbrella. "Now, before I would have not even mentioned it. I would have told myself it was no big deal; I could and would buy another. This time, I realized I left it, told my friend I would be right back, and went in search of it. I know this is such a little thing but I cannot tell you how good it felt inside to do this."

I did not think this was a small thing at all. Samantha had allowed herself to value herself long enough to retrieve a lost item, and in symbolic fashion integrate taking care of herself into her Self. Who she is and what she needs was important enough to ask for the extra time.

As more time went by, Samantha found herself standing up for her needs in many more circumstances, all with the same quiet inner glow of satisfaction and congruency. "For the first time in my life I have the same relationship with myself that I have with everyone in my life. I don't feel that I am pretending to be someone else depending on who I am with." Retrieving lost items was showing up in Samantha's inner and outer life. She was reclaiming parts of herself long subdued into the unconscious.

Into this scene, and on the rebound from the breakup with her boyfriend, arrived the new man in Samantha's life. In the very beginning she continued her integritous behavior. She would come into my office with a radiance borne out of quiet self-assurance in every area of her life. On the day I told the Lady Ragnell story, she had come in and sunk a bit deeper into the softly upholstered sofa.

"I feel pretty good overall, but I have the beginnings of feeling heavy. Stewart and I are getting along well; we did have a small tiff, but I told him how strongly I felt about something and we worked it out."

"Is that when you began to feel heavy?" I asked her. She replied:

> Actually, no. Stewart and I had a good weekend after that, and then he went out of town for business. When he got to his hotel room he left me a message saying he had a wonderful time with me these last few days, and he gave me his cell phone number to check in with him. The next day I called him back and left him a message.

> That was three days ago and I have not heard from him since.
>
> I have been feeling so strong, so centered in who I am and what makes me tick; I can't believe this matters so much to me, but it does. I have lost immeasurable ground since he hasn't called!

Looking deeper into this dichotomy, Samantha discovered, when he did not call her, the *feeling* that she had no recourse. As any child waiting, sometimes patiently and sometimes without patience, for her father to notice her and having no say if or when that would happen; as an old-fashioned woman depending on her mate or family for news from the outside world; Samantha felt relegated to the waiting game with Stewart. She saw, felt, believed, and assumed no choice in this matter, and that drove her crazy. And thank goodness it did.

It takes courage to transcend fear and habit stemming from the collective unconscious of being oppressed and dependent. Our long history of being subjugated is akin to Lady Ragnell's evil spell. Her stepbrother hated her and rendered her helpless to help herself. While it is not explicitly mentioned in the tale, I wonder if he didn't hate her for being strong, opinionated, and willing to speak out loud. The spell-breaker is sovereignty—the choice to want what you want. The voice, the fortitude, the responsibility, the courage to say it like it is and stand for what you want, need, and believe in.

Samantha's bent to wait for or on Stewart is unnatural, grotesque. It leaves her unhappy and painfully reminds her of her early years when she attempted to turn herself into a pretzel to get her father to notice her and keep her mother from overwhelming her with her mother's own need for closeness. As Samantha allows herself to feel the pain of trying to be something she is not, her genuine need to be loved and to love comes to the surface.

And now, as an adult, looking for love in the wrong places, Samantha can face the early demons of not being correctly met. James Hollis in *The Swamplands of the Soul* indicates that looking for love in all the wrong places has its roots in childhood, where we were "summoned to confront the very thing that was too large for the child to bear or assimilate." He further reassures us that the "adult is capable of bearing the unbearable. To wit: 'I am alone, really alone. No one is really there for me.' 'I can be hurt, powerfully hurt.' 'They will not take care of me, or meet my needs.'"

Samantha is discovering that she can bear the unbearable as she allows herself to contain the strong emotions left over from childhood instead of being ruled by these obsolete feelings, and she looks with new eyes to find ways to assert her needs in the intimacy of present-day relationships. As she discovered in the delicious moments before giving herself away to Stewart, forming her own identity was natural (instead of grotesque) and brought her deeper satisfaction, contentment, and relaxation. Discovering, in a deep way, that she is lovable paves the way for her to find ways to fill this need in a constructive and healthy fashion.

Shortly after these discoveries, she broke up with Stewart and allowed herself to "hang out with herself" over a prolonged period of time. She faced being uncomfortable and at times very lonely, but found she could bear it. When Michael entered her life she was feeling strong. And then, their time together brought Samantha to even deeper levels of insecurity: interestingly enough, because it appeared that Michael was the person she had been waiting for all along. Even though she felt more comfortable with him than she had felt with anyone else, and even though they could laugh easily and spend lots and lots of easy time together, she was unsettled: "He does not seem attentive enough, which, needless to say, worries me greatly. I came back from an important work week and he did not even ask me how it went. I spend most of our time together asking him about his days and how he feels about things." She had many such examples (they run out of things to say when having dinner together), all the while running up the reasons why he is not the person for her. "When I tell my friends about why I am not totally happy with Michael they want to know why I am not breaking it off. Why I am 'wasting time' with him."

As Samantha took her needs seriously and found the courage to say something to Michael, she was delighted and surprised with each new talk they had. Michael was very receptive to her concerns and showed how much she mattered to him by changing his behavior and paying closer attention to what she needed. And each time they talked, they forged a deeper and more intimate connection.

This would bring up more insecurity in Samantha, which she would bring to our meetings together. She knew she was dealing with a backlog of not being taken seriously and did not want to sabotage this fledgling and positive relationship. Over time, with much work on her part and tremendous receptivity on Michael's, Samantha developed a healthy and deeply satisfying relationship, one where her needs were as important as her partner's. She fell more and more in love with him, all the while holding onto her own sense of who she was. Within this context, she discovered she could know what she needed, she could find the courage to forge new territory by telling Michael what she needed, and gradually she formed a new and sustaining pattern of taking herself seriously.

Samantha's story is not unique. Collectively, we as women have forged an unnatural shape from years of dependence and oppression. We, in order to cultivate a deeper and deeper well-being of resilience, are *required* to ask ourselves what we need. Ask the questions:

- ▶ How will I sing the praises of Lady Ragnell and exercise my freedom of choice?
- ▶ Who am I, and what voice and choices do I need to exercise?
- ▶ What is my natural shape, and how will I fulfill my destiny?

The face of shame has made us grotesque and unnatural. It is grotesque to fall and not take the time to make sure we are okay. It is grotesque to have the natural urge to pee and not take it seriously! To be resilient we are called back to our natural shape; to be resilient we can no longer cooperate with the age-old role of the scapegoat and exile ourselves to the invisible.

As resilient women we are called into the sun; we are called to discover our natural shape by being true to our natures and needs. The stronger we are in fulfilling our genuine needs the more visible and accountable we will become; and the more natural we are, as with anything deeply rooted, the easier it is to bend and bounce—or bounce back.

exercise

HONOR YOUR NEEDS

Every day for one week, commit yourself to be open to knowing what needs you have been unaware of.

Set aside 15-20 minutes. Ideally, sit with a trusted friend or family member. If no one is available, sit quietly with paper and pencil.

Have your friend ask you, "What do you need?"

As you speak of needs, have your friend write down all you say. When you have reached the end of the free association of needs, your friend will once again ask you, "What do you need?" Continue in this vein for the 15-20 minutes. Have your friend read your list to you.

If you do this exercise on your own, ask yourself, "What do I need?" and write down what comes to you. Ask yourself the question over and over until the full time has elapsed, and then read back the list.

Starting with the easier of the needs, begin to meet it. In your own rhythm, find ways to get each of your newly acknowledged needs met. You might find it helpful to keep a journal of the process of discovery and action.

look ma, i am dancing on my toes 5

It is a joy to be hidden but a disaster not to be found.
—David Winnicot, psychoanalyst

how do you make a difference?
How do you distinguish yourself?

Well-known people have that one figured out, their faces and names standing out because of their talents and gifts. When Barbra Streisand's voice sings across the airways, we instantly recognize her natural gifts and finely honed skills. When we think of Mother Teresa opening her heart to the least fortunate, and see pictures of her standing over a frail woman who's dying, holding the woman's hand and smiling down at her, we know she was a woman who knew how to offer herself. But for many of us it is not as obvious, and, because knowing our worth and being accomplished at something are so important to our ability to be resilient, it behooves us to take time to recognize what we are good at, what talents we would like to generate, and what gifts we can access.

What fools us is that we often take our talents for granted. They come so easily, or we're so good at them, that we don't recognize them for what they are. How many times have you heard a woman friend say something like, "Oh, that (for example, growing prize tomatoes). That is not a talent. I do that *without thinking!*"

Talents like: gardening, gourmet cooking, writing poetry, loving cats, meeting people on the bus, creating occasions out of fiascos, jumping naked in the ocean, putting colors and designs together, building furniture, adding numbers in your head, doing craft and hand work, making order out of chaos, capturing nature or a person's soul on canvas, sculpting a gracious movement, climbing mountains, recognizing plants and flowers, nursing someone sick, knowing how to jitterbug, writing letters, humming while working, knowing the names of the planets and constellations, pulling needles out of haystacks, finding nutrition in the wilderness, singing in tune, making people laugh, sewing clothing with or without patterns, seeing patterns in nature and life, scuba diving, tree climbing, riding a wild horse, mastering a craft, trade, or business.

And gifts: having a sense of humor, being up for an adventure, saying what you think when it is really important, liking windy days, making someone smile, putting a friend before friendship, knowing how to groan and forget it, having loads of stories in your head and liking to tell them, being comfortable with who you are and what you have to contribute, being friends with your family, knowing how to disturb the peace for good cause, renewing yourself, being a good kisser, relishing the feel of a child's hand in your own, appreciating how you are different, following current events, having good taste, knowing how to walk into a room, creating conversation, being a leader in society, being comfortable with mistakes, knowing how and when to follow, trusting your intuition, valuing competency and excellence, retaining a beginner's mind and continuing to learn new things, fostering your integrity, interiority and vitality, knowing how to argue and analyze, taking other people into consideration.

Talents and gifts hold several benefits for traversing adversity and being resilient. First of all, to know you are good at something, to be centered in an accomplishment, creates a sense of well-being and esteem. When life throws us a curve ball or a disaster, it is easy enough to be thrown off center and wonder at our abilities and possibly even our worth. We might know enough to not take a hurricane personally, but the breakup of a relationship or even the diagnosis of a severe illness can and often does send some of us into self-doubt and possibly self-pity. Let me illustrate this point with two stories:

Monique is a multifaceted and multi-talented woman, but she is unaware of her own abilities and qualities. She is athletic, dynamite at refurbishing antiques, and a sumptuous cook with a clean eye for setting a table to enhance her meals. She takes these talents for granted, not claiming her expertise and not enhancing them with concentrated practice. She did, though, throughout the years, invest her full sense of herself into her family.

When her son and daughter left home and her husband had an affair, not only did Monique's life fall apart, so did the image she held of herself. She wondered if she were not beautiful enough, thin enough, talented enough, smart enough, young enough, and on and on. She not only blamed herself for her husband's affair, she spiraled downward into a deep pit of feeling unworthy and without value.

For years after her husband returned and they reestablished their relationship, Monique continued to hold herself in poor image and found it nearly impossible to get on with her life. Not having other personal resources at her beck and call, she was virtually held hostage to believing that the hardships in her life resulted from being innately flawed. This also kept her from being able to face how she might have contributed to her troubled relationship and rebuild a new level of intimacy.

Genuinely appreciating herself and her gifts and talents could enable Monique to have more bounce and fortitude. With greater esteem she could have more energy to find the other resources she needs to patch up her relationship with renewed vigor, honesty, and determination.

On another side of the fence is Kelley. Kelley learned to be generous from her father. Her dad was a simple man who had a natural talent for giving. He loved his family and the customers in his store knew his charity firsthand; if a mother did not have sufficient cash for the week's groceries, he found a way to help her maintain her dignity and give her necessary supplies. He had a knack for quietly seeing a need and helping someone out, and the best part, according to Kelley, is that he did not sacrifice himself in the act of giving. He was generous to himself as well.

Kelley knows she is also generous. She likes that in herself, and because it is an accepted and cultivated part of her, she does not have to think about it very much. She allows the natural flow and finds ways to give and be available to others, and allows herself to reap the self-fulfillment she feels as a result. She knows the people around her respect this aspect in her, and this affords her increased self-confidence.

She is also very aware of her immense capacity for organization, getting things started when and where needed, and her contribution to any project she is passionate about undertaking. When Kelley's husband Martin had an affair with a younger woman, and when the music store she had birthed and nurtured had to close permanently because of skyrocketing rent increases, and when her uncle (her favorite person on the planet) died, Kelley's world shook in its orbit. With this happening all at the same time, it was more loss than she could withstand.

Kelley was shocked and devastated; she loved Martin with all her heart and wanted to be married "until death did us part." The music store had been a treasure for her and the community, and she knew she would never be the same again without the comfort, love, and companionship of her uncle. Kelley herself, though, remained intact, rooting herself in her deeply held knowledge that she was valuable. She cried, grieved, and raged, but the absorbing losses and ends of her dreams did not rob her of selfhood. In fact, believing in herself allowed her to look at the ways she had turned a blind eye to the problems in her relationship with Martin. Martin was the obvious "problem" in the equation, but why hadn't she seen this coming, and was there any way she had contributed to the demise of what she held so dear?

Staying grounded in her own self-worth, knowing she was valuable and talented, Kelley did not succumb to self-destruction and looked for ways she could be more aware of her surroundings, especially things she might not want to see. She began to notice her propensity to believe only good things about people and how blind she was to her own and other people's darker thoughts and feelings. In this light she was able to discern how she had inadvertently ignored her husband's unhappiness and restlessness, even though he had been giving her signals for a long time.

Kelley, devastated, did not need to lose all her bearings when her world fell apart. Not losing sight of her innate worthiness, she surveyed her destroyed world and could pick up the pieces in a constructive and forward motion. She could confront Martin on his "stupidity" in dealing with the problems they faced. She could keep her uncle's counsel close to her heart, and begin to look for other ventures or projects that would suit her and offer her the satisfaction she likes to feel when she invests her time and money. Her sense of herself gave her the solid ground to rebuild her relationship with Martin with integrity and maturity. She and her husband could both face themselves and consciously choose how they wanted to relate and how they desired to move forward.

• creative outlets

A second benefit of talents and gifts to riding the waves of hard times is that they give us creative outlets to relieve tension and hold us while we go through the pain and difficulties. We offer ourselves, unself-consciously, in the gardening we so love; we find solace in poetry, in cooking, in looking for an undiscovered constellation.

Kelley and her husband agreed to a separation, a very painful decision for both of them. Kelley relates how turning to her music brought her certain equanimity:

> There are always certain songs that will express how I am feeling. When my husband and I broke up there was a song I played over and over again. I cried and cried, even as I plucked the strings of my guitar. It helped me that I could take the pain and do something with it. That is why music is so great. It does that for me. I played and played the painful song and without consciously realizing it, the music moved into a song that was upbeat.

It can be helpful to develop skills and abilities at times other than crisis, so when something painful happens (like the loss of a loved one) the skill can act as a salve and buffer. The ease with which Kelley turned to her music was due in part to the fact that she didn't have to think about strumming the strings or remembering the words of the song. Instead, her talent gave her the time and grace to be carried along, her body and spirit moved by the vibrations of the music. She was held within a skill that had already become second nature.

Psychologist Kate Hays, Ph.D., of the Performing Edge in Toronto, looks specifically at aerobic exercises (running, biking, swimming, skating, walking, and yoga) for evidence of the significant gains we can derive from immersing ourselves in a skill. The action of exercise, along with the absence of interpersonal competition and repetitive activities that do not require much attention, allow "the opportunity to tune out and tune in. Exercise offers antidepressant effects, a sense of mastery and a potent tool for stress management." Not only can we lose ourselves in running or swimming (or any talent and gift that is without competition and is repeated), but if we have also recently experienced a trauma or major disappointment of sorts, these activities will give us the added benefit of holding stress and depression at bay.

When we practice at our skill, we also get a sense of mastery, which can be a powerful antidote to feeling badly about oneself. Most talents and gifts, especially when practiced to the point of mastery, speak to creativity: the ability to see old things new; to make something into something else; to express ourselves in different forms; to bring disparate ideas, concepts, articles, and materials into a new unifying whole.

Cultivating our creativity, through gifts and talents, allows us an original way of dealing with adversity and creative outlets to traverse difficult paths. It opens us to more and more possibilities. Rather than feel stuck, trapped, or held hostage to victimization, being creative shines a light on other ways of seeing and dealing with situations and circumstances.

Carmen had devoted her life to the practice of original thinking. When a young man, waving a gun, walked into her garage and threatened to harm her if she didn't give him all her money, she turned to him deliberately and said, "Don't I know your mother?" He was so rattled by this unexpected response to his aggression that he ran out of the garage empty-handed. Her creativity obviously helped her out of a tight spot.

● "that? that's easy! anyone could do it"

Recently I led a presentation on resilience to a room full of men and women mental health workers. The conversation swam along as people shared their personal difficulties and their reasons for being interested in learning more about resilience. When the topic moved into vulnerabilities, everyone looked at their shoes and the floor for several minutes until one brave soul began talking about a personal failing. As soon as he opened the gate, the others began to think deeply about their own vulnerabilities, and pretty soon all the participants nodded in agreement with each other as they shared their personal sensitivities.

Halfway through the evening I asked them about their talents and strengths. What did they have to contribute to their worlds—what were they really good at, and what difference did it make that they showed up to this presentation? There was dead silence. I made note of the unusual reticence (different from the rest of the evening's discussion), and they nervously laughed.

One woman mentioned that she brings different things to different places. She would bring one thing to this group and something else to her family holiday gatherings. She did not mention what these gifts might be. Another woman spoke of a colleague who she admires for her straight talking. She spent considerable time describing this colleague's talent. This woman, however, said nothing about herself. Again I asked, "What are your particular strengths?" The discussion veered into another direction.

I'm used to it by now. I lead groups with the expressed purpose of cultivating resilience. By the time we reach this step of the process, the group has been together for a long enough time to know each other and see each other's weaknesses and strengths. But I almost always have to do specific exercises to grease the wheels of recognizing personal talents and gifts.

I will ask each person in the group to go around and describe the talents and gifts he or she sees in every other person in the group. Every person has an opportunity to offer their perception to the other participants and to hear from each person in the room what talents, gifts, and strengths they see in him or her.

When I do women's groups the reticence is even more pronounced. In large part, women in this culture are not used to singing their own praises. We are more accustomed to boosting others, and, coming from a long history of second-class citizenship, often lack the feelings of deservability required to be straightforward about our own gifts and talents. But there is something else operating here, and that is the issue of personal responsibility. It is a statement of accountability to stand tall and declare oneself good at something, strong in an area and capable enough to be taken seriously.

Instead, a great deal of projection goes on. We are accustomed to hearing about projections of dark, ugly, and undesirable traits. But there is also projection of positive traits, seeing the other person as good at something, strong and capable, when we will not recognize the traits in ourselves. We are called to end idealizing someone else for their talents and gifts. Why not withdraw the projection and take responsibility for it yourself?

The way of individuation, becoming whole, can be through acknowledging and making use of our talents and gifts. We can become and express our full selves through art or cooking, in the midst of technology or politics, being a businesswoman or grandmother. We can foster greater resilience by accepting our abilities, using them to aid our strength. The more confidence we acquire from authentic gifts and talents, the less likely we will be to go down for the count.

My friend Ellen is an accomplished woman. She is a respected accountant for a nonprofit philanthropic organization. She has lived on her own for close to twenty years, ever since her marriage ended in divorce. She is loved by her friends and is the first person there whenever something is out of whack or someone is in need. Her generosity is legendary, and she can be counted on for a smile and an encouraging word. But it has never occurred to her to stop and notice when she has accomplished something unusual or particularly well done.

For many, many years the organization she worked for had been behind on its recordkeeping for accounts receivable because of an outdated in-house accounting system. By working overtime for many months, Ellen managed to get all the books in order for the first time in the history of the organization. But when she finished she simply inserted the final number and closed the last page of the last book, then moved on to the next project. Her coworkers and boss might even have noticed this feat, but Ellen's deft movement onto the next project left no room for any exclamations.

A few days later Ellen had a dream that she was leisurely and comfortably walking in the forest when a very large moose walked up to her and deliberately whacked his butt into hers. She, more surprised than anything, straightened herself out and walked around and away from the moose. He looked her straight in the eye as if he was attempting to get her attention, and once again walked over to her and, harder this time, whacked her butt with his. By now Ellen was getting exasperated and looked at him levelly and said, "Okay. What exactly is it you want?"

The moose continued to look directly into her eyes until she appeared to understand. She reached out to the moose, whereupon he became very small; she gently placed him into a small treasure box and placed him inside her heart.

After waking from the dream, Ellen did some thinking and realized that the moose probably symbolized self-esteem and feeling good about one's accomplishments and deeds. She felt a bit breathless to realize that she was seeing a pattern of her own behavior. She was so accustomed to ignoring what she did well (and not ignoring what she did not do well) and not allowing herself to reap the satisfaction of being good at something.

She knew she did not feel that good about herself in some situations, and she knew that she looked to the outside world for confirmation and validation. What she did not know was that she'd been robbing herself of the mature awareness of a job well done, a talent well honed, and a gift taken seriously enough that it could give her a sense of who she was, distinct from anyone else. Recognizing this for herself gave her a stronger base, a stronger sense of herself, and greater resilience for the next stumbling block.

Talents aid resilient behavior by:

▶ Sustaining our self-esteem
▶ Supporting us through the hard times
▶ Fostering our creative abilities in dealing with the harder times of life

Denise came to me wanting to leave her husband, who was many years older than she. They had met when Denise was a freshman in college. She had not had any other dating experience, was painfully shy, and had lived most of her childhood and adolescence alone, preferring not to be noticed. The thought of separating filled her with guilt, self-doubt, and fear. But she was not happy in the marriage and was no longer willing to put her uneasiness on hold.

Denise was one of three children; her parents were "nice enough" people who, to Denise's eye, had dozens and dozens of unfulfilled dreams. They had never seemed happy with each other, and Denise had heard often how unhappy her father was with his job. Because he had always had a deep pride in being loyal and principled, he had "chosen" a safe career in order to properly care for his family and had never pursued his lifelong dream of becoming a landscape architect. Although he never acknowledged his sacrifice out loud, to Denise it was as palpable as the well-worn carpet in the entryway. And now it was too late for discussion: by the time Denise arrived in my office, her father had passed away, taking all his untried dreams and ambitions with him.

Denise did not experience outward affection between her parents and was left with the vivid impression that their marriage was equally sacrificial for her dad. Her mother was attentive to the children, provided them with good nutrition and proper clothing, and participated in all their activities. She went through all the right motions and seemed to get some satisfaction out of her days, but appeared to nurse some deep, abiding unhappiness that was never acknowledged or discussed.

Denise remembered a few incidents with her father that left a lasting ache. She enjoyed playing soccer and was good at it. It was one of the only activities that she "went out for." At one of her games, after missing a goal, her father yelled at her in front of her teammates. He then stormed off the field, leaving Denise to run after him to the car, desperately trying to hide the tears running down her cheeks. This public humiliation and rejection, in the one area that Denise felt interested enough in to come out of her shell, pushed Denise further into the background.

Marvin was the first man to pay attention to Denise and see past her self-imposed shell. He was in his thirties, working in a retail store near her college when they met, and they had been married for fourteen years when Denise came to see me looking for the courage to leave Marvin. In the previous fourteen years Denise had discovered her facility with computers and had parlayed her father-taught belief in hard work and loyalty to a lucrative position in a Bay Area technology firm. Because of her job, she and Marvin had been able to buy a house and maintain a comfortable lifestyle, and had "settled" into a reasonable day-to-day living.

Denise was well aware that she was going through the motions of living, just like her parents. Her heart was not in it. She felt she had missed out terribly in her early years, and with great difficulty she admitted that she did not love Marvin. He had been convenient in that he had showed up and paid attention to her, but she was not attracted to him, and even more, felt he was pulling her away from herself.

Denise had long ago begun to resent Marvin. He was excessively possessive, wanting to know where she was at all times and jealous of any time she spent with friends or coworkers or doing solo outdoor activities. Marvin did not make as much money as Denise did but had grown very accustomed to their lifestyle and generally spent more money than Denise did.

By the time she came in for therapy, she was caught between her deep sense of loyalty and her increasing unhappiness that was beginning to show up in a depression. Most of all she wanted to be free, free to live her life with the resources she had accumulated. Free to go out with friends, take vacations, go back to hiking, date for the first time in her life, make her job and career more creative, and not feel weighed down by Marvin's dependence and her lack of love for him.

Denise, using therapy to dig down deep within, discovered enough courage and conviction to tell Marvin she wanted a divorce. The following months were very painful and full of conflict, especially because Denise could not find an articulate way of telling Marvin why she wanted to end their marriage. She did not want to hurt his feelings and tell him she was not attracted to him, and she could not convince herself that being unhappy was sufficient cause in itself. She vacillated between believing there was some way of working things out between them and knowing she had been forestalling her leave-taking for many, many years.

Denise did manage to leave Marvin, but the fallout was excruciating for her. Her sense of herself had fallen apart, and much of her early childhood feelings of inadequacy rose to the surface with explosive force. Instead of feeling and being free, Denise became immobile. She would have spurts of activity, but for the most part resumed her old patterns of hiding out. If someone at work suggested going out for dinner she would go; but short of outside invitations she went to work, went home, watched TV, and went to bed.

Her weekends loomed depressively long. She spent many of them staring at the four walls and others frenetically involved in chores and activities, then falling into bed at night exhausted and terribly sad. She would concentrate on what she had walked away from and wonder if she had made a big mistake and should have settled for her lot.

As we noted in chapter 1, the process of becoming resilient often first involves a descent into the thicket of trouble, the loss or tragedy being the catalyst to healing and growth. But there are times when a person is not ready for a powerful dive for a treasured pearl, and instead the psyche repeats the insults and injustices of the adversity. Like a guinea pig running around and around its rotating wheel, the person gets stuck in agony and emotions.

That is what Denise was experiencing. She was not at a point in her life or development to travel deep within herself and was virtually caught in a never-changing cycle—physically gone from her marriage but emotionally stuck in believing she was inadequate and not enough of a person to attempt to catch the gold ring of social and romantic relationships. She still needed to build a stronger ego, a stronger sense of who she is.

In the midst of this anguish, arriving like a knight on a white horse, came karate. Denise had long flirted with the idea of learning karate and finally allowed herself to check it out. She found an instructor and class close to home that suited her to a tee (or should I say black belt?). The beginning classes stretched her to the point of exhaustion, and she came into my office with a glow to her skin. She adored being worked that hard and loved the physical results. She felt in better shape than she had felt in many, many years and was impressed and "pumped" that she could now do 150 pushups.

For the first time in a long time she was willing to learn something new and not ride herself for making mistakes or not learning fast enough. (Remember her father's disappointment on the soccer field?) She found herself getting stronger and stronger and discovered a new ease with reaching her limits and knowing she would have to try again later.

Being naturally athletic enabled her to adapt well and feel a level of confidence toward mastery. The instructor had a great sense of humor and humility, neither of which interfered with his apparent mastery of the mentality and physicality of karate. Denise admired him, felt safe to learn from him, and was inspired by him to work harder and understand both the mechanics and philosophy of karate.

What began to happen to and for Denise was a visible increase in her esteem and self-confidence. She began to view herself as a strong person, something she had wanted since childhood. She is a slight woman, and part of her living in the shadows of life came from her feelings of vulnerability due to her size and demeanor. The mastering of karate increasingly gave her a different experience and view of herself, one that was outwardly corroborated by her interchanges with fellow students and the instructor.

Denise would have been happy and satisfied with these esteem-building results of karate. The involvement and practice pulled her out of her doldrums, energized her, and naturally pushed her to talk with other people. Denise began to show signs of resilience; her periods of depression were grief-related instead of low esteem and anger based. She began to plan for the future by rearranging her job responsibilities to put her closer to where she had always wanted to live, and she was able to find more creative paths for her extra time. She was more emotionally available when friends or coworkers suggested a long hike or climb. She literally had more bounce to her step and her life, which she attributed to the taking on of the demanding practice of karate.

But karate gave her even more than that, with its martial arts philosophy of redirecting and letting go. Marvin was not in a field that paid him much money, and Denise vacillated between being angry at Marvin for the suggestion that she should pay him some alimony and feeling horribly guilty for leaving him when he was not going to be able to afford the lifestyle to which he had become accustomed. Worse still, she was worried he would go bankrupt.

Each week she would come in feeling angry or guilty—either way tied to Marvin. Marvin would call and ask for more money, and Denise would react to him either guiltily or angrily. It is difficult, if not downright impossible, to find flexibility and resilience when you are that tied, unhealthily, to someone else. The energy she needed to bounce back was all knotted up in worrying or resentment.

Through the martial art-based philosophy of absorbing the energy or standing out of the way, Denise began to entertain the possibility that she could learn to redirect her energy and issues with Marvin. She could begin to learn how to detach from Marvin's demands, discuss the laws and financial realities fully with her attorney, and learn how not to react to Marvin. She could literally *feel* how it worked. Having the physical experience and confidence in one area then encouraged her to use her new skills in other areas as well. With the growth of these skills grew her capacity for resilience.

● allowing adversity to forge talent

Adversity is like a strong wind. I don't mean just that it holds us back
from places we might otherwise go. It also tears away from us all
but the things that cannot be torn, so that afterward we see ourselves
as we really are, and not merely as we might like to be.
—ARTHUR GOLDEN

Immersing yourself in an activity like guitar playing, singing, sculpting, karate, or any other that brings the experience of being in the moment and aware of nothing but yourself and the activity allows you to forget yourself—and that can be the greatest feeling of all, akin to the feeling of love. The love of making the best sandwich in the world, the love of meditating on the colors of the sky. When you allow yourself—no, require yourself—to grow your talents, interests, gifts, and contributions, you are indicating your value and being serious about your place in the scheme of things.

By loving yourself and what you are doing, you are then able to radiate that energy out into the world. It is easy to see the value and contribution of a Barbra Streisand or a Mother Teresa. But we all bring something marvelous to this human experiment.

Listen to the dancer Martha Graham (from *Dance to the Piper*):

> There is a vitality, a life force, an energy, a quickening that is translated through you into action. And because there is only one you in all time, this expression is unique. And if you block it, it will never exist through any other medium . . . the world will not have it. It is not your business to determine how good it is, nor how valuable, nor how it compares with other expressions. It is your business to keep it yours clearly and directly, to keep the channel open.

In order to keep our internal house in order and ready for any chaotic winds whipping through, it is important to nurture and cultivate familiar and new talents and gifts. But what Graham is pointing to is a responsibility we have to ourselves and to the world.

What does it mean to truly embrace and act from the realization that you are a unique life force and the world is dependent on you expressing this vitality?

In Native American cosmology every single human being is born with a certain medicine that is needed for the world. It is up to each of us to discover what medicine we bring to the community and offer it for the good of all.

What medicine do you bring to your world?

Sacred Jewish texts invoke the belief that each of us is born with a God-given purpose to our lives.

Why are you here at this time?

Buckminster Fuller—inventor, architect, engineer, mathematician, poet, and cosmologist—is most well known for his invention of the geodesic dome, the lightest, strongest, and most cost-effective structure ever devised. He was a practical philosopher who, at age thirty-two, stopped speaking for two years when he realized he had not had an original thought of his own. He concluded that he would stay quiet long enough to discover his own and true feelings.

He felt a strong need and commitment to discovering what he needed to learn and why he was here. He believed that all humans are a private hotline to God, and we are called to be who we are and contribute what *only we* can. "It is easy to imitate and hard to be original. Nothing is easier than saying what everyone else says. True talent is the moment you feel you are no else but yourself."

What is your true talent?

The ancient Greeks believed that each of us was born attached to a *daemon* (unnamed spirit, felt and sensed as a definite presence) who determined, wholly or in part, our destiny. This can be understood as an image of our soul, the essence of who we are and what we are here for. The idea of a personal daemon determined many great world thinkers' ideas on life and meaning.

Carl Jung, Plato, Socrates, and Plotinus each offered musings on this spirit guide, expressing their personal experiences with a daimonic guide as conscience and transcended. Plotinus maintained that the individual daemon was "not an anthropomorphic daemon, but an inner psychological principle." According to both Jung and Plotinus, daemons are objective phenomena that manifest both inwardly through dreams, inspirations, thoughts, and fantasies as well as outwardly through visions and apparitions. The muse that inspires us, the walk in nature that reminds us, the passion we feel for what we are doing, or the strong intuition that keeps us safe. We might face our daemon in dreams, through an inner voice or a simple presence that is undeniable. When we know we are on the right path, when we know we are on the wrong path, a daemon is at work.

Plato's acorn theory (based on each of us having a daemon) posits that each of us chose our place in this universe before we were born. We chose our families, needing certain experiences and lessons, in order to incarnate our daemon, our personal genius or reason for being. In order to be who we are in the world and weave our thread into the cloth of humanity, we choose our struggles, our learning, and our strengths ahead of time.

This idea turns psychology's theory of pathology on its ear. Rather than look to our childhood to find the causes of our insecurities, neurosis, and lacking, we can look to our childhoods to find the preparations for our life's work.

Carly, a talented healer, was an unwanted child. Over lunch she told me:

> I was forever formed by being unwanted. I carry a deep feeling of being an outsider and the profound taste of disappointment that comes from being betrayed by my mother and father. It took me thirty years to heal the first twenty years of my life. And yet, being a wounded healer not only allows me to feel sincere compassion for myself and my fellow warriors, but I am made aware of my uncanny ability to adapt and thrive in most circumstances and learn how to be more resilient *because of* the cellular awareness of being an outsider and *knowing* disappointment and betrayal. By being an outsider I am freer from the trappings of escalating obligations and expectations that come from being beholden to society's successes. I am free to hear people's stories without a preconceived agenda in one part because I am free to be myself.

What is your daemon?

Knowing who you are and your rightful place in this world enables you to see the bad and the ugly as part of your life. The terrible is an obstacle and needn't be a permanent detour.

Recognizing your own special gifts and talents simply allows you to enhance your sense of self and well-being, which then gives you a wider platform to work from when life hands you difficult turns.

Your gifts and talents can also be a window into the self-exploration of your larger place in the scheme of things. The art of resilience works in favor of strengthening who you are, discovering and polishing your original and very personal pearl.

Who are you and what is your pearl of great price?

exercises

1. SHUFFLE INTO CREATIVITY

You can help cultivate your creativity by writing all the aspects of any problem or situation on a piece of paper. Cut up the paper so each piece includes only one aspect of the problem. (Or use index cards.) Randomly shuffle all the cut-up pieces and pick out two or three to form a new whole. Meditate on this new formation and see what ideas generate from this.

When you feel finished with this formation, shuffle and form another new whole. Continuing in this vein will give you lots of new ideas and ways of seeing one problem or situation.

2. LOOK MA, I'M DANCING ON MY TOES

Take a sheet of paper and a few minutes to make a list of talents and gifts that nurture and nourish you.

Once you have made your list, calculate the amount of time you spend each week involved with these activities.

Now ask yourself another question: What talents and gifts would you like to develop? Which ones are realistic and what do you need to do to bring this joy into your life?

3. LET THE SUN SHINE

For one week write down every compliment you receive. Notice if, when, where, and how you resist taking in a compliment—and if you are not receiving compliments, consider your circle of friends and family (see chapter 2).

For one week write down every compliment you give. Which, if any, of the compliments you give might be a projection of some unrecognized or unappreciated talent or gift of yours?

that's close enough 6

The subject of priorities is at the center of our spiritual pratice.
—RABBI DAVID A. COOPER

as I SIT DOWN to write this chapter I am expecting out-of-town guests who will stay for a week. I would prefer they did not come at this time; when we planned it I wasn't as busy. But I cannot find it within me to say no to them.

What *is* so hard about saying no?

Why do we do this? What is so very hard about saying no, or not getting embroiled in solving everyone else's problems? Life is full of surprises and requests. We live in a time of rapid and accelerating change that impacts us daily—in the ever-present uncertainty of world events, in our work, our physical and emotional health, and the quality of our relationships. We are called upon frequently to be available, to juggle schedules, to answer bosses, partners, children, family, and friends. The world has shrunk, and we are called to at least be aware of current events, the economy, and the impact of this global world on our personal lives. Many of us find ourselves trying to keep up and saying yes to it all. To be resilient in the middle of these changes, we need even deeper resources. And yet, for many women especially, the inability to say no renders us overextended, overcommitted, and depleted. It leaves us without the currency needed to navigate hard times, quality relationships, and the continual change of our time. We must learn how and when to accurately and effectively say no:

- ▶ No to too much work, too little appreciation
- ▶ No to what isn't working
- ▶ No to doing too much for someone else
- ▶ No to living within someone else's rhythm or pace
- ▶ No to abuse and mistreatment
- ▶ No to relationships and jobs that are not healthy
- ▶ No to what is in the way of knowing ourselves deeply and knowing what our lives mean

And we need to figure out to what we are saying yes!

Sound easy or simple? Nothing could be farther from the truth. To begin with, most women are conditioned to be caretakers and consider connection to be fundamental to our lives. This is often a very good thing, enabling us to make the necessary sacrifice of self-interest that raises healthy children, reaches out to family and friends in need, and has something left over for the community at large. How then do we discern when it is a good thing and when it is too much of a sacrifice?

When it comes to speaking up assertively, many women are reluctant to possibly hurt someone else's feelings. This works well when our best friend asks us if she looks fat. But many of us have taken this reluctance (or politeness) to ridiculous extremes. I think of Susan, who, when asked by her hairdresser if the cape she had just tied on was too tight, lied and said no. It *was* too tight, but she did not want to hurt the hairdresser's feelings!

Women tell me that saying no makes them worry that they will disappoint or upset the other person. They speak of fearing that they will end up alone, at a level that feels as if they would not then survive. These feelings and worries are deep; sometimes they are based in reality and sometimes not.

There is also a way that women, collectively, have been psychologically conditioned not to be assertive. When psychologists study individuals who have been mistreated, oppressed, and/or abused, they find that they have lost the ability, awareness, or practice of speaking up for themselves. Most commonly, they have become timid and cowed. Not only have they not had the opportunity to develop this natural skill, but many, even more sadly, have lost the belief that they have the right to assert themselves. Instead they believe there is something wrong with them and, in some aberrant fashion, they "deserve" to be punished or mistreated.

This is also true of groups of people who have been "kept down." Women, having spent generations assumed to be inferior and having experienced years of abuse and oppression, are having to actively, and sometimes painfully, pursue their rightful voices. It is like the elephant that, for years, has been chained to a post so that he can only walk in circles. Once the chain is removed the elephant still walks only in circles—conditioned to that being the only option.

However, to adapt, survive, and thrive, we must put our availability, our caretaking, and our politeness into perspective and remind ourselves that *we have the right to determine* when and how we are available. To be ready for the moments of life that require our resilience, we must overcome our years of conditioning and assert the "no's" of conviction and influence. It is important to exercise the habit of "Not now," "Sorry, cannot help this time," "Stop, you are hurting/bothering me," "I cannot help you," and "I am about my own business now."

It's all well and fine to want to be generous and kind, but the amount of energy we have is limited and needs to be used in balance; we must be sure to leave ourselves enough for that rainy day that calls us to be flexible and resilient for *our own* good. It is up to each of us to learn, through trial and error, how to balance our availability and to make sure we take our selves, our time, our work, and our tasks earnestly. It is important to take our time and energy critically so as not to deplete ourselves, and it is important to value what *we* do enough to limit distractions, set appropriate boundaries, and carve out time and attention *for ourselves.*

● are these women's stories familiar?

Mary Catherine Bateson, writer and cultural anthropologist, writes in her book *Composing a Life:*

> For at least twenty years, whenever I interrupted my husband when he was busy, he finished what he was doing before he responded. When he interrupted me, I would drop what I was doing to respond to him, automatically giving his concerns priority. As time passed, I learned occasionally to say please let me finish here first, but usually this has made me so uncomfortable that my concentration [was] lost. By now, Barkev has learned that both of us need to be on guard against my willingness to sacrifice my time and my space, as if my goals were automatically less important than those of other members of the family.

Theresa came to see me when her husband had an affair and they wanted to save their marriage. Through several years of hard, painful, and constructive work they had recommitted to each other and had had a third child. Both of their lives were busy and overcrowded with responsibilities. When her husband came home he preferred to "take five" and replenish. Theresa's workday did not have a natural cutoff time. The work of caring for three children, preparing meals, and doing laundry and other household chores was more like painting the Golden Gate Bridge: as soon as it is finished the painters begin again at the other end. This was a bone of contention for Theresa, and she fought with her husband for help. He would tune her out and get lost in his hobbies. The sadder truth here, though, is Theresa's deeper feeling that her time and job was not as worthy as her husband's, her lack of true conviction that he should help her.

In fact, on one typically busy day she received a call from her husband, asking her to drive into the city to bring him something he'd forgotten at home. Not something related to his job, mind you, but a hobby project that he had hoped to show to an expert over lunch. Theresa did not think twice about getting in the car and delivering this item to her husband. It did not matter to her that she had three kids in the car and dozens of errands to finish. Or that she was meeting a friend for a play date with all the children. "Oh well, we can always get together another day."

What about telling her husband she was not able to bring him his hobby?

Marie Louise Von Franz, analyst and respected elder of the Jungian community before her death, calls forth a familiar tune when she wrote about her knee-jerk reaction to saying yes when she wanted to say no:

> In general, life is so complicated that if one has to think about things one is always too late. I am hopeless in that respect. If someone telephones me and says they must see me that evening, or they need an hour tomorrow, I am not quick enough in deciding whether to say Yes or No, or to find an excuse by saying I am not free. My nature sweeps me away, my inferior function; I say yes and afterwards am caught in it, it is all wrong. And then I say: "Confound it all, I was too slow again!". . .Then comes a bad dream which gives me a good blow on the head and I wonder if I will ever get out of that stage and be quick enough to not always get caught in the same trap.

Her unconscious helps her out her by giving her a blow on the head as a reminder. Many of us, not used to saying and meaning no end up ill and shriveled.

And now I will admit a story of my own. I was walking through the Presidio (a breathtakingly beautiful former military base in San Francisco) on an early morning. As I walked past the tennis courts a man, holding a tennis racket and a can of balls, asked me if I had the time. "It is 10:15," I said. He muttered, "Oh, maybe my team is not showing up. I am so disappointed. I have been waiting all week to get outside and have a good game." My immediate and instinctive response was to ask him if he would like me to play with him. I felt strongly inclined to help him out.

Even though this man was a complete stranger and I don't even know how to play the game, my strong impulse was to rescue, to help this man out of his quandary, to find a ready solution for him, to be available to give him a helping hand. How utterly ridiculous! But such is our conditioning as women.

● what makes it so hard?

People often ask me whether women or men are the more naturally resilient. Most people believe that women are, that we're tougher, more inclined to come back up after a long fall, more accustomed to pain (this said in reference to childbirth), more able to withstand emotional pain, anguish, and being alone. Does that really hold up to scrutiny?

A friend of mine went on a rigorous trek in Bhutan that turned very bad when the guides got in over their heads and left the camp unaccompanied. My friend observed how much more quickly the men took ill and became physically weak than the women. In her study of girls, Harvard psychologist Carol Gilligan came to the conclusion that boys are more emotionally fragile because they are forced out of their mother's arms at a much too early age.

Both of these may be true, but the road toward flourishing and making usable lemonade out of lemons is not an easy one for women. Despite obvious gains in visibility and esteem, the world we live in continues to relay the message that girls are inferior to boys. In Taiwan, daughters are referred to as "water spilled on the ground." In Uganda, they are "prostitutes" to be exchanged for cattle at the time of marriage; in China they are "maggots in the rice"; among the Zulus of South Africa they are "only weed." A common Arabic insult is to call someone the "father of a daughter." A Korean phrase states, "A girl lets you down twice, once at birth and second time when she marries." In Colombia only male members inherit land, and most girls are not expected to study beyond primary school.

In a Chicago-based clinical study, researcher Bernice Lott found a striking percentage of middle-class mothers favored boys over girls. Parents in Britain spend considerably more money to celebrate the birth of a son than to celebrate the birth of a daughter, according to British scholar Sue Lees. The birth of a prince earns a twenty-one-gun salute, a princess only ten. The devaluing of girls is not random; it is systematic, and it is inherited from generation to generation.

Added to this is the alarming statistics of girls incested, raped, molested, and otherwise oppressed into second-class citizenship. Eve Ensler, in her *Vagina Monologues*, tells of going to Bosnia to help women. She had read that 70,000 women had been raped as a result of the civil war. She came back to this country incensed that we weren't doing anything about it. "Do you know why we are not doing anything about it in this country?" asked her friend. "There are 700,000 women raped a year in the United States and we are not at war."

A friend of mine recently returned from Israel and met a small group of Orthodox women who are reporting awful truths. According to these underground women, there is a high incidence of sexual abuse and incest in many Orthodox families, but no one speaks about it. It is being kept a big secret because, if it were known, these families would not find husbands for the abused girls. "No one would want a spoiled woman."

Harriet Lerner is a therapist and author whose voice has reached women all over the country in the hope of moving us past a history of oppression. She writes:

> We have to challenge the tyranny of the biblical Eve depicted as a temptress with a profane and unclean body, held responsible by mankind for original sin for thousands of years. This myth has reinforced the stand that women should always have second-class citizenship because they were created after Adam from his rib. In all prohibitions placed on women, Eve is used as a validation.

Is there any question why we believe we are here to please, why we think we have to prove ourselves worthy, and why it is difficult for many women to say no and assert themselves?

● psyche speaks up

Since our reticence can be this deep, it helps to look to mythology for the compensatory response. In the story of Psyche and Eros, Psyche is married to Eros but must live by constraining rules of not ever seeing her husband or knowing who he is. When Psyche is talked into disobeying and learns she is living with a god, Eros flees. The rest, and bulk of the story, shows Psyche having to go through difficult obstacles so she may become whole in her own right. The challenges presented to her increase in difficulty as she ascends the journey, her intuition helping her all along the way.

Her last task is to go to the underworld to find and bring back Aphrodite's beauty cream. She is given what she needs to get past the three-headed dogs guarding the cave in the underworld, but she is given a much more arduous task before even arriving at the cave. She is told she will meet a very frail old lady who is carrying a terribly heavy burden of kindling and logs on her back. The woman will ask for Psyche's help, but she is to refuse and say to the woman, "I am about my own business." She is told that, as she crosses the river to get to the cave, she will see a drowning man who will implore her to save him. She is to refuse and say, "Sorry, I am about my business."

"Sorry, I am about my business." Can you even imagine? I suppose very few modern women are called upon for anything that dramatic, but I posit that for many of us speaking up or saying no to someone genuinely in need when it conflicts with "our own business" feels just like that. It can take courage to develop proper and healthy boundaries:

- ▶ The courage to know how and when to say no, the courage to stand for yourself, the courage to stand alone
- ▶ The courage to face the upset, anger, disapproval, or disappointment of another
- ▶ The courage to end a friendship when the friend is unrelentingly self-absorbed
- ▶ The courage to know who you cannot be vulnerable with
- ▶ The courage to not have holidays with family members who are hurtful and judgmental
- ▶ The courage to tell an authority figure you disagree

First of all, because women are not that familiar with the behaviors called for in saying no, there can be a clumsiness involved that can exacerbate misunderstandings. How do we say we are "about our own business"? Do we ignore the request from the other person? Do we blame them for asking? Do we pander and apologize profusely, bringing attention and embarrassment to our discomfort? Do we overexplain why we are "forced" to be about our own business? And on and on. It might never be comfortable to refuse another's request in favor of setting healthy and necessary boundaries, but it can be accomplished in a courteous and constructive fashion. It is possible to take the other person into account as we gently but firmly say, "Sorry, in this instance I cannot help you out." If the matter includes mistreatment or abuse, saying no not only sets up proper boundaries for the mistreated party but also does not allow the perpetrator to "get away with it." It is possible to leave the other person *and* ourselves whole and dignified by the end of the transaction. By saying no to another person or situation, we allow someone else to step in, we allow something creative to fill a hole, we allow recognition that we are not the center of the universe or the only one who can help, and we allow both parties to possibly experience the vulnerability of disappointment, a part of life that's here to stay.

Second of all, we need to ask what we are saying "yes" to when we say "no." While it can take immense courage to rock the boat, knowing why and for what we are doing it can be the difference between a constructive and a destructive encounter. Psyche's first order of business all through her ordeal was to do what she needed to do to enable her to be reunited with Love, in the form of Eros. The result of Psyche's courage and willingness to stay about her business was becoming whole. She discovered parts of herself that were previously unfulfilled. She had been living unconsciously, willing to be completely taken care of without any contribution or awareness on her part, including awareness of her husband's true nature. By going through the tasks and by doing things that stretched her to her limits and many tears, she became equal to Eros and was then able to partner with him as a developed and full person in her own right.

Although the myth does not say, I can imagine Psyche being willing to set hard limits because she was about nothing short of transformation. She said yes to waking up from her sleepwalk existence. She said yes to knowing who she was and what she wanted—consciously, not because others were telling her what she should have. Not that any of her journey was easy or smooth. She cried through most of her ordeals and acted more on faith than on confidence. Nonetheless she persevered.

Do you know to what you are saying yes?

Let me introduce Pamela. When Pamela came to see me, her rage was palpable and her depression and anxiety were debilitating. It didn't take long to notice how creative and imaginative she was, although she mostly used her vivid, colorful imagination to detail all the horrible images that haunted her and spelled disaster. In other words, her imagination fed her anxiety.

Pamela had been in and out of therapy for most of her life, beginning in childhood. Both of her parents were eccentric in their own way—in quite opposite ways, as a matter of fact—and they divorced when Pamela was seven. Pamela adored her father; he could do no wrong. By contrast, Pamela detested living with her mother. She considered her mother loud, obnoxious, and hell-bent for personal destruction. It was the 1960s, and Pamela's mother was determined to find herself and her freedom. She dated, experimented with drugs, and stridently took up the cause of women's liberation.

Her father, on the other hand, was properly civilized, and his tightly held schedule (breakfast at 6 A.M. with the newspaper and dinner promptly at 7 P.M.—workday or weekend, rain or shine) gave Pamela a sense of security and devotion. She adored the fact that he wore a hat, freshly pressed suit, and spit-shined shoes every day of the week. He never embarrassed Pamela.

Pamela's anger toward her mother—about the divorce, toward herself, and about the hundreds of daily upsets—was all mixed together in one large mass and left her emotionally immobilized. Pamela told me weekly that she firmly believed her anger was caused by being neurotic; she considered herself so off kilter, she believed she was holding dearly to her sanity. From where I sat things looked different.

She was a first-rate physical therapist, and in her work with patients her imagination and creativity blossomed. She had several specialties and hundreds of success stories with hard-to-help conditions. The hospital was a place where she felt empowered, in charge, and passionate. This zest, though, stopped at the hospital door. In the rest of her life she lived with no voice; she had no strong opinions and was seriously timid in the face of daily encounters.

When our work began, most of her anger was directed toward her husband. She was resentful of everything he did and everything that represented the reality of marriage. He was receiving a great deal of the anger Pamela felt toward her mother. After some time the complaints she had about her husband came through with more clarity and validity. She had been attracted to him and his family for their contrast to her family, and now she was feeling overdosed on the difference.

Her family was emotionally distant, and her husband's family showered everyone with affection at each greeting and departure. She was convinced it was because she was neurotic that she felt intolerant of so much closeness. Pamela used our sessions to let her feelings out and to say things she would never have dreamt of saying elsewhere. "Isn't it possible you have a valid point here, Pamela?" I would ask with regularity. "Even ecstasy (in the form of affection) has its limit; anything that goes too far in extreme invites its balance," I would suggest.

Eventually matters between Pamela and her husband reached a serious low, and they agreed to go into marriage counseling. Although Pamela professed to wanting to end her marriage and go live by herself in a small town, answering to no one, much of this sentiment was coming from being bottled up and living with a build-up of unspoken ideas, beliefs, and disagreements.

As our work continued, Pamela found the strength to know her own mind and believe in herself; and as she used the laboratory of marriage counseling to speak her mind with her husband, I watched as her depression began to lift and she found herself having many good days in a row.

Then one day Pamela came into my office bluer than I had seen her in months. She was furious, and the anger was all knotted up in a ball. It took the bulk of our time together to unravel—there was so much bothering her. Her husband's family had always demanded more physical affection than she was comfortable with. She liked them and genuinely appreciated their kindness, attention, and devotion to their family, but she was keenly uncomfortable with the amount of physical touching. "This time, when my brother-in-law held my face in his hands and kissed me on the lips, I really didn't like it," Pamela said rather shyly.

She struggled with judging her discomfort, worrying that she was so "messed up" she couldn't maturely accept her brother-in-law's affection for her. As she experienced it, his affection was sincere and had no ill intent, however inappropriate for her. On the other hand, she was fully aware how uncomfortable this made her and how it could result in her avoiding him and beginning to dislike him. She wanted better boundaries but wasn't sure she was entitled to them.

We discussed what she would like to do about this. I reminded her that she could be the captain of her own ship and had the right to say no when she was uncomfortable or wanted to decline something offered, no matter what it was or how innocently, or freely (or inappropriately!) it had been given.

What came out was that she wanted to tell her husband. She wanted him to hear her, understand how she felt, and be supportive. She was not sure how he would react; she would bring it up in therapy. She wasn't sure what she wanted to do about her brother-in-law, but she was clear what she hoped for from her husband.

When we met again the following week her mood was elevated. Her husband had been receptive and had even helped her problem-solve how to handle the situation. Pamela was relieved and a bit giddy at his support. For most of their marriage they had both agreed that it was his family that "worked well" and that her discomfort was her problem, her own terror of intimacy. She was finally open to the idea that her desire for a bit of balance was all right, and she was pleased that she had learned how to communicate this to her husband.

For his part, her husband was also willing to change the way he saw the situation with his folks, and was only too happy to help chart a course of boundary setting that would be more comfortable for his wife. What was so striking to me was how much lighter and happier she seemed once she had singled out the problem and dealt with it directly. Cause and effect is rarely linear; there are more often many causes to the effect. In Pamela's case, it appeared that at least one of the reasons for her depression was an inability to assert herself and an inability to know, trust, and use her authentic voice. She had begun to figure out her boundaries, her level of comfort, and was beginning to challenge herself to use her voice for her own good.

She did not like rocking the boat, and she was uncomfortable with conflict and confrontation, but she had become more uncomfortable having to live with the unspoken. She was deeply desirous of saying yes to more honesty between herself and her husband, saying yes to both liberating and respecting her feelings, and saying yes to perceiving herself having strength, conviction, and deserving to be heard. As a result she was willing to learn and practice how to use her voice. She was willing to look at what was affecting her mood and see if she needed to speak up, change changeable circumstances, and take responsibility for what she was feeling.

She continued speaking up for herself. In fact, sometimes it happened so naturally that she didn't even notice a change in her behavior or attitude. When she wanted something badly enough, she began to find ways to assert her desires and opinions and noticed how often people were willing to accept them or make changes accordingly. Of course, there were also times when she found a particular situation too daunting or difficult to "rock the boat," and she shied away from causing any dissension, and other times when she was not even aware that she was caving in until she felt the repercussions in her mood. And so it goes as we attempt to flex new muscles and define and redefine our strengths and weaknesses. And so it goes as we attempt to discover the art form of setting proper limits and boundaries that works for all involved.

● learning to set proper limits and boundaries

Where do we turn to relearn the natural inclination for proper lines in the sand? One day I was sitting at a peaceful pond, reflecting on the quietude, when a stray cat wandered by. The cat walked along the rocks and sand, hugging the edge of the water, but did not go into the pond, even though it was home to its preferred food: fish. Most cats are uncomfortable with water; they will not voluntarily enter a body of water. This line in the sand, drawn by some unseen creator of cats and ducks and fish, is purposeful when it comes to protecting the ducks and the fish from danger and ensuring their survival. We can look to nature to understand that limits have a purpose and there are boundaries that offer structure and assurance that the world is in its proper place. Nature is full of examples that show that boundaries, personal protection in the way of limit setting, is appropriate and necessary.

We can also learn from each other. One of my favorite role models is Maya Angelou, poet and woman extraordinaire. I have learned much from her through the years—reading her books, standing inside her poetry, and gaining courage from her personal life story. Ms. Angelou has written about her own traumatic rape as a child, so she speaks with great authority when she counsels other women to begin to learn to stand up for themselves. Her style is feisty. Her courage is of the no-nonsense version: Don't even think of messing with me. She tells other women to speak up immediately. If you wait, says she, the oppressor, the critic, the not-on-your-side person will peck at you like a duck. They will bite off a piece of your ear—not enough for you to even notice. Then they will turn to your hand and peck off a piece of skin—then they will blow on the bite to soften the hurt and peck again. Blow-bite-blow. Until we've been pecked to death. As Angelou says, if a person pulls out one patch of your hair and you do not say anything, the next thing you know you will be bald.

In a conversation with Oprah on the Oprah Winfrey Show, Maya Angelou declared, "The first time a man tells me I look fat in the dress, he is gone. We must develop the courage to do this for ourselves and do the other a favor by stopping them in their track." We must stop as soon as we feel it, hear it, or sense that we are in danger. We must deal with this dynamic with forthright directness and say, "Stop it—not me—stop it."

> The greatest accomplishment is / say it isn't so. They say you are
> weak / say it isn't so. They say you are . . . / say it isn't so

One of the reasons many women do not speak up for themselves or do not easily come to the same strength and tone of Maya Angelou is that they have swallowed the blame for the transgressions laid at their feet.

● it is not your fault

I heard a story about Jacqueline. Jacqueline grew up with a very disturbed mother. Her mother would hit and beat her and call her names. Because her mother was living in her own world of horrors, she would lash out at Jacqueline with horrible sexual assaults, calling her names and screaming sexually graphic expletives and behaviors. One day, when Jacqueline was eight she and her mother were on a bus in a busy urban downtown. As her mother "went off" on her, screaming obscenities and calling Jacqueline vile names, Jacqueline hid her face in her chest, holding her breath and waiting for the tirade to end. A woman seated nearby managed to place a piece of paper in Jacqueline's tightly held fist. Jacqueline held her hand closed until, a few hours later, she was alone.

"It is not your fault," the note read.

Jacqueline kept that note for the rest of her life. She hid it carefully in her treasure box, and whenever she was alone and afraid she took it out for comfort and solace.

It is not your fault.

It is not your fault.

The erroneous belief that "the grown-up is hurting me, therefore I must be a bad girl" lingers in adulthood as low self-esteem and lack of confidence about one's own opinions, ideas, and competencies. Adults do it, too. We wrongly indict ourselves for being gay, black, fat, poor, or a woman, having internalized the phobias of our society and harbored the belief that "they" are right and we are intrinsically wrong. Resilience requires that we learn what to take responsibility for and what is not our fault.

Maya Angelou counsels immediate response: "Speak up immediately!" This implies not letting the displeasures, the crossing of the lines build up until you are ready to explode. In order to be in a position to know in the moment that you are being wrongly treated, to recognize in the moment that the other person is out of line, can require inner healing of early traumas or violations. Healing of the wound that takes all blame, swallows all transgressions, and assumes center of the universe, including the problem. Finding the voice that was quieted, shut out, shut down, and listening to the sound of muffled screams and cries, giving light to the instinct that was stamped upon, and making room for the anguish of loosened moans and outrage.

Jacqueline held onto her note from the stranger who bore witness to her humiliation and offered another view. Until Jacqueline was ready to discover a fuller understanding of her experience and until she could speak on her own behalf, she held tightly to another's voice. Until she found her own voice, until she could learn to use her voice, she nourished herself on the generosity of a stranger.

Losing your voice obliges you to find your voice. Finding your voice obliges you to use your voice.

● inner boundaries

Boundaries—the line drawn between one thing and another; that which indicates or fixes a limit; the often abstract space where one person, like Pamela, begins and the other, her brother-in-law, ends. This is the line that helps us understand what needs to be said, when it needs to be spoken and what can be let go. But there is an inner boundary we are responsible for as well. The line between feeling something and acting it out. The line between your own unknown feelings and thoughts and projection—what is mine and what is yours? The line between assumption and checking things out. The line between blame and personal responsibility and the line between the hurt from the past and the reality of the present.

Vicky walked shyly up to me at the end of a workshop I was facilitating. "Are you taking any new clients?"

As we spoke, Vicky disclosed that when she was three and her sister was two, their mother went into the garage and shot herself. This is a loss beyond words, beyond comprehension, and beyond imagination. Three is an age too young to absorb or even have a semblance of understanding of such a loss. For Vicky the violence of this experience left her with a deep, long-lasting rip in her connection to life itself.

When she and I began working together, this contradictory timid and vivacious eighteen-year-old woman, with devil-may-care orange streaks in her hair, lived at an edge of not-wanting-to-be-here all too often. She came into therapy because her boyfriend had recently broken off their two-year relationship, and Vicky was devastated to a level that easily resembled the loss of one's mother, through violent means, at age three. We worked together for the four years it took for her to find a modicum of recovery.

For four years, she hissed, screamed, and shouted her rage of loss, deeply believing she would never again find another "right" person for her. Her tirades often left her spent and having to clean up after herself, in that other people didn't want to be around her and disagreements with bosses and managers left her chronically worried about her job or place in the company store. She was prone to accidents and wracked up several body injuries during the four-year upset with life. In the quiet privacy of our work together, Vicky was not happy with herself or her behavior, but the depth of her abandonment often rendered her hostage to her emotional outbursts and waves of rage and terror.

Then Timmy entered her life, quite unexpectantly. Vicky entered and lived in this relationship differently than any other. She went slowly, where in the past she would have dived headlong into the throes of passion and lost herself. She kept communication open, and was willing to share herself, especially her doubts and fears, and felt overjoyed when Timmy reciprocated.

In retrospect, there were some signs of trouble all along, but none that were all that predictable, so Vicky opened her heart and was well into being in love when Timmy indicated that he really could not sustain a healthy connection and needed to end things. The "Dear Joan" letter was delivered in person with considerable sensitivity, but nonetheless . . .

After Timmy left, I think we both held our breath as we waited for the proverbial shit to hit the fan. We both knew, with every fiber in our beings that, as with every other leave-taking, she could fall big, fall hard, and be lost for a long time. Vicky consciously chose to do things differently this time. She knew only too well the deep abyss waiting for her. She said, *"No, not this time."*

Vicky is a talented artist. She knows how to bring deep emotions and vivid images alive on canvas. She has had several paintings accepted for viewing in prestigious galleries and had, many times in her young life, gained the hard-earned respect of colleagues and the public. She was recognized for a willingness to tell the raw truth, as only someone who knew such rawness could. But, for the past four years she had been unable and unwilling to create or offer herself to a project. When she met Timmy she got involved in some of his projects but remained inattentive to her own voice and expression.

At this significant crossroad in her life and her psychological and spiritual development, Vicky lifted herself up and turned her attention to her art form. She began to envision images, stories, and angles of light as she prepared to discipline herself to creating a painting in time for a gallery opening. She would throw herself into the project and allow it to hold her through the breakup.

She could imagine coming out of this experience with a new piece of art and a different way of dealing with the hated dragon of rejection that she couldn't help but experience as abandonment. The very act of working on the painting, of spending hours immersed in the ideas and the creation could be a container for her pain, anger, and the familiar feelings of being unworthy for love. With the project containing her in this way, she could learn to ride the waves of emotions instead of drowning in them. She will forever know the exacting nature that her early loss left her with; she cannot be free from the hole in her heart, but she can be free to discover ways of connecting to her life and continue contributing the riches only she can contribute.

I once heard that Carl Jung believed the only appropriate prayer was, "Enough!" He believed that the unconscious is unaware and uninterested in time and space and will, like the Energizer Bunny, keep on giving. It is up to the strength of the conscious awareness of each of us to draw the line in the sand when needed. We all live with inner tensions, conflicts, and stored-up memories. It is up to us to learn to modulate the boundary and know ourselves well enough to say *"Enough!"* when we are facing the possibility of hurting ourselves or hurting someone else. It is up to us to discover the same effective line for safety and survival as the cat and fish have with the natural boundary of the water's edge.

Vicky will most likely not stop feeling terror or rage, especially when she experiences being left or hurt or mistreated. It is unrealistic to imagine that the tension she lives with will be eliminated; it is part of the human condition to be conflicted and sometimes ambivalent. But to increase her resilience and repertoire of ways of dealing with her relationships and demons, she can continue building a stronger and more firm center of being by practicing the art of "enough," not repressing the strong feelings but finding constructive ways of channeling the forceful energy. She can practice the art of choosing her feelings instead of being held hostage by them.

● choosing feelings and perception

I read and hear dozens of heroic stories each year, the stories of men and women who stretch our imaginations and make us wonder at their ability to face life and adversity with a mighty hand. Viktor Frankl, Nelson Mandela, and the Dalai Lama offer us examples not only of staying their course during horrific measures but aligning their way to match and overcome the tragedies bestowed upon them. Through their profound demonstration we see that their critics and torturers would not have the final word or their souls.

"I am not one of those who left the land to the mercy of its enemies," writes Russian poet Anna Akhmatova, who lived in Leningrad during the Yezhov terror and bore witness as Stalin rode destruction and evil over her beloved countrymen.

> No foreign sky protected me,
> No stranger's wing shielded my face.
> I stand as witness to the common lot,
> Survivor of that time, that place.

Anna would join hundred of others waiting in line outside the prison in Leningrad, waiting for any word of family members. Might they catch a glimpse of their loved one, offer a morsel of food, hear any word of their plight? She, a well-known and loved poet, was recognized by a woman in line, shivering in the cold, whispering through blue lips. "Can you describe this?" the woman asked. "I can," Akhmatova replied. "Then something like a smile passed fleetingly over what had once been her face."

As Akhmatova's reign of bearing witness came to an end in Russia, Etty Hillesum's began in Amsterdam. Etty Hillesum died at age twenty-nine. "I want to be sent to every one of the camps," she declared to her friends as they all watched their world crumble. Just before the war Etty had moved to a large home in South Amsterdam, among an interesting circle of academics and spiritualists. First and foremost, Etty was moved by an inner life—the war was secondary. A feisty, deep, and inquisitive woman, Etty watched as her friends and neighbors were carted off to prisons and concentration camps. In her educated and sophisticated circle there was no denial of the severity of the situation. The war and its consequences were very real; Etty experienced genuine fear and terrors, but she felt moved by something deeper, something that insisted she walk into the camps tall and dignified:

> I shall become the chronicler of our adventures. I shall forge them into a new language and store them inside me should I have no chance to write things down. I shall grow dull and come to life again, fall down and rise up again and one day I may perhaps discover a peaceful space round me which is mine alone and then I shall sit there for as long as it takes, even if it should be a year, until life begins to bubble up in me again and I find the words that bear witness where witness needs to be borne.

Two women choosing to bear witness where many would understandably turn their face or tremble in horror. Choosing not to give into fear, loneliness, disbelief, or hatred. Both women demonstrated quiet practicality and common sense in situations of dark, unimaginable forces, but stayed their course. Both women were questioned by others and were often misunderstood in their motivation. Etty writes:

> I shall always be able to stand on my own two feet even when they are planted on the hardest soil of the harshest reality. And my acceptance is not indifference or helplessness. I feel deep moral indignation at a regime that treats human beings in such a way. But events have become too overwhelming and too demonic to be stemmed with personal resentment and bitterness. These responses strike me as being utterly childish and unequal to the fateful course of events.

Two women gave their lives for a greater voice to be sounded. Two women quieted their personal grievances and used their cries to be heard around the world and throughout time.

- ▶ What do we learn from their example?
- ▶ How does their fortitude translate to our lives and our use of voice?
- ▶ How does their profound "no" to hatred and "yes" to bearing its witness for the world move us?
- ▶ What does their strong voice of personal responsibility inspire when each had reasonable justification for blaming their villains and looking for some means of rescue?

Each woman expanded her consciousness and her perception of the world to include things that should not happen. The evils of their day *were* happening. Each adjusted their expectations to include what to do when the unforgivable occurs. Neither woman was *silenced* by the circumstances, the atrocities, the wrongness, or the injustices even as these horrors ran under their feet and swallowed them whole. Both women found a way to scream and resist when there was no avenue for direct altering. Both women chose to feel the global and diminish the personal. Both women chose to perceive their place in hell as effective, meaningful, and dignified. Both women found the power and the urging of the soul to bear witness, to bear witness when all else failed.

We are obliged, especially in the name of resilience, to using our voice whenever and however we find it.

exercise

REFLECTION

Use a journal, artwork, and/or imagination to help you connect with your answers to the questions below (see the exercise in chapter 1 for more explanation).

Reflect upon a time (or times) you felt taken for granted, bullied, unappreciated, or unfairly judged:

▶ If you spoke up, how did you feel?
▶ If you did not speak up, how did you feel?

Design an ideal interchange coming out of those times you felt taken for granted, bullied, unappreciated, or unfairly judged:

▶ What might be in the way of achieving the ideal?
▶ What can you do, one action at a time, to become more constructively assertive?

poison or pearls 7

*To make peace with an enemy one must work with that enemy,
and that enemy becomes one's partner.*
—NELSON MANDELA TO GERRY ADAMS

LIFE IS DIFFICULT, and we hurt each other often and in all sorts of ways and degrees. And we hurt ourselves. In our sometimes clumsy, sometimes cruel, sometimes selfish ways, we step over each other, put each other down so we can feel better, beat each other, compete to the death with each other, oppress each other, violate and rape each other, murder someone we personally hate or feel threatened by, and create torture and murder on a global scale.

Given a basic human condition of aggressiveness, egocentric points of view, the inevitability of unmet needs over the course of our lives, and survival at all costs, is it any wonder that we harm each other and ourselves? Given the difficult lives most of us live, given the thousands of existential and day-to-day situations and circumstances to be afraid of, and anxious about, is it any wonder we push each other out of the way to find some security? Given our tendencies to fear what we don't understand and feel threatened by those who are different, is it any wonder that we discriminate and polarize?

This may sound like a very dark view of humanity, and I certainly don't mean to condone or "normalize" such behavior, but it is important that we understand the historical and global scope of the hurt and injury we heap on each other and give voice to a larger perspective. In the name of finding creative, nonharmful solutions to the effects of human cruelty, we must be sure not to take everything unduly personally and to broaden our understanding of this darkness and of forgiveness.

Of course, when we are aggrieved, it is and feels personal. Whether we were injured long ago in childhood, recently in adult relationships, or a combination of both, we are subject to an intense and strong inner cry of "It should not have happened." Whether we are the recipient of something terrible or the perpetrator of hurting someone we care for, we are faced with the reality of a harmful rupture that is ours, and ours alone, to deal with—to stitch back to some semblance of normalcy so that we can continue to live a life of relative well-being. That's where shadow work and forgiveness come in.

● transforming resentment: shadow work

No matter how much parents and grandparents may have sinned against
the child, the man who is really adult will accept these sins as his own condition
which has to be reckoned with. Only a fool is interested in other people's guilt,
since he cannot alter it. The wise man learns only from his own guilt.
He will ask himself: Who am I that all this should have happened to me?
To find the answer to this fateful question he will look into his own heart.
—C .G. JUNG

I am convinced that shadow work is one of the most important challenges of our individual lives, as well as for society. I am continually struck by the seemingly automatic response our citizens have to the horrific nature of violence in our society. "He seemed like such a nice person." The naïve idea that monsters will look and act differently than we do, rendering us surprised when the next "nice" guy commits a heinous crime. We live in a pretty psychologically sophisticated time, and yet we generally project our shadow on others on a regular basis. We project our darkness on ourselves as well, assuming we are the worst person alive, and move into a spiral that has nothing to do with the deeper pains and anguish.

We get into a fight with a coworker, loved one, or authority figure, and we are sure the other person is the enemy. Or perhaps *we* are the enemy and look to how to eradicate ourselves. Rather than face our own devils and saints, we assume we are in the right and the other person is suspicious. Rather than face our own fears, we assume the other person is evil. Rather than face that we all have inner lives and unconscious material, we take too many people and circumstances at face value, again showing great surprise when a seemingly mild-mannered person loses it and opens fire, takes his or her own life, strikes his wife, or batters her child. Or we are taken off guard when someone we trusted turns on us, as if we did not remember that feelings could change on a dime.

Rather than face our own darkness and motives we look to another country, culture, or people to scapegoat and blame. Collectively we appear to find a sense of relief when we can discover the "enemy" outside of ourselves and direct our hostilities toward a worthy evil opponent. I wonder often what our world would be like if each one of us committed ourselves to the inner shadow work, the work of looking for, admitting, and consciously integrating the darker aspects we all carry.

What is shadow? And what effect does it have for us in our day-in-and-day-out living? We all have a shadow. We all house darkness and evils. I have the honor of being with people as they lift their personal veils and explore their lives and inner worlds. Between the daily readings of the news of the world and this work, I continually believe I have heard all there is to hear about the evils of our world. And I am continually proven wrong. We hurt each other terribly and in awful ways. One of the reasons for this continual violating is our conditioning to deny our shadow. All through our lives we hear what is deemed acceptable to do, to think, to feel, and to say. This is how we are supposed to be, and this how we should not be.

We hear what is inappropriate, immoral, and never to be done. We need to find some steady ground to stand on, and we don't want to believe we are anything we do not respect or want to be. What has been unsavory to the image we hold of ourselves was sent packing into the darker alleys and corners of our unconscious. The particular tune is different in different families and for different individuals. For some, being emotional is acceptable, for others it is not. For some, being envious was part of the family's picture; for others, being angry was allowed. For many, having needs is akin to being greedy and merciless.

Some families pride themselves on cheating the government at tax time; other people rely on their upright morals to feel worthy. Some families require that everyone like each other; jealousy, conflicts, and negative feelings about the members of the family get swallowed and lost in the dark. Some families feel it is unseemly to think too highly of yourself, so confidence, pride, and desire for accomplishments become shameful. Some cultures see eye contact as a sign of trustworthiness; others believe behind-the-scenes deals are signs of intelligence. And, since the realm of the whole psyche contains all, whatever we are conscious of has its counterpart in the unconscious.

The person with abiding faith in the goodness of the universe will have doubt hidden far below. The person who insistently relies on the rational will undoubtedly house irrational beliefs and assumptions in the unconscious. All thinking and no feeling? Look under the rug and find a highly underdeveloped, but potent, feeling state.

The particulars differ, but the dark corners of the unconscious are common. What we don't like, what is threatening to our sense of who we are, what is unbearable in our view is tucked far away. It is tucked away, kept in a very dark place, but contrary to our desire, the shadow qualities are not necessarily quiescent, obedient, or invisible. And, *the shadow is negative only from the point of view of consciousness.*

MEETING THE SHADOW

The shadow is not to be taken lightly; the domain of the unconscious requires the same respectful approach as does traveling to outer space or underwater. By its very nature it is difficult to apprehend. Possibly for sanity's sake, we cannot look directly into its face or domain; it is forever in hiding and asks a lifetime commitment to its ongoing discovery. Inviting our shadow requires a humble attitude, a dedication, and a genuine willingness. It is not cute, funny, and perhaps not even benign. It exacts a price of shifting the perception we have of ourselves and making room for the unpleasant, the undesirable, the unpopular, and the ugly.

By the mere fact that we have denied our shadow aspects, the light of day renders it wild and worthy of a respectful attitude. If you kept an animal on a short leash for years and years, forgetting to feed it or pay attention to it in any meaningful way, it is likely you would have a ferocious animal on your hands. It is not hard to imagine the animal fiercely growling, tugging, and lunging to get free and biting the hand that feeds it. It would take gentle, consistent, and cautious daily feeding to regain the animal's trust and help it become civilized enough to let it off its leash and welcome it back into the family.

The same can be said for uncovering and integrating the shadow into our conscious life and attitude.

To begin with, our friends and family are likely to be familiar with our shadow qualities. Anyone coming into our home would certainly notice a wild animal tied up in some corner. Some people might directly mention what they see: "You seem a bit controlling." "Why are you so jealous (arrogant, regretful) when you are around X, Y, or Z?" Others might walk around your home, and you notice they are not comfortable when they go anywhere near that corner. They find ways of avoiding you or certain issues whenever relating to you. Others might find sport in directly engaging the beast, and before you know it you are in a sparring or confrontational match. To know more about your shadow, pay attention to how your close circle relates to you, watch how acquaintances and strangers interact with you, and look especially closely at how people who don't like you or who take exception to how you treat them relate to you.

The shadow resides in the unconscious, which reveals itself to us in many forms and ways. To meet our hidden selves, we need to turn our sights to the unconscious and show an interest and willingness in the revelations offered. Often, meeting the shadow calls for slowing our pace of life, listening to our body, and allowing ourselves to be alone or quiet long enough to digest the cryptic messages from the underworld.

Slowing down allows us to follow the subtle routes and see where they lead us. Slowing down offers us the time and space to take our dreams, projections, and associations seriously and unravel the symbols and meaning they are delivering. We can watch our dreams and learn the symbolic language to understand parts of us that are unknown. Many times we will experience a strong emotion with a dream, signaling how we feel about the situation or person or part of us that is showing up. Many times the dream shows strangers, unfamiliar territory, and scary, dangerous circumstances; fairly strong images to indicate unknown and possibly threatening material. One young woman I work with, during a particularly hard time attempting to feel what it was like for her when she was young and deeply invisible in her home, dreamt of a young child who hurt so badly, carrying all the pain in her stomach, that she could not be touched. The built-up pain tucked away in her unconscious revealed its enormity and its tenderness as well as its fear and distrustfulness. What child does not need and want to be held and comforted when they have a terrible stomachache? And yet this little girl had to guard herself against wanting to be taken care of, because being taken care of had never happened.

Projection (associating qualities to someone else that are not factually theirs or are more intense than warranted) is often thought of as negative. But the extent that we are willing to "take back" our projections is the extent to which projecting can be informative and valuable. Say you become livid each time a particular person enters your life. Is this strong reaction indicating unfinished business between you, an unmet need you are unaware of, a quality about you that you do not like or perhaps detest?

Another woman I work with, Valerie, became completely upset whenever her friend went after something the friend wanted. The friend often got what she wanted, and Valerie considered her friend selfish, which was unbearable for Valerie. Upon reflection, Valerie, who believed she was facing her own shadow of selfishness, came upon another reality. She did not know how to get what she wanted because she held a deep belief that to be assertive meant being selfish, and being selfish was on par with being mean or uncaring. She faced an irony of having to be "selfish" and finding ways to figure out what she wanted and allowing herself to get what she wanted. This required her to rethink the issue of selfishness.

Being selfish was negative from the point of view of her consciousness. On another level, in order to be more complete, whole, and integrated, Valerie needed to embrace this shadow aspect and find ways to be more assertive.

Her strong reactions to her friend were an indicator of what had been too long held outside of consciousness and not available for fuller functioning.

Or, as another woman I work with discovered, projection can tell us more about ourselves than the other person. Lydia had not seen her good friend for a couple of weeks. She was recalling their last conversation and beginning to believe that her friend was upset with her and was staying away because of hurt feelings, not too busy a schedule. Lydia called her friend to check out her worrisome feelings. Lydia's friend assured her that she did not have hurt feelings and was truly overly busy at this time and was having a hard time keeping up with her schedule.

Lydia felt an immense burden lift off her shoulder and, in further reflection, realized she was missing her friend quite a bit and that was the source of her discomfort. Not being aware of this vulnerability and not being comfortable with relying on someone else, she projected her unease onto her friend and assumed she was harboring hurt feelings.

Another time, while working with a woman who was out of touch with her feelings, I inquired how her partner might be feeling in this situation. The woman was quick to say what her partner might be feeling. When she checked it out and found her partner not feeling fearful, she correctly looked inside herself for the possibility of fear. Projections and dreams can be complex and might require talking over with someone else, but they can be valuable sources of detecting shadow material.

Even as we devote time and energy to our dreams and projections, it is good to keep in mind that we are up against a worthy partner that can be like quicksilver. We can be open, willing, and strong enough to face and embrace our shadow qualities as we move through life and the varying phases and developments confronting us, but the shadow recedes very quickly. No matter how strong and ready we perceive ourselves—it can be an unpleasant, shocking, and frightening thing to experience a shift in our self-image. We might so quickly move into denial that we fail to recognize the murderous fantasy, suicidal thought, or embarrassing envy that is revealing a part of our darkness. One day we might see with vivid clarity the truth of a trauma, the next day it will be as faded as last year's rose. The next thing we know we are being tripped and surprised by some unpleasant aspect of our personality and needing to look afresh. It is reasonable and smart to be cautious with the shadow; it is foolish and shortsighted to ignore it.

Anger and Rage
Frequently, especially for women, anger, murderous fantasy, and rage are shadow material and, from the point of view of our consciousness, an

unpleasant, nasty, and potentially destructive emotion. Not that we do not show signs of being angry, but how aware of our anger are we is the question. Not that we do not know we are angry, but how comfortable are we with the full force of rage, and what do we do about it?

What do you know about your anger? How do you typically express angry feelings?

- ▶ Do you hold onto it?
- ▶ Do you ignore your angry feelings and say it doesn't really matter nor have anything to do with you?
- ▶ Do you ignore daily angers and then fall victim to overpowering anger or rage?
- ▶ Do you use sweet words to punish or demean?
- ▶ Force your will on those dependent on you, gossip to a thrilled audience, and threaten with ending a relationship or affection?
- ▶ Do you go over and over the grievance, massaging it in your mind?
- ▶ Withhold praise or giving of credit where credit is due or perhaps take it out on someone other than the person who "faulted" you?
- ▶ Keep it unconscious and stay mad at the world?
- ▶ Project it onto other people, politics, causes, or injustices?

Learning to express anger without being a victim
is a key to your empowerment.

Often, because anger and rage are shadow material, either hidden from view or shameful to admit, their force is uncontrolled, unfocused, and can be randomly felt and directed. I will never forget the visceral experience of touching and feeling the rage I held toward somebody who had hurt me very badly. It was a force I did not know I was capable of, and I knew in that moment that I had the ability to destroy.

What if anger were not relegated to the dark alleys? What if instead of striving for politeness or even sainthood, you chose to discover where to allow right anger and when not. It is healthy, and in many instances necessary, to have deep reactions to disrespect, threat, and injury, so anger needs to be freed from its bondage; we need to benefit from learning to be angry in a mindful and integrated way:

▶ Becoming more familiar and comfortable with anger and rage offers the ability to harness its energy and use it when the deep reactions to disrespect, threat, and injury call it forward.

▶ Being at home with anger allows us to express being upset, angry, miffed, and furious in the moment in ways that are constructive and forward moving.

▶ Taking responsibility for being angry allows us to express it, knowing we are not motivated by power or desire to annihilate.

▶ Becoming more aware and accepting of angry feelings and how to use this energy wisely gives us the opportunity to integrate this energy into our conscious personalities, thereby knowing ourselves more fully and having a stronger sense of self.

When we know ourselves, when we are committed to a full picture of who we are, we also have the power of understanding others and having access to creative possibilities for redemption and reconciliation. People who have looked evil in the eye and chose to fight through constructive change in society have founded organizations to take on drunk drivers, child molesters, animal preservation, and prison reform. For four centuries of women's history, we have a collection of stories of women who lacked household goods, moral support, and role models but who took matters into their own hands, channeled their frustration to free the slaves, and pioneer the right to vote. And we have thousands who do not make history but daily change the course of life around them.

THE SEAT OF THE PEARL

One does not become enlightened by imagining figures of light,
but by making the darkness conscious. The latter procedure,
however, is disagreeable and therefore not popular.
—CARL JUNG

According to Jung, we are called to make the darkness conscious. The process of cultivating resilience is discovering the gem in the midst of the darkness and mining its value for your life. Oysters make a pearl in the dark. Pearls are the result of an irritant—an irritant housed and moistened in the dark. After a period of time, the shell opens to reveal that the irritant has become a pearl—a pearl of great price from a grain of sand irritating the membrane of the mollusk. The shadow, the dark, the discarded, the unknown, and undesired is the seat of the pearl.

What is not remembered cannot be reconciled. What is not available cannot be used, and what is not seen cannot be known. We would not attempt to plant our garden without the shovels, hoes, and fertilizer needed for a good harvest. We would not attempt to travel without adequate resources and skills needed according to our plans and goals; and yet we live our life without the full use of our history and personality. We keep ourselves under wrap, even given the fact that there are "positive" qualities in our underworld. For those who were not allowed to feel good, develop a sense of wellbeing, build confidence, talents, and gifts, *these* are relegated to the unconscious and no more available for everyday use than the qualities we more commonly think of as shadow material.

It is not only rabid jealousy, destructive rage, terrifying vulnerability, and boundless greed that are hidden from view; healthy responses to conflict, abilities to enter tough situations with dignity, self-respect in the face of mistakes are also out of reach if they have been sent packing into the unconscious. As Jungian analyst Liliane Frey-Rohn says, "The shadow retains contact with the lost depths of the soul, with life and vitality—the superior, the universally human, yes, even the creative can be sensed there."

Many have learned, through hard work, that all they had repressed held a tremendous amount of energy, with a great positive potential. As with the leashed animal discussed earlier, releasing memories and feelings showered them with the energy the animal had to give when reintegrated into the psyche. To forgive, to have a future, requires us to look into the eyes of the beast, befriend it, and harness its energy for creative, productive use. As one of my patients said, "I forgave my parents by becoming them. The archetypal powers in their psyche are in mine as well." And in all of ours.

She continued,

> It leads nowhere to rail against my mother and father ad infinitum; it does not help matters to project these powerful feelings against other men and women or against society for that matter. Instead I concentrated on remembering, remembering my past in deeper and deeper feeling states. It is a painful voyage that admittedly requires deeper and deeper courage, but one that I discovered has the potential for ending the cycle of hatred, violence and vengeance. It takes courage to stand in the vast sea and recall, with exquisite tenderness and full body present feeling, that I did experience something awful, something that felt evil, and something that should not happen to anyone.
>
> Through dreams and body memories I can now feel what it was like to be completely alone during and after the trauma because my parents did not have the fortitude, maturity or consciousness

to know how to handle the circumstances, themselves or me. I can now feel what it was like to have no support, no friends, family or teachers to turn to. I now know what it feels like to hold unimaginable horror all by myself. I can remember, I can feel, and I can integrate each layer into my present awareness.

It is a voyage towards genuine healing—and as I feel deeper and deeper and hold the reality as a truth not to be denied or tucked back under, I am rewarded with an incomparable knowing of the light and dark in humankind. I am rewarded with a discovery of a redeeming power in the human spirit—a redeeming power in my capacity to forgive, love and know compassion.

● forgiveness

Perhaps all the dragons in our lives are but princesses that are waiting to see us act just once with beauty and courage. Perhaps everything terrible is in its deepest essence, something helpless that needs our love.
—RILKE

Forgiveness is about letting go, *really* letting go of resentment and bitterness—both personal and global. Forgiveness requires strength of character, it requires courage, a courage that needs to be replenished daily and rekindled when it falters. Forgiveness requires a commitment to something other than revenge and the natural desire for retribution and/or an apology. It requires, since there are events and behaviors that are unforgivable, ultimate compassion.

To forgive someone or something implies that there has been a transgression. You have been violated, hurt, insulted, treated badly or inhumanely, or somehow suffered greatly by another's actions. Something very valuable has been taken away; there has been grievous harm. Sometimes the transgression is factual; someone has been murdered, tortured, raped, neglected, beaten, publicly humiliated, or oppressed. Sometimes the transgression is subjective; we get our feelings hurt in ways that would not necessarily hurt someone else's feelings. Someone forgot your name at a party, your child was overlooked for a scholarship, someone assaulted your leadership style, or your boss did not pick up your ideas. As author and Buddhist meditation teacher Sylvia Boorstein says, "We all have tucked away in our unconscious a little list of people who have hurt us in some way in our lives. And we keep the list even though they can no longer hurt us, as if forgiving them will give us amnesia, and we'll get hurt by them again."

When we have been hurt, we show a feverish intensity to the situation, we hold a magnifying glass on the person or people who hurt us, and we are exquisitely aware of the effect the injury has had on us. Whether objective or subjective, we are faced with similar feelings of being upset and resentful of being treated wrongly. Whether subjective or objective, whether it is a slight or a grievous transgression, when the hurt and insult has created a bur in our psyche we are faced with the heroic task of being responsible for the resulting psychic pain.

Hatred, resentment, and a desire for revenge and getting even are heavy emotions that weigh us down. Heavy emotions, reliving the trauma or fight, and being tied to the past robs creativity, spontaneity, fun, and any semblance of a free life. We become virtual prisoners caged inside our own moods and dark thoughts, whether we are painfully tied to the traumatic insults waged against our bodies and spirits or fueling the flames of everyday grudges and insults. We instinctively know holding hate and resentment is not good for us, but being willing to let it go, knowing we are so justified in feeling a sense of outrage and a desire for justice, is another kettle of fish altogether.

It is understandable and instinctive to experience the strong negative feelings associated with being harmed, insulted, and injured. We want to blame the person or people who hurt us; we want to see them suffer. We want them to hurt every bit as much as we have been hurt. We instinctively look for ways to make ourselves feel better, stronger, back to center. We don't want to view ourselves as the hurt, the weak, and the one under. It feels further humiliating to be unable to right the situation, protect ourselves, or stop the aggression or injustices. Even when we have been victimized, we dislike being the victim.

Resentment creates a heavy heart and fuzzy thinking for the one carrying it. It can result in obsessing and ruminating on what has been done to us or what we have done to someone else. Or, in so many cases, putting childhood events and stored-up hatred and resentment out of mind, only to have them appear as unrelated depression and irritability.

It is not unusual for resentment to keep us awake at night, invade other healthier thoughts, interfere in other relationships, and create distractions at work. This is costly and counterproductive, to *you,* not the person who harmed you. As the adage says, resentment is taking poison and waiting for the other person to die. We who hold the memory, consciously or not, the thoughts and the feelings of the transgression, are the ones who are suffering, and we are the only ones who have the power to transcend the heaviness.

Through forgiving and cultivating genuine compassion, we take our power back; we open the door to freedom. We discover the freedom to be inventive in relating to others, to handling traumatic experiences in a strong and firm manner and standing up for ourselves without damaging anyone else. Being resilient, weathering the next storm or navigating the present upheaval requires an open heart and a clear mind that results from forgiving and having compassion.

To be resilient requires a lightness of step and the flexibility to move and not stay stuck or mired in yesterday. It is through accepting the reality of what has been done, accepting the reality of having been hurt, betrayed, wronged; working through the layers and layers of difficult emotions and thoughts accompanying the injury, and finding ways to improve our life and state of mind that gives us the best opportunity for true freedom from insult and trauma. It is through admitting, feeling, and letting go of the negative emotions associated with the egregious act that we transcend victimization.

Many people are under the illusion that forgiveness lets the misdoer off the hook; it does not. Genuine forgiveness is not about condoning awful behavior. Forgiveness and compassion do not green light what has been done. There's no question that perpetrators who are in a position to hurt again need to be stopped. Ironically, the clearer we are, the less saddled with the negativity of previous transgressions, the more creative and effective we can be in stopping further violations. The fewer resentment blocks you have, the more access you have to saying no; cursing the behavior appropriately and in a resilient fashion protects you or anyone else who needs it.

The Courage of Forgiveness

Before outlining the process of transforming these resentments, let's take a few moments to look further into the idea of forgiveness, what it means and what it does not mean.

To forgive, to transform resentment, is a process; I do not want to imply or indicate otherwise. In the lives of people who come to see me, it can take many years to understand the effect, much less transform the wound of having been wounded by mother, father, sibling, or life. Many people bury childhood experiences and concomitant feelings for years of adulthood. This can result in living on a couple of cylinders instead of running full throttle, and experiencing much of adult life through an anxiety that had no relation to present life or circumstances. And despite all the healing work one does, one most likely will still go to one's deathbed with some effects of being wounded. There are pain and permanent effects of being mistreated.

Forgiveness does *not* mean extinction of the experience. It does *not* mean what happened is all right, and it does *not* mean we personally and collectively do not have to deal with the realities of injustices and evil.

What it *does* mean is finding ways of standing up for yourself:

- ▶ It *does* mean being angry and proactive in the face of violations and wrongdoing.
- ▶ It *does* mean being willing to let go of resentment and hatred *for your own sense of well-being* and freed-up energy.
- ▶ It *does* mean putting down the self-imposed burden of negativity in order to lighten your load. Forgiveness and compassion are health food for the victim.

These heroic tasks of transforming resentment and forgiving can be a life's work. Because facing our deepest pains and traumas cannot happen all at once and because the psyche has many, many layers, resentments can show up unexpected, unplanned, and years later. The best we can do at any one time is have the conviction and make a true commitment to the process of transforming resentment and forgiving.

Forgiveness asks a great deal from us. It does not come cheaply or easily. Forgiveness implies a letting go of hate, negativity, grudges, and moving into a state of not waiting for the transgressor to change, make repairs, or soothe our troubled waters. Forgiveness implies letting go of certain images we hold of ourselves: the one who has been wrongly treated and/or taken advantage of, the one who needs to be taken care of or given retribution or seen as needing special treatment as a direct result of being harmed. The one who has been done to and cannot be expected to pull our own weight fully or grow up completely. The one who will never forget, so the violator will be held accountable. These are indirect gains that could prove hard to give up because they appear to be a just reward for the transgression, and they often cover up a deep fear or inadequacy of not having sufficient strength to deal directly with the world and the ugliness that can accompany being related to one another. Instead, forgiveness implies not waiting for life or someone else to remedy the problem or our wounding, instead taking the bull by the horns and finding ways to let go so we may be in charge of our life again and become stronger for the work.

Ideally the person or persons who harmed you *will* take responsibility. He or she might apologize, seek ways to repair the damage, and work with you to resolve any remaining issues. Ideally the person who has harmed would be accountable and find ways or be required to pay penance. I certainly see this voluntary taking of personal responsibility often enough in couples who struggle with infidelities. I have seen parents maturely work with adult children to heal what went wrong in the earlier days. Unfortunately, this does not happen that regularly with most other transgressions, and mostly the victim is left with a legacy of pain, remorse, and harm. For the most part, it is up to the victim to create and seek help to accomplish peace of mind and healing.

DEFENSES AGAINST FORGIVENESS

There are many strong reasons women give for not wanting to forgive. They are waiting for that apology, they believe forgiving condones the behavior, they are too angry and hurt, they desire some revenge or retribution. Underlying many, if not most, of the resistance is a deeply held belief that they will be in a weakened position by forgiving the wrongdoer. That they will lose something of value and be less than they are. On one level, it is against all reason that anger, mistrust, and fury are offering power and strength. (Or as Sylvia Boorstein remarked, forgiving will give amnesia and allow others to hurt us again.) On another level, the assumption holds water. We build up defenses of anger and righteousness to guard against being hurt again, to puff ourselves up as if to say, "I am no longer prey to your intents," creating distance between ourselves and others with the hope and belief that no one would dare touch or hurt us again. We are tough; we are not to be trifled with. We believe that if we give up this defensive posture we will be reduced to the puddle of weakness that allowed us to be sinned against in the first place.

While there is use for anger and rage, being fueled by stored-up bitterness is not power, strength, or resilience; it is a superficial defense that can be cracked and broken. It is a faulty defense against further harm and it is in itself toxic to closeness, flexibility, and consciousness. The irony is that willingness to let go of resentment and developing creative ways of using your vulnerability are both protective and a seat of real strength, or, as a modern advertising slogan decries, "One day you realize that being soft is actually a sign of strength."

When our personality is not brittle from false defenses, as we learn to accept more and more reality that includes the dark and evil of life, as we free up energy used to hate and blame and plot revenge, we are more open to exploring and fostering genuine strength and means to constructive solutions and resolutions. For example, learning more and more ways of taking care of yourself, discovering creative, healthy, and original ways of protecting yourself, and accruing the resources needed to stop further wrongs from happening add effective and necessary tools for growing from adversity. How much better off we are when, instead of concentrating on getting even and seeking vengeance, we put our attention and efforts into building a stronger personality and becoming a force to be respected and valued.

False and Premature Forgiveness

Sometimes second chances *are* possible. A woman I work with lived in anguish that her husband would have another affair. The pain and suspicion she lived with ate at her, leaving her tired and losing pleasure in her daily life. When she created the inner conviction (through a great deal of trust-building work) that she was willing to give him another chance and that if he did have another affair she would leave him, she found a peace of mind and communicated a clarity to her husband that left them both feeling more secure and able to piece together a new level of intimacy.

She could not rest easily nor genuinely forgive until she repeatedly expressed her distrust, felt that her pain and anger were heard in an abiding way, and found grounding from knowing her limits of tolerance and needs for reassurance. Over time, as this was ironed out, and she and her husband understood her needs, she came to the clarity that allowed a second chance.

We can even give third and fourth and fifth chances. The key is having the conviction come from a place of integrity and not the place of making nice, being polite, or not speaking up. Forgiveness does not mean overlooking the situation or the person's ill intent; it is not to act as though the problem or event has not occurred. To forgive, to transform the resentment and be ready to give second chances, requires us to truly heal. To truly heal we must say what is true for us, not only our regret and suffering but also what harm was caused, what anger, what disgust, and also what desire for self-punishment or vengeance was evoked in us. When this process of reconciliation comes from an authentic understanding and from evidence that we are not being harmed and we have solid reason to believe in the other person, it is generous to forgive and move on.

So how do we distinguish between false forgiveness and the genuine article, between premature forgiveness and a timelier one? Genuine and timely forgiveness is not about being saintly or turning the other cheek; it's not about wanting to ignore the painful vicissitudes of being hurt; it's not about desiring to move summarily into a pasture of everything is all right. Genuine and timely forgiveness asks that we look deeply into our soul and express the darkness, the shame, and the reality of our wounded pride, psyche, and human beingness. When we have done that—and feel a sense of freedom and equanimity, knowing that we are able to look *into* the harsh light and not away from it—we can trust that we have done the hard work of forgiving.

But Doesn't It Require Reconciliation?

Many people also hold the idea that forgiveness requires reconciliation. This is not the case. Many times it does not even have to include the other person.

We can choose to have nothing to do with the other person and still forgive, let go of the negativity we hold, and let go of the desire for revenge.

A woman I work with was immensely pained to cut off contact with her family, but she felt she had no choice because her parents lived in denial of the physical and sexual abuse she had lived through as a child. She, through great and courageous work, was willing to enter into a process of transforming her resentment and work toward forgiveness, but she was not willing to endure the continual trauma of her parent's denial. Her process of forgiving and letting go needed to include room for the grief, sadness, and rage she felt at the loss of hope of ever having a supportive family, making her work of forgiveness doublefold. But she gained a deep sense of personal integrity for having the wherewithal to free up enough energy and creativity to make a new family from friends and to use her time to devote to her painting.

Sandra, another woman I work with, is anguished that she cannot have reconciliation with her mother, who died many years ago. Given this young woman's capacity for psychological growth and her desire to discover an authentic sense of herself, I am encouraged that she will ultimately be able to let go of her fury and built-up grievances. Her process helps inform the ups and downs of learning to let go and how strongly we can be bound by a deep, deep urge for justifiable justice.

Sandra's mother was ill throughout Sandra's childhood, and Sandra was her mother's primary caretaker. Her stepfather left the home when Sandra was ten, leaving her to grow up exceedingly fast and terribly prematurely. Her sister got lost in alcohol and drugs, also leaving Sandra to bear the entire burden. Her mother was unable to see outside of her own troubles and looked to Sandra as a live-in nurse, housekeeper, bill-payer, cook, and bridge to the rest of the world. Sandra coped and learned more about survival than any young child should know.

Now as an adult, when her resentment flares, Sandra finds herself bound to a narrow life, as narrow as she experienced growing up and caring for her sick mother. She desperately wants to confront her mother about her lost childhood and her mother's culpability in their confined relationship. She longs for an apology and a "real" place to vent her years and years of frustration. At times, this desire to be finally heard by her mother consumes much of her energy, many times robbing her of the time or opportunity to develop a level of trust that other people are not always wanting to "use" her, not leaving time or taking interest in being with friends, meeting the someone special she would love to meet, or engaging in the traveling she has wanted to do most of her life.

Ironically, she moves in and out of living the self-same life she did as a child, without her mother's presence or illness. Her stored-up negativity periodically weighs her down and keeps her in a restricted lifestyle. I am struck by the sadness of this when I spend time with a couple of my friends who are straddled with chronic pain from an illness and an accident. They are seriously limited in their activities and need to prioritize everything they do in order to economize their limited amount of energy and time free from pain. They have no choice in their circumstances other than accepting the limitations. They cannot obtain more, extra, or different energy or abilities. On the other hand, when we live with a desire for revenge, we are sentenced to a life of inordinate limitation when there *is* a choice.

Sandra does not need a face-to-face reconciliation with her mother to heal her deep wounds and long history of oppression. She works with an older woman who has many personal problems that she brings into the office, and Sandra found herself feeling familiar feelings of subjugating her own needs as this woman spent inordinate amounts of time talking with coworkers about what was troubling her. Sandra, who is included in the circle of workers listening to the daily trials facing this woman, began to feel uncomfortable with the amount of time this was taking from the job and began to question how professional or appropriate these conversations were.

Within the context of therapy, she was able to distinguish the past and the present sufficiently to be able to speak to her boss about her discomfort with the work situation. Her boss was receptive and effective and suggested that Sandra speak with the other woman as well, to tell the other woman exactly why the situation was not working.

It was a difficult challenge for Sandra, but she rose to the task. She was clear and direct with the other woman, giving her examples of how her personal problems were intruding upon their work world and how projects were suffering. Sandra was no longer angry when confronting the woman and was able to speak calmly and firmly.

An interesting byproduct resulted from this interaction. Not only did Sandra feel like a million dollars for directly confronting the woman who was problematic and her challenging work situation, but also she experienced an empowerment that was sorely lacking in her childhood interaction with her mother. She was learning how to speak up for herself; she was discovering resources of self-confidence and belief in her needs, even when they were incompatible with someone else's needs. She had learned the diplomacy of office politics and had pushed herself to confront her problem directly, not waiting for someone else to remedy the situation. She risked the dynamics of "whistle blower" and learned how to reconnect with the woman she confronted.

For several weeks after this incident, Sandra was not angry with her mother. She felt a level of peace about her relationship to her mother and had energy to engage in her present life. Nothing had changed about her childhood; her mother did not reappear to offer solace, but the experience in the present and her ability to deal with it gave her the strength and vigor she assumed she would feel if her mother had apologized.

Just as research shows resilient children and adults having reasonable expectations about themselves and their environment, not spending much time denying or embellishing their problems and wishing things were different, Sandra is finding ways to help herself. She is learning to accept the painful reality of her mother's death, her lost childhood. She is slowly allowing herself to experience the layers of feelings of profound sadness and deep anger, she can mourn and grieve what she did not have, and she can pound life for the injustice of what she missed and what was required of her. She is giving up excuses.

As she peeks behind the thick walls she has erected to protect herself from the years of neglect of her needs and the absurdity of having life and death adult responsibilities as a child, Sandra is discovering all the feelings she hid from herself, some terribly frightening and dark. Each time another life situation presents itself to her, she is digging deep inside herself to discover her authentic voice as she accommodates her present life one step at a time.

As she remolds her life, she is faced with meeting people she can trust, which frightens her as much as it comforts her. She is confronting these new realities and developing the tools and resources she did not receive as a child. She is finding and using her voice to make her presence known so she can more often enter a full life with freed-up energy and wide choices of where to go and who to relate to. One step at a time, she is learning to care for herself so she feels strong enough and valuable enough to put down her defended walls of resentments.

GIVING UP EXCUSES

Holding onto resentments can be a form of resistance against deeper pain. Not staying angry with someone, not blaming someone else for the way things are or were, and giving up excuses opens the door to the deeper and more intense feelings of the actual hurt and violation. As with a flower opening up and revealing the deeper layers, the psyche reveals its secrets a bit at a time. In some higher wisdom we can know our pain in sufficient dosage to open into consciousness a few layers at a time—not be overwhelmed with too much at once—and yet be capable of discovering ourselves at deeper and deeper layers, including our pain and suffering.

As people go deeper and deeper into the excruciating pain of suffering, betrayals, and loneliness, they often experience a vanishing of hatred and the desire for getting even. What I often witness is a pure and intense feeling of pain that leads to deeper healing. While not distracted by blame or hatred or desires of wishing someone else ill, the person uses energy to be with herself fully. While the pain is more intense and fully felt, the relief and healing that results is sustained at the same deep and intense level, and the energy that is freed up is more pure of toxins.

The deeper we are willing to go into the lion's den of the pain we swallowed and ignored, the more honest we are with ourselves about the cost of the big and small transgressions of our life, the more we hold the flashlight on our own experience instead of projecting it out, the deeper our healing will be. The deeper our healing is, the more natural will be our ability to forgive and feel compassion, for ourselves and for others, the more resilient we will be in the face of hard times.

Forgetting does not make it go away and have no effect on our daily lives. This is a journey, not a goal, and for many of us the inner conflict is simmering in our psyches. Sandra battles not wanting to remember. She closes her eyes and sees herself at seven years old and knows her world is about to crash around her. Her mother is sick and her stepfather is leaving. Because it takes time to face remembering, and because a large part of us does not want to remember and face the gruesome reality, Sandra goes slowly and cautiously to the place where she knows the world she had known was coming to a brutal halt.

As difficult as remembering is, as much courage as it takes to face and accept the reality of our story and our emotional storehouse, it is in the remembering that transformation can take place. Sandra longs for someone to truly know what she went through, and she knows she needs to bear witness for herself as well. She needs to know she is not out of touch with reality; her coming up was treacherous and painful. As she allows herself to accept and bear witness to her childhood, she can release the energy bound to the defense against knowing. She can free up the energy and discover a reservoir of understanding and compassion for what she went through, for the hardships demanded of every person in her family. She can discover an amazement of the resilience of the human spirit that lies in wait, in the darkness, under and around the bound-up resentments, fears, and pain.

For myself, and for so many women with whom I have had the honor of working, there is a profound treasure in the recollection of the self. When we are willing to forge into the journey of self-acceptance through knowing ourselves fully (including and especially the shadow, the unknown), we are afforded the gift of being in our full power, even for a moment in time. What I know and what I have seen in others is that extraordinary moment literally and fully eclipses resentments and any traces that might have remained. It is a moment of now that transcends any trauma, pain, and transgression you have experienced.

We are called to restoring memory; we are called to our full power. We are called to the seat of the pearl. We are called to transform victimization, transform resentment, and transform blame and irresponsibility. We are called to cultivate ultimate compassion. It is said when all is understood there will be nothing to forgive. Ultimate compassion.

Look beyond, underneath and around all the shame, negativity, and shadow material to the land of compassion; the geography of unity and the knowing that we desire and have a connection to each other and it is possible to understand and feel someone else's pain and troubles, even to someone who hurt us.

To be resilient, to restore our equilibrium during and after the rupture, we need to restore balance. In ancient times people restored balance and attempted a cleansing through rituals. To establish a fresh start and a spirit of renewal, they used fire, ceremonies, chasing scapegoats from the midst, and symbolic meanings. These ceremonies and cleansing helped individuals feel whole again and the community intact, bringing them back to the geography of unity and connection to each other.

Today, why not light a candle, remember your dreams, and diligently take back your projections in order to restore personal and collective balance and unity? A conscious and purposeful "spring cleaning of our mind" offers us an understanding and compassion of our own suffering as well as the pain and trouble of the other.

exercise

(with gratitude to Clare Morris)

STEP 1

Do this exercise as it is written. Do not read to the end first.

Draw a circle.

In the inside of the circle write the names of the people you know who you would want to come to your home for an evening.

On the outside write the names of the people you would *not* invite and would not want to be there.

On a separate piece of paper, write out the qualities of the people inside the circle. Then write out the qualities of the people outside the circle. Put the qualities side by side and reflect on this comparison.

STEP 2

Pick one of the persons from the outside of the circle. We are going to spend some time getting to know this person more intimately and perhaps get the chance to walk in his or her shoes for a short time.

Using what you know about this person, imagine yourself going through his or her day.

- ▶ What is it like awakening in the morning?
- ▶ What do you see when you look in the mirror?
- ▶ What type of foods will you be eating through the day?
- ▶ Who will be in your life? Who are your closer friends? What is the rest of your support system like?
- ▶ What are your strengths? What are your weaknesses?
- ▶ What is your work life like? What about your family? Are you close, supportive of each other? What is it like for you in this family?
- ▶ What wounds do you carry?

STEP 3

Imagine that you are that person. Be inside their body and mind. Through these eyes see *you*—who you are in fact. What do you see?

now *that's* funny! 8

*Everybody's got a laughing place. Trouble is, most folks
won't take the time to look for it.*
—BR'ER RABBIT

I HAVE A DEAR FRIEND who was a nun for twenty-five years. She tells
the story of sitting under an oak tree near a pristine creek. She was
dressed in her habit and had a sketch or writing pad with her. She was lost in
her work when she noticed a naked man walking by her, from left to right.
Seemingly out of nowhere, this naked man was walking directly in front of
her. He was ambling, as a matter of fact, and since she was sitting down she
was eye level with his genitals. She watched as he strutted past her, turned
around when he had walked beyond her sight and walked back past her to
wherever he had come from.

She didn't even have enough time to react before a second man, also naked,
walked the same path, nay, sauntered past her. Left to right, genitals at eye
level, stopped and walked back again. By the third naked man she figured it
out: some group of men was most likely daring each other to walk naked in
front of "the nun."

Not your typical bashful or retiring nun, when the fourth man's slow and
naked walk crossed directly in front of her she was prepared. She held up
her sketchpad: "5."

● laughter

Many years ago, when my former father-in-law was diagnosed with lung cancer, I was studying shamanistic healing. Laughter is known to be very beneficial in bringing balance to an overwhelmed emotional system. Laughter
allows us to take deeper breaths. My father-in-law was a serious man prone
to depression, and, not having seen him laugh out loud in the decades I had
known him, I was unsure how to begin to use humor to help him and the
family cope with this terminal illness.

I told him my idea: He would listen to comedy 1 to 2 hours a week, and every Friday I would visit him loaded with one-liners to make us both laugh. The thing was, though, he needed to tell me what made him laugh. Humor is so subjective (as I am all too well aware, having compiled jokes and stories for this chapter) and for this time to have any meaning we needed to be gathering stories and jokes that would make him laugh. He looked straight at me as I laid out my enthusiasm for this journey and sat quietly when I finished speaking. He, with a straight face, told me the funniest thing he had ever heard was my suggesting this idea. (And then he laughed.)

We talked it through and did discover what made him laugh. We scoured old record stores and collected dozens of records of old comedians. Comedians from my father-in-law's past, his culture, his way of looking at the world. His favorite was Mel Brooks's and Carl Reiner's dialogue in the skit "The 2,000-Year-Old Man." He listened to the jokes, smiled, and relaxed. Pretty soon the rest of the family began to listen with him, and by the time I would arrive at the end of the week with hordes of corny jokes we were all primed to laugh at very little.

A man was coming home after work one day when he noticed a snail on his front porch. He picked it up and threw it far into his front yard. The man walked into his house and put away his briefcase and hung up his coat. Fifteen months later, the man once again returned home and, once inside his home, put away his briefcase and hung up his coat. This evening there was a knock on his door. When he opened it and looked around he did not see anyone until he looked down. There at his feet was the snail. "What was that all about?" wondered the snail.

Humor can work that way. We can grease the wheel. There is a Buddhist meditation of sitting in a circle in silence. Someone will begin to laugh out loud, usually without much gusto, but as a starting point. Someone else will join in, and a third, fourth, and fifth. Pretty soon everyone in the circle has joined in, and over time the laughing deepens, people's shoulders begin to join the fun and then, by the by, everyone in the room is engaged in deep belly laughs. Someone might throw in a funny story or a joke and, if even a shard of it is funny, the tears of hard laughing begin to fall.

If you are willing to let yourself go, laughter is contagious and delightfully intoxicating. Did you ever play the game with your friends where everyone lies on the floor, each person's head on someone else's stomach, and, in turn, everyone begins to laugh by starting with a *ha* and a *ho* and a *ha-ha*—slowly at first but building to guffaws. Can you remember the sensation of having your head on a belly jiggling from laughter? Can you remember the unrestrained giggles? Even the vision of this can bring a smile to our face. When was the last time you did anything so silly?

● humor and resilience

What matters is whether you can make yourself laugh.
—MICHELLE G. NEWMAN, PH.D.

Laughing breaks the barrier we use to keep life restricted and orderly. Sometimes our contained world needs a jiggle. By lightening up and getting a humorous perspective, we can give room to tolerate and cope with stress and hardships and calamities. For years Erma Bombeck offered stay-at-home moms relief from the ordinary, the drudgery, and the thankless chores that went with the territory. With each hilarious story Ms. Bombeck offered, women knew they were not alone; there was a great deal that was funny about what they were doing, and they could release tension by standing back and seeing the absurdity of the white-glove approach of discovering dust on the tabletops or their adorable and well-behaved child dragging dirty underpants into the living room as soon as company arrived.

Laughter and resilience follows upon the heels of transforming resentment, a likely next quality. Laughter has been studied for its positive effects on our physical health and our emotional well-being. Whereas resentment and anger and hatred have been shown to diminish our quality of life as well as possibly contribute to a shorter life, laughter and mirth, giggles and sidesplitting guffaws can counteract the physical distress of the more distressing emotions and physical ailments. Just as we can be in control of enhancing our physical immune system through good nutrition, exercise, and appropriate rest we can help our psychological immune system through healthy attitudes, beliefs, thoughts, and feelings. According to Steven M. Sultanoff, Ph.D., who specializes in the psychology of humor:

> After each stressful event in our lives our immune systems contain fewer antibodies and, therefore, antibodies need to be regenerated. If a sufficient quantity and/or intensity of stressors persist, and there is no opportunity for the immune systems to recharge, a "breakdown" occurs. Breakdowns may be in the form of distressing emotions, rumination, inability to work, physical ailments, etc. When our immune systems are compromised, emotional

distress (such as excessive anger, depression, anxiety, guilt, or resentment) or physical distress (such as colds, headaches, or stomach aches) often occur. Humor not only helps relieve distress and fights environmental toxins when they occur, it also regenerates our "antibodies" so that the impact of the toxins is minimal. This regeneration bolsters antibody levels and helps sustain resilience. As we experience humor, we "stock up" on psychological antibodies. When a potentially stressful event occurs, psychological antibodies are then "activated" to address our emotional distress.

Why not bring good laughs into our lives? It is known that we cannot be depressed, angry, or anxious at the same time we are laughing. Sure, the negative emotions can return, but why not find as many ways as we can to laugh instead? Why not enhance our immune systems?

You do not need to be a comedian in order to laugh; you do not need to insult your intelligence or sophisticated ideas of life and hard times. What makes you or you and your friends laugh might not even be funny to someone else. What is important, though, is to be able to find the humor and make yourself laugh. Find the funny, use it, allow it, and cultivate it. Learning to laugh at ourselves (when it is reasonable and not hurtful or results in being put down), not take situations overly seriously, and enjoy a hearty laugh all bring a levity, resiliency, and balance to our personality and the circumstance. The more we can break through boundaries with an appropriate light and playful attitude, the less we take things too seriously and the more we allow for curious and detached observation.

> *Life does not cease to be funny when someone dies,*
> *anymore than it ceases to be serious when someone laughs.*
> —GEORGE BERNARD SHAW

Humor both needs and gives perspective. Whether the perspective comes from time passing or being able to view the situation from afar or outside, humor can bring a lift and a sigh to life's difficulties and atrocities. Fifty years after the Holocaust, the Italian director, Roberto Benigni, made the movie *Life Is Beautiful,* using the Fool archetype to bring a lighter step to this horrific time in history. Through his thoughtful sensibilities and long-distance perspective the tone of the movie, while not insulting the seriousness of deliberate mass torture and murder, gave the audience the images of the Fool mocking the order of the day.

The holocaust of plagues, like AIDS, are not and never have been funny, and yet many people and groups intimately involved are finding humor in its T-cell count, its needles and condoms, and its heart-defying number of deaths. In the *Doonesbury* cartoon, when someone asks how can you joke about AIDS, someone with the disease answers, "How can you not?"

Shortly after September 11, 2001, Shazia Mirza, a Muslim woman comedian, used humor to deflect some of the profound fear, distrust, and even hatred she and other Muslims were experiencing from Westerners. She was looking for ways to offer perspective and bring us some breathing room at a frightening time. Using precarious timing (a few months after 9/11), she successfully allowed her audiences to release some of the pressure and tension by telling stories about her personal experiences. Upon sitting down on an airplane, obviously Muslim by her clothing, she watched as the woman seated next to her requested another seat, further away from Shazia. Mirza waits a beat as she tells her audience, "So if I am going to blow up this airplane you are safer sitting three seats behind me?!"

In order to be able to laugh at something, one must be able to gain some distance from the situation and the time, and within this perspective secure the vision needed to see adversity as situational and changeable instead of global and permanent. For adversities that are longer lasting and seemingly irresolvable, humor offers the possibility of finding a lighter and easier-to-bear handle on the suffering. The lighter touch can allow other creative solutions to come to the forefront that might not have been obvious before. As has been poignantly stated many times, comedy equals tragedy plus time. Can you see the upcoming joke as a possible relief from the frustration that had built up from women's years and years of servitude?

> The frog pleaded with the beautiful lass to kiss him and return him to his rightful form of a handsome prince. "In return for one kiss from you I will promise you my hand in marriage. You will come with me to my castle rich with great temptations. You will oversee my cook and prepare luscious meals for me, learn to get the royal clothes pristine clean and spend your leisure time learning from my domineering, but interesting mother, the Queen. You will bear my children who will inherit all I have. What say you, fair maiden?"
>
> The young woman reminisced these words as she licked her fingers clean, having feasted on frog's legs. "I don't bloody think so!"

Humor can help lighten loads, chronic difficulties, injustices, and horrible experiences by bringing in an incongruity that pokes fun at whatever life is dishing out. Doctors and nurses wearing red noses or bunny ears when working in children's intensive care units communicate this incongruity without saying a word.

I met Laura on a shuttle going to the airport. We began talking about women and resiliency and she wanted to know if my work included a light touch to life's hardships. She had a story to tell about her mother, who had lived until the age of ninety-four. Her mother married the man of her young dreams and in quick order gave birth to eight children. When the oldest was eight, her husband suffered a heart attack and died, leaving her widowed with eight small children. She never remarried, saying no one in their right mind would take on this large a brood. Laura describes a very feisty, independent, strong-willed woman who lived and breathed her Catholic faith into practical survival. With a steady undercurrent of respect for the mystery of God's will, she went about her business of living and supporting her family, enhancing God's will. They were very poor, but that did not stop her from making sure each child had the best of private educations.

Because they were the poorest of her own large family, every time someone died they left her some money. "Ma, have you looked at Aunt Tilly lately? She doesn't look so well." And they would all burst out laughing, waiting for the next relative to die so they could send the next younger child to school.

Humor gives us a broader perspective that allows us not to take life and ourselves so seriously. Sarah, a lover of off-the-beaten-path, took a journey through the jungle in South America with several friends and many guides. By the time she emerged from the density of forest she was covered, from head to toe, with mosquito bites. As she tells the story she is out of her mind with itching, jumping up and down trying to scratch every part of her body. Sarah prides herself on being dressed well and being socially appropriate! As soon as she gets the lotion for relief, she rips off her clothes and begins to bathe herself in the potion. She is standing there stark naked, dousing herself "like a crazy woman" and realizes that everyone in her party has stopped what they are doing and are watching her with complete amusement and disbelief. Everyone burst out laughing.

THE "IT COULD BE WORSE" GAME

Knowing that much of our distress about life's hard times is the interpretation, meaning, and perception we bring to it, humor and a comic way of looking at things offer us many resilient qualities for coping. They can:

- ▶ Lift our spirits
- ▶ Relax us

- ▶ Increase our energy
- ▶ Allow us to let down our guard
- ▶ Give a different perspective
- ▶ Outwit the inner censor
- ▶ Turn meanings upside down and inside out
- ▶ Expand our options for coping and resolution
- ▶ Break rigid ways of perceiving
- ▶ Give a felt sense of joy and pleasure
- ▶ Increase our abilities to laugh at life and ourselves
- ▶ Create bonds and relationships—we're more likely to connect when laughing
- ▶ Help communicate and connect, especially with harder issues
- ▶ Be a less or nonthreatening way to communicate—can signal benign intent
- ▶ Lessen the intensity of life's challenges
- ▶ Change and manage our emotional distress
- ▶ Rearrange our thoughts and emotions
- ▶ Open the door to creativity—new ways of looking at adversities

A *New Yorker* article tells the story of a woman who was having a very difficult and stressful time at work. Her husband gave her a card that made her laugh and showed her that he understood what she was going through in her job. The card showed a burning building marked "Crisis Center" going over a waterfall. It could be worse!

John and Carol require and treasure their orderly way of life. They believe they could not keep all the balls in the air if they were not vigilant to everything and everyone being in its proper place. They laugh at themselves, knowing how their lifestyle borders on being nuts. When they find themselves close to a chaotic moment, they shorthand their chuckle by bringing up a beloved friend who is so absentminded that he once took the wrong airplane and ended up in the Soviet Union. It could be worse!

Sally spent a month in residential treatment learning how to get along with and maneuver her new guide dog. It was a huge acceptance in Sally's life; she had worked around and diminished her disability for most of her life. The training included living with twelve other people who were also coming to terms with disabilities and new ways of living in the world. Sally's roommate during the training was blind, unable to hear, and had a roaring sense of humor. Losing her makeup (Oh, well, it's not like anyone here can actually see me), mixing up kibble in her soaps and creams (Maybe I will discover a new skin enhancer), mixing up her white dog with another person's black dog (Like how could we possibly know this), she and her humorous way of looking at many of the frustrations helped Sally's stressful time both during the residential stay and her adjustment at home. During her first week home, she and a friend attended the symphony for the first time with Sally's new seeing-eye guru. When Sally and her dog almost walked into a person wielding an oxygen tank she laughed, wondering the protocol on who goes first. As this first night became stranger than fiction, she and her also-new-at-this dog found themselves arriving at the door at the same time as an over 6-foot man on crutches, having lost a limb. Who needs to watch out for whom? As the medium-sized dog attempted to find some comfort squished in the aisle, the dog nonchalantly licked the ears of the couple sitting in front of her. They, appropriating civil symphony and seeing-eye-dog behavior, said nothing and did not turn around. Sally found humor and absurdity eclipsing her very difficult adjustment. It could be worse!

A bone got caught in Terry's throat at a "fine" restaurant. It took many people, staff and otherwise, to keep her from choking to death. When the paramedics arrived and took her to the hospital, most believed the worst. They were happy and surprised when she called the restaurant the next day to thank them and apologize for the mess she left behind. "I have been battling cancer for eight months now; I'll be damned if I was going to die choking on a bone, for God's sakes!" It could be worse!

THE JOKE'S ON US

There is an art form to using humor. It can be misused; it can be an attack, a put-down. It can be mean; it can be used to cover up insecurities and hatred. It can be sarcastic. The teller risks being rejected. There is a danger in not taking some situation or person seriously enough. There is the possibility of not being sensitive enough to the emotional state of the receiver. It can be negatively used to create distance from an emotional experience. *A secret ingredient to making humor effective and constructive (feeling good, bringing us closer together as well as reducing stress and enhancing the immune system) is kindness.* Kindness as the motivation, as the intention, and as the awareness all contribute to the laughter's helpfulness. When the comedian Bill Cosby tells funny stories about his father worshiping the god within the toilet bowl whenever he comes staggering home late, he offers these revelations with a sense of tenderness. Even comedians with a sharper edge, the Chris Rocks and the Paula Poundstones of the world, are not unkind. (I am not suggesting that all comedians or comedy are kind. That is not true. I am suggesting kindness is the glue for resilient and therapeutic humor.) Using kindness as the barometer helps keep the humor and jokes beneficial instead of harmful, bring us closer instead of further apart, reduce our stress levels as well as lessen our depressions and anxieties, help our esteem and creativity instead of adding to our burdens, and create an environment of trust and openness instead of defensiveness and barriers.

Another general rule about helpful humor is to aim the humor at ourselves. Politicians who are successful are seriously aware of this. When George W. Bush was running for president in 2000, he appeared on the *David Letterman* show. He came on armed with several jokes about David Letterman. The audience booed at every joke. He learned quickly, and for his next appearance on the show he used jokes and funny stories where he was the brunt of the joke. The audience was much warmer.

The most difficult humor to pull off is aimed at the other person. When two or more people are very close, very confident in their positive feelings for each other, and know how to work their way through disagreements and conflicts they can tease and rib each other pretty effectively. For example, Nancy Mairs in her book *Ordinary Time* describes a time when she felt very out of sorts because someone else had just written a book very similar to hers. The conversation with her husband of many years:

> "Aaaaah. . . . and some other woman has written my book, only her time is virginal whereas mine is ordinary."
>
> "That's her book," George says. "You're writing your book. Some people might want to read them both."
>
> "Oh no they won't. They'll want to read hers. She's a certified genius. Really. A MacArthur Fellow. I'm just a frivolous writer, inconsequential."
>
> "That's not what those letters you get say. Those people take you seriously."
>
> "Ha, what do they know? They're undiscriminating, tasteless. . . ."
>
> "A bunch of boobies," he finishes for me. "The kind of club you wouldn't be caught dead joining . . ."
>
> ". . . if they'd have me for a member."
>
> I can't keep up my petulance a moment longer. I have to giggle. He's done it again. He's entered, with perfect sobriety, into my mood of fantastic despair, helping me spin it out to its inevitably ludicrous end. In more than thirty years, I don't think he's ever ridiculed me. But he laughs companionably when I

finally reach the point of hooting at myself. Then he makes me a cup of raspberry-flavored coffee. . . .

Short of knowing and loving someone that well, the possibility of hurting the other person, rendering them feeling very unsafe in your company, and causing a serious rift in the friendship or relationship is large. People's humor quotient can be tested, gently and gradually to begin and again, with kindness, find the ways to include and increase humor's use for resilience. Does your friend, spouse, or partner easily laugh when you approach a particular subject? Do they "see" the situation in equally ridiculous ways? Can they laugh at themselves? Look for what does make them laugh. Are they offended by certain topics? Do you know where they are thin-skinned?

Having seen too much violence and meanness in my life, I was very turned-off by physical humor. I could not understand, in any way, shape, or form, what was funny about *The Three Stooges* or *Laverne & Shirley*. I sat perplexed while others howled with laughter. Fast forward many decades, and one of my grandsons opens my eyes to the hilarity and innocuousness of physical humor. From a very young age he found toy cars bumping into walls and falling off tables laugh-out-loud funny. As young as ten months he would laugh out loud by the mere mention of the word, *whoops*. He continued this leaning to finding all physical humor very funny, and I began to find myself laughing along and finding what was genuinely funny about this topsy-turvy worldview. I still don't see what is funny about sticking one's finger into another person's eye as Mo or Curly might do, but I can say that a sense of humor can be developed and advanced, especially if one so desires and commits.

● we don't laugh enough

Several years ago the *New York Times* published an article on risibility (the ability or inclination to laugh). First, the article quoted scientists' conclusions on the health factors of chuckles to bend-over hysterics. "Robust laughter increases circulation, works the abdominal muscles, raises the heart rate and cleanses the lungs of stale air. Your blood pressure drops to a lower, healthier level than before the buoyancy began." In fact, a positive emotional state like laughing can equal time spent on the rowing machine or stationary bicycle. Exposure to humor increases the immune system and increases the body's defense mechanisms against viral and bacterial infections; and even more wonderfully, the effects of a good laugh last well into the next day. Laughing is good for our health.

In fact, in at least one study a Canadian psychology professor, Herbert Lefcourt, Ph.D., discovered that women reap health benefits from humor more than men. Women who scored high on a sense of humor scale (intentional use of humor as a means of coping with stress) had lower systolic blood pressure than women who scored lower in coping humor. For men, the opposite was true. Men who scored higher in coping humor had higher systolic blood pressure than men who scored lower. "Our suspicion is that women's coping humor takes the form of laughing at themselves which restores social closeness. Men's coping humor takes the form of attacking others, which represents an attempt to maintain their position in the social hierarchy."

So far, so good. Laughing is good for our health, and women especially benefit from using humor as a coping device. Knowing this, why wouldn't we engage in such healthy and fun behavior? Dr. William F. Fry, a Stanford psychiatrist, responds to this with a sobering reality. He tells us that babies begin laughing at two or three months and increase their chuckle rate until they are six years old, when an average child laughs three hundred times a day. After that, sadly, we begin to lose this natural ability. Fry estimates that adult laughs range from a high of about a hundred a day to a low of only fifteen. I wonder if some of us even laugh fifteen times during a day.

Perhaps that is why there is an official World Laughter Day, celebrated with events around the globe. People around the world are making funny faces, silly postures, and telling each other we need laughter more now than ever.

THE ABSURD

Life is so full of challenges, struggles, and pain that it behooves us to look for the absurd. We can find humor in the irony, in disobedience, and in tragedy. When the laughter lightens, when a chuckle reminds us of better times, when shared laughter brings us closer together, when the laughter of history strengthens love, when a hearty smile or belly laugh dissolves anxiety, it offers us health and well-being. When laughter allows us to play, when comedy enhances a group belonging, it sets a relaxed and positive emotional tone to whatever is happening. When we are able to stand back from ourselves and see the humor in what we are doing, how we are reacting and how the shadow trips us, we have the bountiful advantage of using the absurd as resolution.

There is a lesser-known tale of Demeter's anguish after her daughter Persephone was abducted to the underworld by Hades. Demeter, in her screaming grief, had caused all life to halt, allowing nothing to grow or be born. She herself is famished and deteriorated in her unrelenting sorrows. In *Women Who Run with the Wolves,* Clarissa Pinkola Estés paints a colorful portrait, as Demeter meets a most unusual person.

> Even though the pain in her (Demeter's) heart was staggering, she would not surrender. After many askings, pleadings, and episodes, all leading to nothing, she finally slumped down at the side of a well in a village where she was unknown. And as she leaned her aching body against the cool stone of the well, along came a woman, or rather a sort of woman. And this woman danced up to Demeter wiggling her hips in a way suggesting sexual intercourse, and shaking her breasts in her little dance. And when Demeter saw her, she could not help but smile just a little.
>
> The dancing female was very magical indeed, for she had no head whatsoever, and her nipples were her eyes and her vulva was her mouth. It was through this lovely mouth that she began to regale Demeter with some nice juicy jokes. Demeter began to smile, and then chuckled, and then gave a full belly laugh. And together the two women laughed, the little belly Goddess Baubo and the powerful Mother Earth Goddess, Demeter.
>
> And it was just this laughing that drew Demeter out of her depression and gave her the energy to continue her search for her daughter, which, with the help of Baubo, and the crone Hecate, and the sun Helios, was ultimately successful. Persephone was restored to her mother. The world, the land, and the bellies of women thrived again.

Maybe Baubo told Demeter the following joke:

> A woman went for plastic surgery and discovered the newest treatment. As the continuing years took its toll on her face she could, with a slight wind of the knob inserted in her temple, gently, but firmly keep lifting her face. After several years and many turnings of the knob she noticed, to her despair, that she was developing bags beneath her eyes. She went to the doctor with her concerns. The doctor examined her and told her, "These are not bags under your eyes; they are breasts!"
>
> "Oh, my gosh," she responded, "which would account for the goatee."

The unexpected, the totally delightful that reveals the curious, the flexibility, and sometimes the bawdy. Being willing to be surprised, include the outrageous to bring comfort and emotional release when the tension and despair mount. Do you know what makes you laugh? Are you willing to expand your horizons of the absurd? We can and need to develop our sense of humor and make sure we see and delight in the funny, the unexpected, the absurd, the ironic, the silly, the goofy, and (without malice) the joke on us.

LIFE "LITE"

Laughter is the shortest distance between two people.
—VICTOR BORGE

Given that laughter and a lighter way of perceiving life helps us feel better, connects us more easily with each other, puts us in a better mood that can help us open up and be more adventurous to different possibilities in life, it makes sense that we cultivate this ability on a regular basis. Don't rely on the laugh-'til-your-sides-hurt. As marvelous as these times are, they do not happen frequently enough. Read the comics in the papers, listen for and collect jokes you find funny, visit comedy clubs, watch comedians on TV, keep on eye on the absurdities in life (they are bountiful). As with my father-in-law, find out what is funny to you and mine it. Discover who shares which aspects of your humor. Discover your favorite comedians. Hang out with carefree and playful children. Show your children you can laugh and laugh. Teach your children healthy humor. Allow the humor and joy within you to emerge. Watch for opportunities and share your laughter and light moments with others. Use humor to relieve depression and anxiety. There is a reason many public speaking trainers tell the nervous presenter to imagine everyone in the audience naked or in their underwear. Hang out with humor daily, so it is more accessible and useful when hard times come to call.

I heard this story on the radio when one of the talk show hosts returned from vacation in Italy, where different regions can be across the road from each other. This host had a glass of wine with dinner one evening that he particularly enjoyed. The following evening he was dining across the road and inquired about getting the wine he had drunk the night before. The owner told him he could not provide this wine for him. "The wine does not travel well."

The Secretary of Housing and Urban Development moved to Washington, D.C., to begin his new job. He, in buying his own home, went to the bank for a loan. He filled out the appropriate paperwork and was led into the loan officer's office for the final negotiations.

"Where do you work?" inquired the loan officer.

"At HUD," responded the new Secretary.

"What do you do there?"

"I'm the Secretary."

The loan officer thinks about it for awhile and responds, "Why don't we say clerk—that sounds more impressive."

A friend of mine's mother was a psychiatric nurse at the time when Elizabeth Kübler-Ross's work on death and dying became well known and widely discussed. Her mother's hospital staff was "picked" to have the honor of being trained by Kübler-Ross herself. This was also the time when "getting out your anger" was deemed advisable, and since being angry was a step toward the acceptance of death this workshop included screaming, crying, and batting the floor with plastic bats. "Let it all out, reach down and feel it." My friend, with high regard and sincere interest, asked her mother how it felt to be with Kübler-Ross. "Oh," replied her mother, "I don't have that much anger. I made out my shopping list."

With a friend, I was traveling through Europe, proudly driving us from city to village and stopping where our hearts desired. After much difficulty we finally arrived inside the city of Nuremberg and having had so much trouble finding the route into town, we were happy to find a parking place and finally get out of the car. Many, many hours later we were weary and looking forward to returning to the pension. The only problem was we could not find the car. I remembered the street we had parked on, but we could not seem to find our way back to it. After a long fruitless search we decided to enlist the police's help. Through the language barrier we were able to convey that we could not find our car, but I proudly announced I did know the name of the street where we left it. The car was parked on EinBeinStrasse. The policeman looked askance at me and muttered to his coworker under his breath, "Dumpkoff." I declared I knew that much German and did not appreciate being called a dumbbell. My friend had a rudimentary grasp of German and had a conversation with the policemen. "My dear Americans, einbeinstrasse means one-way street."

THE HOLY FOOL

I met a Holy Fool at a conference of very serious-minded people attempting to fine-tune their intuition. Susan was older than everyone else, in fact, elderly. She was annoying, interrupting poignant serious moments with superficial and nonsensible questions. You know this experience? It even seemed as if everyone in the room spoke at a certain decibel, and everything she said was louder. She became, in a civilized and polite fashion, a persona non gratis for most of the participants and the facilitator as well. One got the feeling that she had been at previous workshops led by this particular leader, since the leader reminded her several times that her "task" was to listen more and ask fewer questions. She appeared to be there to learn but was quite candid in her disbeliefs about most of what was being taught. It was a conference on intuition and she believed, from her experience, that we are solely made up of minds and bodies. When we were sent off into groups of threes to, using crayons or colored pencils, draw the other person using our ability to "see" his or her "invisible" life force, she joined our group as a fourth. Given that she had trouble seeing and hearing, it took our group a bit longer to settle in and know that we were all clear on the instructions. We all drew her first and then she drew everyone else. She showed all of us what she had drawn. Her insight was stunning, in fact even more so since so little was expected of her. Her drawings were a mass of color and scribbles—not the popular soft, everything is harmonious and beautiful type. In her unique and uninhibited way she proceeded to reflect back an essence she saw that was eerily accurate. By the time she had told all of us what she had seen I was breathtaken by her ability to see deeply and clearly. She had crossed a boundary of sight. And her response to what she had seen? "Don't you think this is all a projection. I am only drawing what is inside me."

Society has long been graced with trickster figures, Hermes, the Holy Fool, Coyote, the court jester, Raven; the figure who crosses thresholds, doorways, and crossroads. The one who enlivens with mischief, the one who runs from one place to another, from one town to another, the one who can move between heaven and earth. Since every group, every institution, every family, and every nation has its edge, the trickster as a boundary-crosser is hard at work. Here is humor, levity at an archetypal level—ever-present to shake things up, bring things to consciousness, draw the line or cross, erase, or move it. The god of thresholds, the cultural hero of the trickster is a resilient figure extraordinaire. The seemingly asocial ways of appearing and working can be counted on to keep our worlds lively and give it the flexibility to flourish.

For resilience's sake, look for and stay open as you encounter the Holy Fool on the open road, during ambiguity, as she steals your thunder or fire and invents new ways of being, as she plays with your boundaries, both inner and outer, as she bends your fingers back, as she shows up in the least expected people and places. Greet her with a smile and greet her at the edge.

LASTING IMAGES
Sometimes we can, while standing in line at the bank or store or theatre, remember a funny image and bring a smile to our lips.

Lucille Ball working the conveyer belt at a candy factory. When the belt moves faster than her fingers she starts to "pop" the chocolates in her mouth, faster and faster. Then in her pockets and down her blouse.

A friend standing on the kitchen counter, wallpapering. Watching the top of the wallpaper, without enough glue, slowly disengage from the wall and drape over her head, over her torso, and cover her body.

Lily Tomlin playing Edith Ann, sitting on the huge chair. Edith Ann in her pig-tails swinging her feet back and forth, licking on a lollipop, reminding all of us of the timeless feeling of being a child in an adult world.

Lily Tomlin working the telephone switchboard as the calls come in faster than she can plug in the receiver and regaling the callers with straight talk.

TRUE STORIES?

When I was a child there was a popular advertisement for toothpaste. Its jingle ended with "You'll wonder where the yellow went." One time my father was coming home too late to have dinner with my mother and me. She saved his dinner, which included a large salad. There were hard boiled eggs in the salad. My mother removed the yolks of the eggs and wrapped them separately in the refrigerator. On cue, when my father asked where the yellow of the egg was, my mother and I broke into song: "You wonder where the yellow went; brush your teeth with Pepsodent!"

Josh's grandmother was used to the borders of her country changing with the political climate. Sometimes her address was in Poland and sometimes in Russia. Then one day the officials came to tell her that the border was being drawn directly through the middle of her house. She was being given the choice of whether to call Russia or Poland her home. Without any hesitation and with great force she said, "Poland." The officials, taken aback by her swift and intense response, moved out of their official demeanor long enough to ask her why living in Poland was so important to her. "I am sick and tired of going through those god awful Russian winters!" she replied.

From a news item in an Ohio newspaper:

> A housewife was doing her laundry in the basement, and impulsively decided to take off the soiled housedress she was wearing and throw it into the machine.

Her hair had just been set in pin-curls, and the pipes overhead were leaking. She spotted her son's football helmet, and put it on her head. There she was, stark naked (except for the football helmet), when she heard a cough. The woman turned around, and found herself staring into the face of the meter-reader from the gas and electric company.

As he headed for the door, his only comment was, "I hope your team wins, lady."'

Ann Landers

Now it is your turn.

exercises

1. GET READY . . .
Begin to discover or increase what makes you laugh.

- ▶ Think back through your life, reflecting on times you laughed out loud.
- ▶ Pay attention to comedy routines, comic strips, jokes on the Internet. If they make you laugh, keep it up. Or use this to figure out what does make you laugh.
- ▶ Observe what makes other people laugh—discover what was funny.

2. GET SET . . .
Laugh at yourself. Think back to some situation where you took yourself very seriously. With some perspective, can you see any humor in it? Practice. Find the times and places you can have a kind and generous laugh on you! Someone does not "get you," you were caught with your pantyhose down, someone good naturedly poked fun at your way of peeling carrots.

3. GO!
Laugh—more—harder—sillier—deeper.

4. AND BRING THE GANG ALONG
Have a joke party.

staying power, leaving power 9

Pick yourself up, dust yourself off and start all over again.
—JEROME KERN AND DOROTHY FIELDS

mANY YEARS AGO I went on a rigorous two-week bicycle trip. There were about fourteen of us, most of whom were novice bike riders, and two talented and skilled leaders keeping us on the straight and narrow and indicating when it might be fun to get off the straight and narrow. We all became quite reliant on these leaders in learning how to care for ourselves as we discovered aches and pains in areas of our bodies we didn't know existed before.

"I have cramps in my calf muscles and can't walk when I wake up in the morning."

"No, problem," one of the leaders would reassure, "just raise your seat a bit and the cramps will disappear."

"My back is sore from leaning over the handlebars all day long."

"You will get more flexibility in your back if you raise your seat," our wise leader would intone.

"I don't feel very secure racing down hill; can't seem to get the right adjustment."

"Give yourself some extra height; raise your seat a bit," came the response from the leaders.

By now we had caught on. Whatever the problem, "raise the seat" was the solution. When fellow bikers were getting testy with each other, we would suggest raising the seat; when people were in danger of missing the next ferry or being on time for the day's starting ride, no problem, raise the seat. As we got cockier about our riding skills and more comfortable with the miles traversed all day we sang our mantra with the zeal of new converts. I can do anything, watch me soar, catch the wind on my back; all I need to do is "raise my seat."

Fine for bike riding and comic relief, but one-stop shopping will not get you flexibility and malleability, hallmarks for resilience.

In researching natural resilience skills in children, two siblings were observed when their father was diagnosed with cancer. One of the daughters sought information from the doctors, went to radiation treatment with her father, and took on more chores around the house to help her mother. The other daughter (the younger one) rode her bicycle, read, watched television, and played with the family cat. The younger daughter fared significantly more poorly than the older daughter. What worked for the older daughter was having a range of responses, being flexible enough to discover and use many ways of dealing with the trauma. The younger daughter's attempt to only use forms of distraction left her vulnerable to depression and anxiety.

People who are good at crises often drum up emergencies and drama, knowing they can handle that type of situation. They are less inclined to know what to do with day-to-day stresses or conflicts. Women who shy away from conflict are vulnerable to ending relationships and friendships for the sole reason of not knowing how to tolerate or move through tough times and differences of strong feelings. Others who are accustomed to relying on fighting the world cannot recognize and utilize a wait-and-see approach. These narrowing of problem-solving strategies are destructive in the long term, an example being the young daughter who became seriously depressed and anxious.

● flexible thinking

If the sun never shines again hold fireflies in your hands to keep warm.
—COOPER EDENS

Humpty Dumpty sat on a wall
Humpty Dumpty had a great fall
All the King's Horses
And all the King's Men
Couldn't put Humpty Dumpty Together Again.

They should have asked the women,
We would have made an omelet.
—JUNE SINGER

People who are resilient know how to be flexible. They have broad and varied interests, which, in turn, call on them to develop complex strategies and new coping skills. They render themselves stronger, somehow knowing that if they used the same coping skill over and over without discriminating the circumstances and their needs they would be weaker and less resilient. They discriminate and select the most appropriate response to a given situation. They do not follow formulas. How they act depends on the occasion. They widen their lens to include a variety of possibilities in whatever they do, looking for lots of solutions to bring to the alchemical vessel of life's requirements as well as many opinions to enrich their decisions. Or several mentors and role models, as Mary Catherine Bateson discovered: "I have never looked for single role models, I believe in the need for multiple models, so that it is possible to weave something new from many different threads."

It is important to learn and develop a wide repertoire of responses, especially if we are habitually accustomed to a narrow band. When Marlene came into therapy, she unfortunately used going to bed with the covers drawn up over her head as we bikers used raising our seats. When she felt inadequate at work, she took the day off and stayed in bed. When she felt depleted by the end of her week, she spent the weekends in bed. When she and her husband had a fight, she retreated to the darkened bedroom and sought comfort under the blankets. When she could not face the realities of living creatively and with vitality, she regressed by sleeping. She narrowed her life to the bare minimum requirements of earning a living and relating to her husband on a superficial level. Her repertoire was fixed and rigid, cutting her off from dozens of possibilities when she was laid off and needed to find another job.

Marlene challenged herself to looking for a variety of relevant solutions to her daily life struggles as well as to learn to think about her own feelings as well as her husband's and fellow workers'. In looking for available options, and in understanding what she and her husband were both feeling, she began to name a variety of ways she could respond to having a fight with her husband. She could tell him how upset she is, she could go for a walk or a run to clear her head, she could cut out newspaper articles that communicate her point of view, and she could utilize communication tools in constructive arguing. She could find a movie or poem or image that presented a bigger or lighter perspective to the current difficulty. She could reflect on her coping styles to recognize that ignoring her husband and the fight they are having or burrowing under her blankets were the same coping skill. She could also reflect on the fact that it is natural for she and her husband to feel differently about the same thing, and conflicts are part of intimate relationships.

Sarah, on the other hand, was full of ideas and creativity when she was rebuilding the home she lost in a fire. Her inflexible thinking cut her off in a different way, though. This home was going to be *perfect*, not only in terms of resisting future fires but in everything being just right for the family's lifestyle. In her search for the Holy Grail of houses she found herself exhausted, irritable with the workers, and losing sleep worrying about all the details that were wrong, out of place, and not happening as they needed to be. The home she planned to love became an albatross around her neck. In her desire for perfection she lost sight of a reality. By limiting our options in service of perfection, we rob ourselves of surprises, better ideas, alternate paths, and possible transformations. For any problem there are dozens of answers, and if we tackle the problem on a variety of fronts we can be surprised at the creativity that will emerge.

Coloring Outside the Lines

Adversity, big and small, can be a time for rejoicing in falling down the rabbit hole, thinking way outside the box, or coloring outside the lines. Perfection and too narrow a range of responses grossly limit the playing field. Sometime you just must include outrageous ideas like parachute jumping or giving up all worldly goods. I know of two people who inspired all who knew them when they were diagnosed with life-threatening illnesses. One woman, having successfully gone through treatment for breast cancer, took seriously the possibility of five clean years, and used that time to rethink her life. She had been an accomplished teacher and artist, finding great satisfaction in her work and the exchanges with students. And yet, when looking at her life from her death backward, she rearranged her entire world and became a Buddhist nun in the Far East.

She is doing something that had not occurred to her at any other time in her life; it was the realization of her life ending sooner than she had anticipated that spurred her to think in a completely upside-down fashion. Another person, a man diagnosed with AIDS, shook up his world and friends by cashing in on his life insurance policy and buying a villa in the French countryside. For the remaining years of his life he hosted an open house in France. All who knew and loved him spent varying amounts of time with him in the lap of luxury in a romantic setting begging for exploration and investigation.

The goal is to emphasize flexible thinking. Think differently, think widely, and find ways to foster your capacity of creative problem solving. By using your imagination to make constructive (and perhaps colorful) decisions and to envision alternate ways to seeing problems and hardships, you can learn to master the changed environment that came about because of an adversity or developmental phase. If you approach most problems in your life with strong reason and calculated ideas, perhaps you can step out of the box and wonder about the next dilemma through your feelings or intuition. Are you in a rut?

Even exercise regimes can stand a breath of fresh and different air. Only a runner? What about basketball? Take all your vacations at the beach? With family and close friends? Off the beaten path? What if you tried something different, perhaps wild? According to Carl Jung's concept of typology (the qualities of thinking, feeling, intuition, and sensation in both introverted and extraverted forms), we all have an inferior function that begs for expression as we approach midlife. Is intuition hidden in your closet? Is categorizing objects the last thing you think to do? What if you took the time, in a non-stressful time, to exercise the parts of your personality you use more infrequently and gave yourself the gift of rounding out your problem-solving capacity?

GIVING UP

Giving up too soon, being too quick to throw in the towel can get in our way of creative and flexible thinking. While we might get frustrated, lose tolerance, or feel inadequate to the task at hand, giving up too soon curtails the creative process, disallowing the active mind to ferment new and different possibilities. There is a poetic dance of knowing when it is too soon to quit and when we are doing ourselves a major disservice by staying at the dance too long.

Let's take a look at the dynamics involved in quitting prematurely. What do you know about your own tolerance level for hard times and difficult problems?

- ▶ Do you know what causes you to want to quit too soon?
- ▶ Do you recognize the telltale signs or uncomfortable emotions?
- ▶ When you look back, do you wonder if you were too shortsighted?

Read these quotations and see if any sound familiar to you:

"I ate ¾ cup of steamed broccoli instead of ½ cup, felt I had blown my diet so I ate a donut."

"I skipped aerobics class one day, decided it was pointless to go for the remainder of the year."

"I neglected to match receipts with one Visa bill. Declared my whole accounting system a failure and stuffed the next five months of receipts into a shoebox."

"I did something embarrassing on a date. Immediately began avoiding all contact with the person, letting the weirdness grow until it smothered all remaining sparks of interest in the relationship."

These quotations are all from a cartoon character named Cathy. She goes on to declare, "Time after time I've given up the whole effort because of some minuscule setback! Year after year I've looked back only to see how well I was really doing at the exact moment I quit trying." I remember a friend of mine looking back on her life with tender remorse, realizing she would know how to play the piano and speak Spanish today if she had not given in to the belief at that time that learning to read music or finding time to practice speaking Spanish was more than she could handle. She knows now that it was not too much; it's just that at that time she did not know how to apply herself and she did not have the necessary support to guide her to keep at it. This knowledge does guide her presently; when she is in the midst of learning something new now, this lesson gives her staying power.

WHAT KEEPS YOU FROM GIVING 10 PERCENT MORE TO . . .

Fear (of failure, of the unknown, and of humiliation) can pull the plug on persistence and perseverance. Desiring perfection, not allowing room for mistakes can result in the minuscule setbacks Cathy reminds us of when she quits at the exact moment her diet, exercise regime, and new relationship could have unfolded or continued. Without fear, and with a healthy attitude about mistakes and failures, more and more is possible; more experimentation, more daring, more creativity can blossom. I remember the first time I approached using filo dough, the very, very thin layers of pastry dough used in Greek dishes. It has a reputation for being difficult, easy to tear, very delicate, and prone for error. I read the directions carefully, plotted out the course, and when it was time to work with the dough itself, went at it undaunted. When it began to fall apart, rip, and prove difficult, I fixed it, worked around it, and kept on going, all the while knowing full well I would complete this task.

I reflected upon this experience because it was different from many other things I try for the first time. I am familiar enough with the fear that can accompany charting new or uncertain territory, even with something as benign as cooking. A secret to diminishing fear is experience. I have been cooking for many, many years, and even though I had never used filo dough before I had confidence in my ability and competence in cooking and enough experience to know that things can be fixed, repaired, thrown away, or started over. Substitutions can be made, and a less than perfect outcome is not horrible.

It is helpful and effective to make room for less than perfect results and mistakes. Many masters of art and spirituality will surprise their students by an enthusiastic response to a "mess." It can prove to be an opportunity for something new, different, and "even better" to emerge. Our most creative experts have discovered a new and improved version by using their mistakes to an advantage. Perspective and a beginner's mind can turn problem solving into invention, improvement, and even genius.

I found it helpful to stand back and see a larger picture than the rips and tears in the filo dough. Within the scope of learning, trying something new and working around mistakes can take on the tone of adventure and spark to activate the imagination. Before I even began the preparation, I imagined what the process and the end product might look like. This enabled me to work swiftly and without hesitation. When I was finished and less than happy with the result, I could evaluate what I did not like and how to improve it the next time. In my mind's eye I began to play with other ways to do it to get more desired results.

Using perspective, imagination, and relying on previous experience for discovering options, alternatives, and staying power is workable for relationships, returning items to stores, or learning a new profession. The same principle can be applied to driving and parallel parking, in other words, learning something new or even addressing starting over in life and learning to live without someone you love. Being able to translate experience from one area of your life to another adds resources to finding creative solutions and can give the necessary juice for going the extra mile and giving the 10 percent more.

"MISTAKES"

A mountaincastle opened its gates for the eagles of Divine Guidance—a meeting-place, a refuge for Angels who by their Loving Kindness return to earth dimension in times of strife and confusion. The mountain is called Great Patience.
—MARIANNA RYDVALD

When "it" is wrong and not to your liking, whether it is filo dough, getting a divorce, or being fired, the larger perspective issue is that you are engaged in the learning process of fully living your life. It is failure and cowardice to give up, not to make mistakes. Developing perspective informs us of who we are in the scope of our whole life and our entire world. What is our journey and how are we going to grow, develop, advance, and love?

Lindsey was a top-notch clinical pharmacist, having graduated at the head of her class and specialized in hormonal replacement treatment. She kept abreast of the most up-to-date information, combining alternative remedies with effective traditional medications. She had grown a clinical practice of such esteem that patients waited several months to get an appointment with her. She was gifted and combined her talents with genuine humility, giving her national recognition.

She came to see me because her marriage was failing and she considered this a personal failure. Her husband was unhappy and spent more of his time outside of the home than with her or their family. Their conversations had become limited to household and family logistics, and Lindsey could not remember the last time she and her husband had been away together. Lindsey came to therapy to have time and a favorable environment in which to reflect on her life and her marriage. Over a period of time, as Lindsey was willing to look at herself from many angles, she began to see how her emotional life and softer side had been sacrificed for the energy she put into being a successful pharmacist. In fact, having free time, relaxing, and not having prescribed projects had not been in her repertoire since she had been a child.

Lindsey was able to save her marriage, which she very much wanted to do, but it required her expanding her view of herself and putting different actions (and non-actions) into her life. She soon began to see her almost-failed marriage as a wake-up call, a near mistake that pushed her to a self-discovery that enriched her life, a perspective of her more full place in the world (her importance as a wife as well as a pharmacist), and her marriage. She valued taking life very seriously and knew she had a calling in the health profession. There was only so much time and so many people to help. Without the troubles in her marriage, she would not have considered that she was out of balance and her life could and probably needed to include fun, coziness, laughter, and light heartedness.

We all have more sides to us than we know at any given time, and sometimes it takes falling on our face or losing something very valuable to push us toward discovering this perspective through bigger and more creative vision. To keep this type of growth and advancement alive and dynamic, it helps to see our mistakes as guidance along this road. Mistakes and failures as a signpost that we are more than we thought we were and/or different than we thought we were and/or there are other ways to look at our circumstances. As Lindsey had learned in graduate school (and could now apply personally), science is described as a paradigm that is not a perfect model, but useful until its inevitable overthrow. She thrived on overthrowing her personal paradigm.

Can, Cannot, Don't Want To

It is important to distinguish between not wanting to do something and not being able to. There are certainly things we cannot accomplish; it is doubtful you will become a world-class downhill skier if you have not learned to ski by the age of sixty, and it is doubtful you will birth a child at the age of sixty-five. What is of importance for this part of the resiliency process is hiding behind a false conviction that you cannot do something when in fact something else is going on in the psyche.

Judy continually runs out of money. She makes a decent salary and yet is in such a sorry state by the end of the month that she goes through an elaborate labyrinth to stop checks, close banking accounts, and scurry back to stores to return items she can little afford. This entire process brings her tremendous shame, and yet it is repeated, with many other added turns, almost on a monthly basis. Granted she is living in an area that is very expensive and many people are having a hard time making ends meet, and granted she did not receive adequate understanding or training about money management from her parents. However, Judy is convinced she *cannot* solve her money problems and uses enormous amounts of energy in being upset with herself and berating her embarrassing end-of-month machinations.

Stephanie is in her early fifties and is in a relationship that causes her serious pain and disappointment. She loves this man dearly, and when things work between them she feels on top of the world. It took her a long time to admit to herself that she did not want to be alone; she had convinced herself that it was important to find in herself all that she was looking for in a man, and she "should" be able to live on her own and not need a man to feel good. She had confused the issues of loving herself fully for who she is (and not needing someone else's validation for her own worth and value) and wanting the companionship and support she could get from an intimate relationship.

Reconciling this distinction and knowing she wanted someone faithful and available in her life left her with a deeper understanding that the relationship she had with this man was causing her more pain than pleasure. She believed she wanted to break it off and leave herself free to find someone else. However, whenever she called to set up a time to talk with this man, the phone would be busy or he was not available at the time she was or he was overrun with important things at work. Stephanie was convinced that these were signs to not break things off with him and the universe was telling her to wait—maybe the lesson she needed to learn was to have patience and allow this man to come around.

Jeanne came from a profoundly neglectful home. With tremendous fortitude she had left a dead-end job in a narrow-minded town and traveled to the West Coast to go to medical school. Having no training, support, or guidance in any area of her life, learning to discipline her time, manage depression while studying, and learning to live in a unfamiliar area while under tremendous pressure took its toll, and yet she managed to keep her head above water.

When it came time to do her residency, she landed a prestigious hospital opening and came to me in tears after her first week there. The other residents came from all over the country and the expectation on these new doctors was tremendous and daunting. Jeanne was overwhelmed and "knew" she was not going to survive the first summer of residency. How could the other people automatically know how to do the procedures required of them when she felt so in the dark? She was required to report to a particular physician when she had figured out the diagnosis of a patient on the surgical floor. She did not know something very basic and it was apparent to the reporting doctor. She felt thoroughly humiliated by the end of her first week and was convinced she was going to fail and wondered what she was doing in this profession. "Why don't I forget the whole thing?"

There is a commonality to these three situations. On the surface all three women have grounds for frustration, aggravation, and painful disappointments because they cannot get hold of their circumstances in an effective manner. Further exploration opens up underlying rebellions because all three women did not want things to be the way they are. Judy found the intense dislike she had for living with any kind of constraint; she does not like being told what she can do and what she cannot do. On the surface what she told herself was the situation was beyond her; there was nothing she could do about it even though she tried so hard.

When she was very honest, though, she realized she wanted to be able to spend money on whatever she wanted with no financial consequences. Strong feelings of rebellion would overtake her because she believed herself deprived and inadequately nurtured, so money would become a substitute for being good to herself. When she found herself deeply in debt or seriously out of control with her spending, she preferred believing it was because it was so expensive to live in the Bay Area. She would then not be responsible for having to move through the problem or coming up with creative solutions to make matters better. She definitely wanted her financial issues to be different, but her rebellious desire was childlike in nature and ran counter to genuine money management and personal responsibility. Without fully realizing the repercussions Judy was living as a victim—oppressed by her own rebellion and unrealistic demands.

Stephanie, giving the universe carte blanche, discovered she was hiding behind not wanting to end her relationship and not wanting to take responsibility for doing something she consciously believed was not good for her. She preferred to believe that it was not meant to be when she attempted to call the man and decided it was up to fate that she was not going to break things off.

Further reflection revealed that she was not psychologically ready to end her relationship because she was dreading being alone and, thinking it was weak to feel that way, she did not want to face that reality. By keeping herself in the bind of not walking away and staying convinced it was out of her hands to control her destiny she co-opted herself into a subtle, but powerful, grasp of victimhood. Looking at the underbelly of faith in the universe and higher powers reveals the way we give away personal power, responsibility, and cooperation in the unfoldment of our lives. By turning over her responsibility to the universe's timing, Stephanie's powerlessness further exacerbated her belief that she could not manage being on her own and doing what she needed to do to find a more suitable partner.

Jeanne was going to quit because she was convinced that her skills were so low that there was no opportunity to improve them. "It's way too hard and difficult." She had also pitted herself against the other residents, sure that they knew more than she and there was nothing she could do to cooperate with or get help from any of them. Her early experiences of neglect manifested in her mind with the punch of a bomb and she reacted as she had always done. She became quite rebellious, saying there was no way she would show her face there again and she did not need any of them anyway. She believed she was being victimized by her ineptitude ("I know I cannot do this"), when in fact she was being held back by her fear and the shock of having to adjust to a new pace of work and attention.

There is probably a familiar ring in all three stories. Haven't we all faced at least a moment or two in our lives when we are sure it is time to throw in the towel? And yet, we are most inspired by others and ourselves when we do things that felt or appeared impossible at first glance. There can be magic in the power of believing in the impossible, wanting it, and making it happen.

In the middle of Dachau, the concentration camp in southern Germany, sits a small chapel erected and maintained by the Carmelite nuns. The camp itself is obscenely large and dark. The energy field around it is potent and can be felt for blocks around its vicinity. The Carmelite nuns, against much disagreement and distrust and after many, many years of trying, secured permission to build a small house of worship within the walls of this site of evil. For several decades they have kept vigilance of chimes, prayer, and music around the clock and through the year. The result of their persistence is inspiring and awesome.

Many years ago I visited Dachau and this chapel. When I came within two blocks of the camp I began to weep and felt as if I had been kicked in the stomach. It took courage and strength to walk through the camp—I had to limit what I saw since I could not take it all in emotionally. And yet, when I arrived at the chapel I experienced a stronger power than I felt in any other part of the camp. The light and love in this tiny little hamlet overpowered the feelings of death and torture and the unspeakable.

I stayed for a while, drinking in the invisible but palpable energies, and when I retraced my steps back to the camps gates it was with an easier step. The felt sense and darkness of the ghosts and memories actually paled and folded into the power of what had been made possible by a small group of persevering, confident, and resilient nuns who changed an atmosphere with their abiding convictions.

● letting go

Earlier I wrote that there is a poetic dance of knowing when it is too soon to quit and when we are doing ourselves a major disservice by staying at the dance too long. While it is easy to recognize the virtue of persistence and focusing, as any entrepreneur will attest, it is also equally important to recognize when it is time to walk away and cut your losses. Being resilient, as earlier stated, means having a wide range of responses and having the moxie to know when to quit is a valuable skill to have under your belt. There comes a time when tenacity becomes rigid and ineffective, when persistence becomes annoying, and trying again is foolish. It takes time, awareness, and experience to know the difference, but I think it is safe to say it is time to walk away when the price has become too high or something of equal or greater value can take its place.

Several years ago Melody Chavis wrote a book about her life and love in a poor and crack-infested part of Berkeley, California. In *Altars in the Street,* Chavis, a private investigator and Buddhist activist, compels her readers with her first-person account of raising her children and grandchildren in a city that faced many devastating downward spirals. She and her neighbors witnessed mothers losing their children to crack; children becoming dealers; neighborhood stores, once treasured, closed, and bloodstains on their sidewalks. Chavis and her neighbors formed committees and fought their uphill battle with conviction and grit. Year after year they won a few and lost many more battles but waged on, as they knew they were fighting for nothing less than the children and grandchildren. And yet, after so many years of staying the course and after experiencing threats and finding themselves exhausted and discouraged, Chavis and her husband made the painful decision to leave the neighborhood and the battle. "Buddhism, teaching me compassion and non-judgment, had up to now helped me to stay, trying harder. Now Buddhism talked to me about the wisdom of knowing when to go. All right. I give up."

The price had become too high, and no one but Chavis could appraise that moment in time. It was time for her to go. In this case the price had become too high—they were frightened and depleted in a deep and harmful way.

A client I see talks of the trapeze swings that the trapeze artist will fly between. They perfect the art of swinging high on one bar as they exquisitely gauge the exact moment to let go and grab the opposing bar. Knowing when to let go can depend on the timing of the second bar. When it is clear that there is something compelling and calling us, we loosen our grip, let go and, with a modicum of faith, reach out for the next rung.

Letting go of a creative project when it is not coming together, letting go of a business that is losing money and is consistently one paycheck away from turning the corner and being a huge success, and letting go of relationships that have just enough good left in them to eclipse the harder reality of its dysfunction. Often the component that will allow us to let go of treasured works of art and love is seeing another possibility, imagining another way, or being offered a provocative alternative.

A young woman with a secure position at a prestigious medical school found herself restlessly awake at night while being in a satisfying relationship with a dashing European man who wanted her to return with him to his country. Her parents had paid for an expensive medical college education, and she had "everything going for her" when she landed a prestigious position that had potential for professional growth and recognition. Could she let go of her conventional image, the plans she held for herself and her parents' pride in her accomplishments? She went with her boyfriend, only to discover they were incompatible.

She spent the next two years traveling a world she had heretofore only read about in books and newspapers. She toured exotic places and developed a facility and a thirst for trying new things and broadening her scope. She returned to her hometown with a new concept of who she is as well as the treasures accumulated through her adventures. She grabbed the flying trapeze, letting go of the familiar and found it to her liking.

By all means, raise your seat. But don't forget to explore the full range of possibilities along the way and enjoy the ride, the scenery, the people you meet, and get the most out of the bumps along the way because they determine your next move.

exercises

1. Color Outside the Lines

This is an exercise to grease the wheels of flexible thinking and creative solution. Write down a central problem or issue that is currently weighing you down. Draw a circle around the problem. In all directions draw lines away from the central issue and freely associate ideas, images, and words that come to your mind. Draw circles around all the ensuing ideas.

When you have exhausted this part, use a second sheet of paper to put one of the associated ideas in the center. Now free associate from this central idea. Do this as many times as you have energy for, and when you are complete, cut out all the encircled associated ideas. Keep the central problem or issue intact.

Keeping them upside down, mix up all the circled associations until you do not know which ideas are written on the opposite side. Randomly pick five ideas and put them around the central issue. Allow your imagination to secure new connections, find crazy combinations, and come up with new suggestions.

Keep mixing up the associations and central issue, allowing your mind free reign and the creative juices room to expand. Completely color outside the lines, and allow yourself to go wild.

2. Discover Your Patterns

Use a journal, artwork, and/or imagination to help you connect with your answers to the questions below (see the exercise in chapter 1 for more explanation).

▶ Reflect upon the pattern you have adopted for solving major issues.
▶ Reflect upon the pattern you have adopted for solving minor issues.
▶ Reflect upon the times you have not quit soon enough.

Using the previous exercise, find new connections and new possibilities to problem solving and to not quitting soon enough.

i can't take any more, or can i?

When two paths open to you at the same time, take the harder.
—HINDU PRAYER

AN IRANIAN ALLEGORY tells us about an immortal bird named Simurgh that makes his nest in the branches at the top of the tree of knowledge. One day one of the Simurgh's silver feathers is found in the middle of China, and the other birds, tired of being without a leader, decide to seek him out so that he can give their lives some direction. They know only that his name means "thirty birds" and that he makes his castle in the Kaf, the range of mountains that rings the Earth.

At the outset, some of the birds lose heart and claim they cannot make the trip. The nightingale pleads his love for the rose; the parrot pleads his beauty for which he lives caged. The partridge cannot leave his home in the hills, the heron his home in the marshes, the owl his ruins. But finally a delegation of birds sets out on this perilous venture. They travel for many days and years to cross through seven valleys and seas, the last two bearing the names Bewilderment and Annihilation. Many of the pilgrims desert, and the journey takes its toll among the rest. Finally thirty birds made pure by their suffering reach the great peak of the Simurgh. At last they behold him, and they realize that they are the Simurgh, and that the Simurgh is each and all of them.

● in the voyage of life

Johanna, a woman in her early forties, was in a relationship with a man who was not particularly reliable. She loved him immensely but would struggle each time he said he would be over for dinner and he wasn't. She had a strong belief that they were meant to be together and was elated when he came forward with a marriage proposal. Everything about marrying him was appealing to Johanna, but she was also aware that she could be setting herself up for repeated disappointments, knowing his proclivity for disappearing into the ether at unpredictable times. She came into my office with several dreams, in the first of which she is on a dock, getting ready to sail the ocean.

She has a sense of calm waters and rough seas but cannot remember whether the sea at her feet was rough and the further waters were serene or was it the other way around.

When we set off on a journey we cannot know what lies ahead. We are positioned to set off without being able to know fully what will be required of us and exactly what type or amount of suffering we will have to endure. Having children or not, changing careers, going back for further education, taking over the care of an elderly parent, getting married or getting divorced, putting your artwork into the public eye—living a conscious life—any circumstance we choose or gets chosen for us brings us face to face with unseen obstacles and unknown waters. Living a full life is equally mysterious; we cannot know what lies in store for us or what obstacles, adversities, or uncontainable joy waits around the corner. Our task is to receive our life and learn what warrants moving through the difficulties and what is extraneous.

● to follow the pain or not: that is the question

People who walk barefoot through much of their lives build up calluses on their feet that allow them to endure rough surfaces and sharp objects. They have suffered through many a blister, cut, and burn. The fact that they endured that type of discomfort and suffering allows them more mobility and flexibility to roam and explore. In our culture, especially this country, we expect things to turn out well, and we take seriously the promised pursuit of happiness in our constitution. Rather than voluntarily enduring rough spots and sharp lessons, much less abide by the notion of being made pure through the suffering, we tend to take pain and suffering as a personal insult, designed to thwart our natural right of being happy and gratified. Suffering is regarded as negative, weak, and contrary to "what happens to 'good' people."

In the Asian culture, on the other hand, life is seen as painful, and people are expected to learn how to deal with pain and disappointment. The Buddha further distinguished between pains and suffering by teaching that on one hand, inevitably, there will be pain in our lives and we are faced with the possibility of a wise and helpful response to it. On the other hand, according to the Buddha, suffering is when we struggle against the hardships and pain in life we cannot change or when we fight, resist, and get angry about not being able to rid ourselves of the pain.

I understand the Buddha's teachings to be in line with Carl Jung's distinction between genuine suffering and what Jung called "neurotic suffering." Jung suggested that neurotic suffering is the attempt to avoid meaningful suffering. Neurotic suffering is our resistance to the pain and suffering that exists by being alive in a sometimes hostile world where we will lose dreams, innocence, and people we love. We attempt to defend ourselves against the pain of these losses or harm by using the defense mechanisms we established in our early years—the same defense mechanisms we used to cope with things we did not want to experience when we were too young and vulnerable to be able to tolerate betrayals, accidents, harm, disappointments, and insufficient love. We developed certain behaviors to protect ourselves from the searing pain, and now as adults when we face the pain and suffering of present-day losses and adversities we regress to using the same behaviors.

We might become ill, engage in destructive behaviors against ourselves and/or other people, distract ourselves through work or other activities, lose ourselves in taking care of others, or become angry, guilty, fearful, depressed, or blame others. Anything to not feel the sting of the loss or harm, we will instead continue the avoidant behavior we have mastered throughout our lives—a type of suffering that winds around itself and renders us brittle, petty, and self-absorbed.

I found the essence of these great teachings on the types of suffering in the precocious words of twenty-year-old Etty Hillesum as she lay writing in the hellhole of a concentration camp during the Second World War. She, observing and experiencing hunger, torture, hatred, and profound uncertainty, expressed repeatedly a philosophy that was growing in unlikely soil:

> Reality is something one shoulders together with all the suffering that goes with it, and with all the difficulties. And as one shoulders them so one's resilience grows stronger. But the *idea* [emphasis in original] of suffering (which is not reality, for real suffering is always fruitful and can turn life into a precious thing) must be destroyed. And if you destroy the ideas behind which life lies imprisoned as behind bars, then you liberate your true life, its real mainsprings, and then you will also have the strength to bear real suffering, your own and the world's.
>
> I am not using the word suffer in its ordinary sense, although we certainly do have pain. But when I say we must choose to suffer, I am using the word in an older sense, in which suffer meant "to be willing to be exposed to an experience that may be disturbing."
> Let ourselves be exposed to the truth about what we have lost, certainly an experience that is disturbing.

I am not talking about masochism or staying in a situation or feeling that is harmful or degrading or stifling. I am not referring to martyrdom, suffering for suffering's sake. I am not talking about roaming the halls of self-pity.

We have the capacity to feel and know wonder, sorrow, excitement, joy, pain, horror, rage, disgust, humiliation, grief, exhilaration, fear, and terror. We have the capacity to feel all emotions, but we stop ourselves from feeling a wide range and often get stuck in a narrow band of emotions. As noted in a Rilke poem, we live emotionally as if our entire world existed on one floorboard in one room in one house—when there is a vast emotional universe to explore and know.

I am using the words *endure suffering* to communicate a way of making ourselves sturdy, hardy, and strong enough to bear the suffering of reality as a result of being willing to be exposed to experiences or feelings that might be disturbing, but experiences and feelings that are *true and genuine* and will bring us to seeds of knowing and the Self hidden deep within us, will "liberate [our] true life, its real mainsprings," will bring us face to face with a wisdom of pure suffering that the teachers and allegories are relating. To be resilient means cultivating the ability to access, feel, and express a wider and wider range of human emotions. It means being able to recognize pain, acknowledge its purpose, tolerate it for a reasonable enough time until the problem can be worked out and conflicts resolved constructively. The premature removal of emotional pain can reduce our motivation for change, and observing pain can reveal the hidden and unrecognized source of distress that are contributing to feelings of depression, disorganization, and victimization. Living with pain and distress gives us time to develop new ideas and patterns for dealing with problems.

The characteristic of a resilient person is one who can bear with the phase of genuine suffering, depression, and disorganization long enough to emerge with thoughts, feelings, insights, and behaviors that will manifest as a furthering integration into the wholeness of her personality and healthier relationships. Make lemonade out of lemons.

We can develop our ability to choose the suffering and endure the dark; we can practice choosing to feel and face the truth about what we have lost and choose to face our pain in order to resolve our conflicts at a higher level, discover patterns to our distress, find new ways of dealing with our problems, and work toward achieving a fruitful and integrated outcome.

● olympic winners

What does it look like to allow genuine feelings and to suffer through them? I have often thought of the value of a gold medal and who should receive them. It seems to me that there are millions of people who are contributing to society by quietly and boldly doing whatever needs to be done to heal, grow, and transform so that not only are they grander for the effort but they have added to society by contributing to a well of health and generosity. There are millions of people who have become strong enough to hold their suffering and the suffering of the world. I believe these millions of unsung heroes and heroines should be recognized.

I have seen dozens of people with stories of abuse and torture. I have listened to scores of men and women spill out their anguish of crippling depression and anxiety. I myself spent many years pondering the abstraction of wholeness. What did it mean for a person to integrate and become whole? What was enlightenment? What was an enlarged personality? Then I met a brave woman whose childhood atrocities had fragmented her into dozens of tiny pieces. She was devoting her life to piecing herself back together again into a functioning adult who could keep steady attendance at her job and manage to drive from San Francisco to Stockton without regressing into a child who couldn't operate an automobile. She met every day as a draconian challenge, mastering her obstacles and demons as wholeheartedly and tenaciously as an Olympian gold medal winner. She brought new meaning to wholeness.

I questioned accomplishments and contributions. Who were the heroes and heroines adding to the wisdom of the ages? I admired the men and women who, with bounding courage, stood for what they believed in the face of controversy and retribution. And then I met a young man who lived with debilitating depression and anorexia. As we worked together I entered his world of tremendous struggle to literally get out of bed in the morning and to eat a nutritious diet. I marveled at this man's courage and strength to find and use the will on a daily basis to not give up. He was in touch with an energy and vitality to heal and mend. He desired more for his life than the shattered remnants of a broken spirit, and he was willing to work for health and salvation. I felt he deserved a prize of distinction. He was living a quiet, unrecognized heroic life.

I have had the honor of working with many of the outsiders of our society. Without glory, without public appreciation, many "invisible medal winners" through enduring what life has dealt them, are adding joy, light, and depth to the collective consciousness. Juanita, for instance, had polio as a very young child. She walked with a limp and slow gait. She needed to use her arms and hands to help move along one of her legs. She suffered from chronic and often debilitating back pain and with the daily awareness that she would ultimately end up in a wheelchair. She relished and utilized her days of mobility.

She was from South America and had come to this country for higher education so she could return to her country and help with her family business. Her family deeply revered her, and her handicap was "taken in stride" throughout her life and her development. But her country was not "handicap aware" and in addition to the trade she had come to master she was learning the ways of wheelchair ramps and handicap accessibilities in this country.

The spirit of this woman literally filled whatever room she entered. She had the charisma of a natural-born leader, and it was easy to see how well treated she had been in her life. It was also obvious that the woman had earned a great deal of wisdom through her handicap and earned easy relationship with everyone in her life. Everyone in her presence felt comfortable and at ease. Rather than her handicap holding center stage and being the source of concern or discomfort, Juanita's personality or "focus of the day" was the reason for social interchanges.

She, with the ease and mastery of an Olympic winner, held her physical pain and the reality of her weakening health and mobility. She endured her situation in such a way that others knew she was not feeling sorry for herself, did not experience her handicap as an injustice, and did not need others to feel badly for being physically whole. And since she had a natural humility, it surprised and delighted others to discover that they were inspired by who she was and how she lived her life. Through her unassumed modeling of strength and vitality in the midst of suffering, she offered a vision of highly developed (and nonmartyred) maturation and resilience.

Shortly after actor Christopher Reeves's devastating accident, I saw him interviewed by Barbara Walters. The accident left him a quadriplegic, and, sitting immobile in a wheelchair hooked up to oxygen so he could breathe and speak, he told the world that he is grateful for his life. He has his thinking capacity and his spirit and saw many viable roads for the rest of his life. At the time of the interview, he spoke of taking on legislation and fighting for the injured. He was planning to return to his extraordinary wife and family and live a full and active life. Several years later we know he has done what he intended.

When Barbara Walters asked him what difficulties remain for him, being paralyzed, he told a spine-chilling story. He was completely dependent on an oxygen pump for his breath and therefore for his life. Sometimes the pump failed for an instant or two and needed to be attended to. He told of waking up in the middle of the night aware that his pump was not working and he was not able to breathe. It sounded an alarm to the nurse's station, but it took about two breaths before it was put back into working order. He would panic until the air came back. That was at the beginning. By the time of this interview he knew what to expect and endured the lifeless moments. He said, "I hold my breath and save my energy. I have faith that the nurses will hear the alarm in time and hook me back up. I lie very still and wait to be able to breathe again. "

Hearing this interview, I was breathless (no pun intended) at this part, imagining what it would be like to not breathe on my own and to have to wait, with hope, for someone else to start me breathing again. Try the experiment. Hold your breath and imagine it. Unimaginable suffering, and yet Christopher Reeves has shown that it is possible to endure. He taught himself to understand the need and endure the existential moments. He taught himself to diminish the natural fears and accept the uncontrollable.

● spinning our wheels

I was afraid of quicksand, tics, boys on the street, the night,
bugs in the bathtub, my father, my mother, falling, hurting myself.
—ANONYMOUS

Change and loss are an integral part of everyone's life. When we go through change, even changing a habit, it raises anxiety, as well as myriad other feelings. If we wish to follow change through its natural course we are required to have responsible mature participation. We are faced with an ending of innocence, childhood longings for life to be easy, to not be hurt, to not fall down or fail, whether real or metaphorically, and come back up with the willingness and developed capacity to accept and live with ambiguities.

Instead, many of us deal with life's integral challenges with tremendous resistances and suffer through self-made agonies. We live with unfinished business. We live with brittleness, forged by denying our deeper feelings. We carry a multitude of tensions, short tempers, loneliness, perhaps headaches, aches, and pains. For many of us certain topics are avoided; we don't "talk about that." Instead we have insomnia and unpleasant dreams, or bouts of tears and depression that seemingly come out of the blue.

Candace is a bubbly redhead with a laugh much larger than her small frame. She was adopted when she was five weeks old. She has not met her biological mother or father and was raised by parents who were distant and cold to her and to each other. She carries a deeply held belief that there is something intrinsically wrong with her. She does not particularly relate this feeling about herself to her early rejection from her mother. She speaks and lives as if this belief is simply true, with no room for other options or possibilities. As the Buddhist philosophy teaches, she lives as if the illusion of being worthless were true.

Candace came into therapy because of immense suffering and feeling as if her life were out of control. She could put productive and satisfying days together, but it was only a matter of time before she would binge with alcohol, drugs, sex, or shopping. She could have days and even weeks of getting along very well with her good friends, but it was only a matter of time before she was irritated and annoyed with a slight or grievance against one of her friends and "hating the whole bunch." "I am sick and tired of all my friends being selfish and not asking me what is going on in my life." Candace feels this as real as the air she is breathing even though two weeks earlier her friends stayed with her around the clock when she had to be hospitalized for pneumonia.

She can gain insight into the destruction of her reactions to her flood of emotions—she understands that when she goes anywhere near frightening feelings she spirals instead into hating her life, blaming everything and everyone else, but she can just as easily lose sight of this knowing and go back to sleep. She has a beautiful soul that shines through at moments of clarity and has realistic desires for making more of her life. She gets frustrated that she does not follow through on her ideas and dreams, and when her friends offer her sage and heartfelt feedback for concrete change Candace will fume that they do not understand her free spirit.

Each setback comes after longer periods of constructive and healthy functioning but, invariably, she gives in to impulses, convincing herself that this is her God-given right to live freely. The overall picture is not of living freely, however; it is one of Candace spinning her wheels and running around in circles, held hostage by her self-imposed illusions and suffering.

It is not uncommon to be in our own way and to watch ourselves and our loved ones repeat painful patterns and spin wheels. In its most positive sense, this meeting ourselves over and over again (in what often seems the exact same place) can be likened to the alchemical process of *rotatio*—a process of repetition. Alchemists, attempting to transform lead into gold, were dedicated to the discovery of transformation for the human soul. As they mixed various materials, believed to be images of the soul, they keenly observed how change came about. In rotatio the materials were heated, mixed, and distilled over and over again and then over and over again. In this process of refinement, introducing the same material in this series of treatments, the alchemists discovered the materials had become subtle and pure. The alchemical process can offer us meaning and purpose to repeating patterns—using the same raw materials and exposing them over and over to the light of day— over and over toward subtlety and purity—a way to understand how and why to endure pain and suffering.

Resilience is not an instant recovery. If we are willing to learn from an experience, we will become astute and aware in other situations right from the beginning. Learning from our experiences and distinguishing suffering can mean a long process of coping and making mistakes on the road toward healing, but not learning can result in remaining depressed and disorganized.

Long after having dealt, many times, with the pain and horror of the violations in her childhood, Sarah, a colleague, over lunch recounts how she experienced meeting her wounds over and over.

> I was dragged into reliving my early traumatic experiences again, at a deeper and more feeling level. At different times, I lived in an altered state of going about my life, all the while carrying raw emotions, feeling twelve years old once again. One day I needed to attend a meeting and I was particularly vulnerable that day, having been awakened by a terrifying dream that left me shaking and feeling very alone.
>
> Even though I could have told the person with whom I was meeting about my real state, I chose not to—I was in too raw a state. But because I could not tell the truth of how I was feeling I had to actively keep my end of the conversation and feelings at a superficial level. An hour seemed like an eternity, and when I left I watched in amazement as I entered a painful zone of self-imposed suffering.
>
> I was upset with the person with whom I had met. I concluded he did not respect my opinions anymore because the meeting had been so flat. "I am so embarrassed. I cannot go back to see him any more. I am so stupid; I didn't make any sense" (completely forgetting that I had chosen to keep things on the surface). The content of my thinking was specious and overblown—a direct quote from my feelings as a child. But the feelings were palpable and felt completely real and valid. I was suffering, but had enough awareness at that moment to recognize that I was distressed because I had not adequately connected with the person and I had not connected because I had not been able to tell him what was genuinely hurting me. Not because I was worthless or he was uncaring.

Going back to Candace—she longs for deep connection, to herself and to the people in her life. But the early wound of not being connected is deep, excruciating, and frightening to her. She works hard and overtime to avoid the rawness of her early rejection. It is like being out in the hot blinding sun—we can only stay so long before we need to take cover. Candace is involved in a powerful push-pull *between* prematurely running from this deep emotional pain straight into victimization *and* getting glimpses of the genuine and sustaining freedom held within the willingness to gradually but seriously look the sun in the eye. Quoting Etty Hillesum, if Candace is able to "destroy the idea behind which her life is imprisoned, she will experience true liberation." The irony is that she, through repeated visits of the raw and painful material of rejection, can free herself from the belief that she is worthless, which is the exact fear she is attempting to avoid by not going near the real suffering.

Because it takes time and time again to rotate, expose the patterns and the feelings to the elixir of transformation, we need to be committed to feeling—to feeling the wide range of human emotions. We need to tolerate intense emotions without caving in or being flooded, backing off or going numb. Choosing to suffer and to endure the darkness is to say, "I am willing to feel. I am willing to face the truth, know what I have lost or never had. I will face whatever I have to face in order to heal, transform, and see clearly. I will permit the feelings to emerge into consciousness."

● feeling

Women certainly have more "permission" to cry, feel, and be vulnerable than men do in our culture, but I contend that we are all given negative messages about crying—ranging from a "nuisance" to an "embarrassment" to "forbidden in this house." Girls are often told that they are too sensitive, overly emotional, and theatrical as the greatest diva of the decade, overreacting, neurotic, or hysterical. A friend told me that her mother would harshly flick her lips to stop her from crying. Another friend, moved to tears by a special gift, said, "Oh my God, I am going to embarrass myself and cry!"

This is more often what we do with our emotions. As with our sorely forgotten dog in the corner in chapter 7, we tie them up, prefer them to be neglected or forgotten in the corner of our "house." We undervalue them and wonder at the spectacle of an overreaction, whether hysteria, minor and major physical illness from repression, or out-of-control violence. And as so many women have discovered when they were ready to feel, previously unacceptable emotions were locked far enough away in the mind and body to become inaccessible. Instead of serving us with helpful and healthy information and expression, feelings not given their natural and proper place will burrow deep into the body or psyche, turning instead into some unrecognizable demon.

Women, in our journey to equality, battle the misconception that crying or showing emotions implies weakness. Coupled with the misconception is the human desire to distance from our vulnerability and any display of helplessness. Admittedly, these are frightening emotions, powerful forces threatening loss of control, feelings and energy that have been leashed for a long time, but this is one of the purposes of the descent.

Each time we allow ourselves to face the powerful emotions we feel less afraid and the feelings are less foreign. As with shadow work, we want to feed the dog very gradually and gently, but with serious nutrition and sustenance, so the dog can ultimately live among the family again as a welcomed part of the household. Becoming friendlier with our emotions and vulnerability, being resilient in this way, gives us the ability to tolerate pain and insight long enough to discover what we need to know in any particular phase of our lives.

SACRED TEARS

Collecting the drops of public sorrow into his volume,
as into a lachrymal vase . . .
—WASHINGTON IRVING

In ancient Rome, archeologists have discovered, in unearthed tombs, a small vase with a narrow neck. This vial, called a lachrymatory, was used to hold the tears of mourners. In her novel *The Divine Secrets of the Ya-Ya Sisterhood*, Rebecca Wells picks up on this unusual idea.

> She reached in and very gently lifted out a tiny glass vessel about the size of a fox-glove blossom. The vial was very old, made of sterling silver over glass, with one jade stone in the center of its little screw-on lid. It's called a lachrymatory. A tiny jar of tear drops. In olden days it was one of the greatest gifts you could give someone. It meant you loved them, that you shared a grief that brought you together.

In the Handless Maiden myth, the young heroine, who will lose both her hands as a sacrifice—a betrayal—stands and cries. Because of a misguided bargain she will be left disabled and distraught. At the beginning of the story she is rendered pure and whole through her continual stream of tears and, most important, because she is crying she is protected from the Devil who has come to claim her as his own. He cannot come near her or own her as long as she cries cleansing tears. As with the lachrymatory, history beckons us to a time that crying is sacred and holy.

This is a concept that has been lost through time. We have lost the numinosity and value of pure grief in the face of loss and separation. Spencer is four years old and his mother told me this story. He had fallen off the jungle gym and lodged his baby tooth back into his gums. The dentist told his mother he would have to give up his pacifier because it would impede the necessary dental work to repair his injury. The pacifier fairy visited Spencer the night before a family vacation and traded his worn treasure with a much-desired Tyrannosaurus Rex. Spencer was impressed that the pacifier fairy knew what he wanted most in the world at that time.

The first night of their vacation proved to be unbearable for Spencer. With his mother lying at his side he wailed for three hours. "I will never be able to sleep again," he lamented. His mother tells me she could feel the depth of his pain, and it felt no different to her than when she lost her father. Spencer was grieving with all his heart and without any reservations. As he lay crying he turned to his mother and said, "So sad, so sad, so sad." His mother recognized this quotation from one of his favorite books where the mother owl loses her child and cries to the heavens, "So sad, so sad, so sad."

"Are you feeling as badly as the mother owl, Spencer?"

"No, not that bad."

He might have lost the beloved comfort of the pacifier, but his mother was right there by his side.

We have moved far away from such unbridled and honest responses. In his brave way of encountering the first major loss of his young life, Spencer found each subsequent night easier and easier. This loss was not something that would have to be tucked away in his unconscious, breeding and brooding sadness to be felt for years and years, all the while forgetting the origin of the pain and loss. I imagine this is what Etty Hillesum meant when she prayed to God to "grant me the great and mighty calm that pervades all nature. If it is Your wish to let me suffer, then let it be one great, all-consuming suffering, not the thousand petty anxieties that can break a human."

● all-consuming suffering

You met Samantha in chapter 4. She was struggling to be in synch with her real needs and not give herself away to the men in her life when she was in relationship with them. When she met Michael she was anxious from the start. "He is so unlike any other man I have dated; I cannot immediately sense his wounds which is a good thing, but I am not sure if he is too busy and ambitious for me." At the time Samantha did not realize this would be the beginning of her enduring her insecurities and anxieties as she navigated her way through the most positive relationship in her life.

Not feeling sure about what she could ask for and what was "too much,"

Samantha kept silent and gave the full reigns of the relationship's pace and meaning to Michael. She complained frequently that she thought he was self-involved and was not all that interested in discovering who she was.

> I came home from this amazing ski trip and he did not even ask me how it was. We go out to dinner and unless I fill in the space with questions about Michael, we sit in silence during the meal. I am definitely more interested in who he is than vice versa and I really cannot be with someone who doesn't share the fundamentals of self-discovery and the zest for a lively give and take in a relationship.

As our work with these issues progressed it became more obvious that Samantha was sitting on many unsaid feelings and thoughts. Rather than act them out by storming Michael about his insensitivities or breaking up with him because he was not, as all her friends said in response to her unhappiness, "right for her," she noticed how she was feeling. Because she was willing and able to sit with her increasing discomfort and express it appropriately, she was able to see more clearly what was bothering her at a deeper level. She felt convinced that her needs were too great and would push him away; when I offered that it was healthy and appropriate to speak up and ask Michael to be more attentive to who she is, she wept. She had felt blind to the balance of what is too much and what is too little.

She came in to the next session positively glowing; Michael had been completely receptive to her concerns and not only genuinely listened to her but also began to ask her more about herself. The relationship deepened and they moved closer as a result.

> Things are really great; we have such a good time together and there are no more silences during meals. He called me from the airport when he got back from his conference and wanted to know how my week had been. He knew I was in a skiing competition and remembered who I was racing against.

Over a period of many months Samantha struggled with deep and free-floating anxieties about the relationship. The pattern developed where she would realize what she wanted was legitimate; she would initiate a discussion with Michael and things would change. However, rather than stem Samantha's feelings of worry, they intensified. She began to worry about the future, the "what if's" and all that could go wrong. She began to look for concrete evidence to validate her worries. "Everything between us is pretty great. We really like each other and the times we spend together are wonderful. His friends are as accomplished as he is and I am beginning to feel insecure. This is really nuts because I am proud of what I am doing in my career and love the actual work."

Samantha is an accomplished, ambitious, and talented freelance artist. The objective reality is mightily at odds with her insecurities. Once again she was willing to sit with the discomfort and self-imposed humiliations of not being good enough for Michael and his circle. She did not like the suffering, looked for ways to remove it, and often felt tremendous judgment that she was "such a mess." In fact, she used how she felt to further indicate her illusion that she was inferior to Michael. He had his life together and did not seem to have any emotional turmoil.

But to her credit, she held the gaze, lived with the messiness, and found that she had not previously been with anyone who "had his act together." She was more accustomed to being the one holding things together while her partner fell into dark and gloomy moods. It was doubtful that Michael was perfect, but he was unlike her previous boyfriends, and that required her to relate differently—to relate as equals.

This allowed her to move into deeper waters. In a discussion with Michael she shared some fears and told him she was concerned he was not happy in the relationship. He was reassuring: "I love being with you. I feel alive, happy to see you when we get together and I always look forward to when we will be together again." Samantha repeated this conversation in my office and then got a faraway look in her eyes. "I don't think my fear is that Michael will leave; I think my fear is that I will throw over my life and needs to be with him. That is what I have always done and now that I am getting more involved and liking him more and more I can feel the terror rising in me."

Samantha's father had been physically and emotionally unavailable, and she had perfected a defense of being ready at all times just in case he would have time for her. The pain, sorrow, and anger at having given herself away year after year were palpably under the surface as she spoke.

This opened a new level of suffering, one she had visited before many times. The fact that she was willing to endure, express, and claim responsibility for these feelings kept them from polluting a present-day relationship that she wanted to sustain and relate to in a newly constructed fashion. By staying with her insecurities and her debilitating anxieties, Samantha was able to look for the deeper meanings and patterns. By containing the ambiguities—were her anxieties pointing to this relationship not being right for her; were her troubled waters showing the path toward further healing; was her mind playing games with her; was she being alerted to calming her mind through meditation so she could enjoy this new, and healthiest, relationship—by containing these uncertainties she could come to clearer thinking and different behaviors. While the outcome is uncertain, the process is evolving and offering Samantha more and varied options as well as allowing her and Michael to get closer. She is uncovering her old patterns of giving herself and her needs away. She is learning to relate to and understand her needs in a new light and have a fresh approach to a healthy give and take in an intimate relationship.

It is not easy to sit with the various intense emotions unleashed as we plumb the depths of the unconscious—behaviors, attitudes, and patterns. More often than not we shy away from pure feeling and suffering.

> Man suffers most through his fears of suffering. The body keeps leading the spirit, when it should be the other way round.
>
> —Etty Hillesum

Especially because fear and refusal will exacerbate and distort genuine suffering. As Samantha worked her way through the layers of feelings that kept her from feeling close to Michael, she came up against fear over and over again. Whenever fear took over, she became convinced she was in deep trouble and needed to dash away from the feelings and/or the situation. When fear enters the picture, our trials and tribulations take on a patina of distorted danger and threat. This is a time we will turn to barbiturates or tranquilizers, alcohol, sex, television, or anything to numb the pain.

We come up with dozens of reasons to avoid the pain. It can seem intolerable—just too much to bear or, since we can't bring back someone we have lost or undo the past, we can believe it makes no sense to grieve, or our families and society tell us to pull ourselves together and get on with our lives, or we become impatient with how long the suffering lasts, or we may be frightened by the strong emotions, or embarrassed by how we feel or worry that it is strange or possibly crazy to feel so strongly. I am sure you can add to this list.

However we do it, it takes courage, enormous courage to be true to our reactions and responses, to face how we feel and not divert our attention to the other person or what should have been or could be. It takes courage to bear the discomfort and admit the cost of our distress, and it takes courage to 'fess up to what we will do with how we feel. And because we have different temperaments we will experience the rush of emotions differently. Some of us will be visibly upset, cry and moan and thrash about. Some of us will scream and rage, some will sit quietly all the while tears continually stream down our faces. Some will cry alone, others will feel the stronger feelings in the company of a safe person. Some will cry and be upset for an intense, short time and feel complete, others will feel the pain for longer periods of time.

● sacrifice

I know you have nothing
That is why I ask you for everything
That way you will have everything.
—ANTONIO PORCHIA

In order to live in the Technicolor of our souls, in order to meet life at its edges and fullness, we must look to the realness of suffering, in ourselves and in the world. Since the beginning of humankind's existence, philosophers, people of the cloth from the East and the West, psychologists and sociologists have grappled with the dark side of life. Bad things happen to good people, and the world at large posits significant doses of injustice and evil.

At the core of survival exists sacrifice of the innocent. When the bird eats the worm, the bird is ingesting nutrition for its survival. But the innocent worm is being sacrificed. In order for the bird to live its life, the worm pays with loss of hers.

Often we prefer to ignore the question of evil and suffering and choose to believe that destiny is indifferent or malevolent rather than admit our helplessness in the face of horrific events and conundrum sacrifices. But the reality of injustice and evil is real, and to live a liberated and conscious life we are called to accept this reality and move to a creative response.

As with the worm's relationship to the bird, there is a theme of sacrifice throughout the conscious life, suffering, asking the difficult questions, and wrestling with the questions of transformation. Recently I saw a theatre piece called *The Laramie Project,* which came about as the result of the death of Matthew Shepard, a young gay man who was inhumanely tortured, beaten, and left to die on a wooden fence in a remote field miles from Laramie, Wyoming. After reading about Shepard's death, a troupe of actors went to Laramie to interview a wide range of townsfolk. They spent months talking with his relatives, the local police, the students and professors at the university Matthew was attending, the young boy who found Matthew, the untiring doctor who treated both Matthew and one of the men who was later found guilty of the crime, and other local residents.

The powerful play utilized these voices to convey a stunning transformation in many of the people of this heretofore private town. One of the young men interviewed over a long period of time was a drama student whose family was homophobic. When he chose a dialogue from *Angels in America*, a play about gays and AIDS, his family refused to come, even though they had attended every single other activity this young man participated in. The young man was confused and wondered how *he* felt about homosexuality.

He had chosen the dialogue for his audition on its theatrical merits, not for any political purposes, but his family's strong reaction made him think deeply about an issue he had not previously given any thought to at all. By the end of the interview process between the actors and the townsfolk, a period of many months, this young man had the lead in the university's production of *Angels in America*. He had recently played Hamlet, and his family had proudly come to see his performance. But when they heard about his role in *Angels*, they told him they would not attend his performance. The young man had had many months to reflect on his own feelings and develop his own ideas about homosexuality. He turned to his folks and confronted them, "You were willing to come see me be a murderer, but you will not show up when I play a gay man?"

A very shy gay woman watched in horror as the media and public eye descended upon her hometown because of Matthew's murder. When a man strongly opposed to homosexuality began to appear everywhere the media was, with large signs indicating the righteousness of Matthew's death because of his lifestyle, this young woman found a voice she did not know she had. She rounded up many friends and made costumes for them all. They dressed as angels with the widest wingspan imaginable and "just happened" to show up wherever this man chose to stand. By circling him, standing in front of him, between him and the cameras or the throngs of people who were mourning at Matthew's funeral, this shy young woman and her friends gently but insistently denied this man his hateful message.

This woman and the young student actor's personal transformation were reflected in dozens of stories in Laramie, Wyoming, and the theatre piece powerfully displayed a new level of consciousness and genuine love that had risen in many of the people in this small town as a result of a sacrifice of an innocent young man. By not turning away from the bigotry, by facing the truth that people you love are harboring prejudice, by standing their ground in the force of hatred (even coming up with creative solutions), many people in this small town bore the gaze long enough to transform their own naiveté and fears.

Hareem and Letitia loved each other through fifteen years of marriage but brought out the worst in each other. Regardless of how they tried, they bumped into each other in ways that inadvertently caused pain and damage to the other person. Letitia had been born with a heart condition, and her parents had isolated her in the hopes of protecting her. She grew up fearful of people coming too close or of feeling too intensely. Hareem, a passionate man, had been orphaned and needed to feel close to people who mattered to him. They both desired to be there for the other, but their opposing needs only clashed. As much as they tried, they only hurt each other and broke their hearts because they loved each other and could not make their relationship close or safe.

After many months of talking, crying, and facing the horribly sharp teeth of despair, they agreed to live apart. When they decided to divorce, they surprisingly discovered an ability to communicate and understand the other person in ways that simply were not available to either of them while married. Sacrificing their marriage and living together gave them a surreal opportunity to be in each other's lives without the expectations that thwarted their mutual desire for closeness.

Lynne's nineteen-year-old son died in an automobile accident. Lynne is a powerhouse entrepreneur who at the time had fifteen people working for her. Her husband and other son (and son before he died) had long ago resigned themselves to her professional priorities and had carved out their own lives, quite separate from her. Many years earlier her family had confronted her about their need of her; she was receptive but appeared hardwired to fulfill her career goals and, even though she is a caring woman, she could not seem to find it within herself to change. When her son died, something shifted in her with no conscious effort. In the midst of anguishing grief, she looked at her husband and remaining son in a new light, and what had previously appeared intractable now shed naturally.

She continued to work but was effortlessly and contentedly there for her family. Her husband and son were hard pressed to have words for the difference they felt in her relationship with them; she was as passionate about her work as ever, but they felt and delighted in her genuine, and now equal, interest in them. As in *The Laramie Project,* the sacrifice of a young man had opened up channels that allowed love to flourish and heal previously closed or bypassed hearts.

These sacrifices, from the worm to marriages and sons, appear unwitting and out of our control. In fact, from the ego's point of view, to sacrifice is nothing short of throwing oneself on the pyre. And yet, we engage in sacrifices all the time. We sacrifice emotions for reason, violence for justice, lives of order and service in lieu of spontaneity and wild outbursts. To achieve a sense of clarity, people will fast for days on end. We give up one thing to have another.

In order to write this book I willingly gave up a great deal of social and family life. To stay home with her family, Clarice sacrificed personal freedom. To study medicine and become a doctor, Jill is giving up a six-figure salary in the high tech industry. To give her sister a longer life, Maxine is donating a kidney. In the novel *The Chosen*, the author Chaim Potok has the young man's father, a rabbi, stop talking to his son. The son has, inadvertently, hurt another young man and does not feel the victim's wound. Through this loud silence the rabbi teaches his son pain, offers him the experience of suffering so he may know compassion. Through the sacrifice of intimacy, the father gives his son a hard look into himself.

An ultimate resilience, the ability to be flexible and creative *within* the reality of our lives, our world, including the injustices and mysteries, requires a confrontation and a sacrifice. A confrontation with feeling the ugliness and horrors that reside within us, the world, and the dark side of life. And a sacrifice of the ego to the Self (in Jungian terms a word to describe the Divine within) to allow the transformation of viewing and living life from the ego's point of view to viewing and living life from the viewpoint of the deeper Self, a place of knowing, wisdom, and timelessness.

Not getting what we want, feeling the loss of someone or something precious, being humiliated or rendered invisible, having been harmed, being robbed and cheated because of injustices are all felt by the ego as a personal insult and time-bound dents in our psyche. Held in this place we stay brittle, superficial, and unprepared to meet further challenges in a large and transformative way. As we listen carefully to the messages from the Self, we will hear the call of the willow, the willow tree that knows how and when to bend and incorporate the mightiest of storms into its fiber.

> Again his taut, avid ego extinguished itself in wide-vaulted order. . . .
> —HERMANN HESSE

The Self is not interested in comfort, safety zones, what other people think, or the social mores of the day, or for that matter, the moral mores of the day. The Self is interested in incarnating and needs the cooperation of the ego. It is as if the mighty gods need the puny human to hold power far surpassing the human's imagination and boundaries. The ego's modus operandi is to protect, build up, and console, but the Self is interested in change, largesse movements, and consciousness at any cost. While the ego is interested in a content and quiet evening where it can reign, the Self is interested in grappling with the hard questions of death, meaning, good and evil, and character.

The ego is invested in being the heroine, in charge of its own life, knowing the answers and being secure. The Self is invested in upsetting the apple cart of status quo, the unknown, the search and the sacrifice for wholeness and consciousness. It is a lifetime process devoted to living an original life, not one designed by the outside world, family, society, or the collective at large. The sacrifice is often immense, more often than not the most essential or valued need, and while there are no guarantees, the result can be nothing less than a precious gem—our Personality and a binding connectedness to life itself. This state of grace can be intuited, in a "Here's a preview allure" during a moment of time. The light in a baby's eyes, a magnificent sunset, viewing a piece of sacred art, tasting the first tomato off the vine can all strike a chord of harmony and give us contact with a spark of divinity—a peek at the promise of a life lived fully.

We are called to live the life sought after and pushed for by the deeper Self—the ground of the original blueprint. Born out of the tempest and suffering of our struggles, without instructions and explanations we are called to an authentic and enlarged life. This is genuine suffering—the sacrifice to become who we are and live our original life regardless of the ego's desire or point of view. A strong and mature ego or sense of self in the world is called upon to cooperate in its demise and collaboration with a larger reality and through this sacrifice raise the life lived to its highest cause.

The perennial question we all face is, Will we listen to the Self? Will we willingly sacrifice our insistences of what is best to a larger reality? I wish I had a nickel for every time I was sure of what I needed or what would be best for me—or my loved ones—only to be shown, after much time elapsed, that a higher wisdom saw more clearly what was in my best interest. Will we abandon ourselves to the out-of-control, sometimes chaotic, and sometimes cruel streams of a larger reality? Would we sacrifice money, time, youthfulness, mobility, freedom, love . . . would we sacrifice being right, being seen in certain lights, the color in our cheeks, the security of a firm grasp or steady step, the image we hold of who we are, what the world is like, and how it should be?

In the mystical tradition of the Kabbalah there is a concept called the *shevirat ha-kelim*, meaning "breaking of the vessels." From the limitless, the unknown, and unknowable God of Kabbalah there came a jet of light that was to fill the empty vessels of the Sephiroth. Instead of being able to hold this light, all but the first three vessels were shattered by it. The shards of the broken vessels fell into the abyss. Most of the light returned to the En Soph, the unknowable God, but some of it remained in the first three vessels.

Somewhere I heard this concept understood as a legend. This legend suggests that we are the vessel, an intricately carved crystal, and we are asked to become strong and sturdy enough to hold the light held forth from the unknown and withstand the intensity and power of the light of God. It is our job, our challenge, our destiny as a vessel, to hold the light so the power and intensity of life itself can be seen and known. I have taken this idea seriously enough that when I went through a depression I despaired I had broken a promise to "not break" and would not be able to uphold my end of the bargain. I was humbled to discover a stronger container for life at the other end of the depression and to discover a larger capacity to hold ecstasy and joy.

Endure suffering, endure sacrifice, and endure ecstasy and joy (the light). Mold and fashion our crystal vessel, strengthen it, caulk its seams and, through courageously bearing direct witness to our struggles, render it sturdy, beautiful, and sacred. From our deepest longings we can create a holy place and experience the fullest awareness of pain and ecstasy—withstand the intensity and power of the light of what is Divine.

exercise

CREATE A SACRED SPACE

Temenos is the Greek word for a sacred place.

Build a temenos for yourself. Using an altar, ritual, meaningful artifacts, close and dear people in your life, art, or music:

Within this temenos, over time, bear direct witness to your struggles. Enduring the dark, choose to feel and face the truth about what you have lost and choose to face the pain.

Within this temenos, over time, bear direct witness to your joys. Enduring the light, choose to feel and face the truth about what you have gained and choose to face your delights and happiness.

diving for the pearl   11

Love is the unfamiliar Name
Behind the hands that wove
The intolerable shirt of flame
Which human power cannot
remove.
We only live, only suspire
Consumed by either fire or fire.
—T. S. ELIOT

WHERE IS THE home of hope, triumph, and miracles?

Maggie and Tim were anxiously awaiting the arrival of their firstborn when Tim found a baby's monogrammed jumper suit in a catalog. As a surprise to Maggie, Tim ordered one with their last name emblazoned on the back. When Maggie miscarried their child, Tim quietly gave the jumper suit to his father, Rich, because the reminder of it in their home added to the pain and grief they felt. Maggie and Tim spent the next seven years trying to have a child. With each ensuing miscarriage their grief deepened and their hopes sank. They watched as brothers and sisters became pregnant and had children; sometimes hiding their sorrow and sometimes feeling they would burst wide open with their losses.

When Maggie became pregnant once again seven years after the original miscarriage, they could hardly hold their glee as she approached her ninth month and the doctor assured them that all was well. Maggie and Tim's baby shower was filled with energy of gratitude surpassing the usual happiness at these events. All of Tim's parents' friends jumped at the opportunity to attend this joyful event and literally shower them with all sorts of baby wonders as well as tearful thanks and appreciation for this healthy pregnancy. Toward the end of the gift giving, Rich, Tim's father, said he had something to give to Maggie and Tim.

Tim opened the tiny package and began to cry. His father had saved the jumper specially monogrammed with their last name. He had put it, wrapped in tissue paper, in the back of a bureau drawer, having not lost faith that one day his son and daughter-in-law would have a baby to wear this long held treasure.

"I thought about this many times through the years," Tim said, "and assumed you had given it to one of your other grandchildren."

"No," said Rich. "It has always been yours and so I waited for this time to give it to you both."

Maggie gave birth to a healthy baby boy.

What do you believe? Where does belief come from?

What do you know? What is unquestionable? What is so strong that it *can* be questioned?

We know that change is a given and that tragedies are woven into the fabric of all of our lives. We know that uncertainty and lack of security is more common than not. We know that, but when change, hardships, uncertainty, and insecurity become real in our lives we shake in our boots. It is then we must know how to find the home of hope, triumph, and miracles—from the small daily graces of solace, gratitude, and resolve to the wings of angels discovered in heroes, altruism, and mysticism.

● meaning and resilience

Finding the home of hope, triumph, and miracles is a matter of awakening to shared hopes that are buried beneath any tragedy and learning how to cultivate this power of the soul. Having meaning in one's life means *knowing* life is worthwhile, even when filled with troubles and adversities. Knowing that life is worth living when the treasured child that brings meaning to your life is taken away from you. Having meaning means believing in something beyond the roles and assumptions we make about who we are. Basing our whole life on being a caretaker or provider only to discover a soaring emptiness when our role is no longer needed. Through the discovery of life's deeper and deeper meanings we become not an ego but a *mensch*, a soulful person who has overcome herself and her sorrow.

I introduced Sandra in chapter 7 as she worked to forgive her mother. Her work on understanding her mother and finding ways to see her growing up more clearly took her to deeper levels within as well as times of great frustration. She felt the pangs of not having parents (her stepfather had also passed away when she was a young adult) and the fears that would arise when she wondered who would take care of her if she could not take care of herself. In the midst of dealing with these issues, both personal as well as existential, she also found herself questioning her faith, which had to this point been stalwart and inherited from her parents. The more she questioned and the more she delved into the meaning of her dreams and her life experiences, the more she discovered tremendous inner strength and boosted self-esteem.

One day she walked into my office with a dream: She was in a cabin on a ship and the cabin was under the sea. She was sitting with her mother and a man and woman she remembered from school. Her mother was being soothing and she recoiled, saying she did not need soothing right now. The man who was sitting next to her, and who she remembered from her past as being very kind to her, asked her why she was eating what she was eating when she did not like it. This brought her up sharp with the realization that she did not need to eat what she did not want to eat, and she went with the man to the ship's kitchen, which was filled with lots of rotten food, and discarded her unwanted meal. Someone came up to her and told her that her father was looking for her. She said she would be there in a minute. She had something to do first.

She then heard a loud, booming, and large voice say, "Where is my daughter?" The voice woke her up and she quietly but firmly replied:

"I am here," consciously answering him and meeting him in intensity and importance.

The powerful dream moved her deeply, and twenty minutes later she told me, "I had always thought security would be in having my parents or having lots and lots of money. Now I feel a sense of security within that surpasses anything I could have on the outside."

MEANING IS THE BOUNCE IN BOUNCING BACK

Resilience is about adaptability and thriving in new soil. To be flexible enough to adapt to continual change and here-to-stay adversity means equipping oneself with the ability to have lots of options, lots of choices, and a hefty dosage of resolve and meaning.

> Finding and living from a place of meaning is the single most important avenue for being resilient.

Finding meaning, purpose, and significance to personal and collective sorrows and tragedy can singularly mean the difference between being lost in the shadow of the crisis and being born of the phoenix out of the ashes. Meaning creates resolve, and resolve brings resilience. Whether we find meaning in the timelessness of the redwood forest, passing on tradition to the next generation, social responsibility, adding to the consciousness of God, or delving into the mysteries of the universe discovered on inner spiritual pilgrimages, meaning has the potential of transcending and transforming tragedy.

The other qualities of the resiliency process add important and necessary skills to affect resilience; cultivating meaning is essential for fully bouncing back. Finding meaning gives us roots and wings to walk and create on the ground of existential uncertainty, temporal impermanence, and redemption possibilities. Cultivating meaning strengthens the inner belief that you can overcome. Not necessarily overcome illness, injustices, or terrible times but overcome fears, giving up, shame, and resistances. Consciously entering into one's life journey as a pilgrimage toward the discovery of personal meaning offers the experience needed to cultivate this precious adaptability and flourishing.

The greatest cause of suffering in so many of our people is their utter lack of inner preparation, which makes them give up long before they even set foot in a camp. They believe our fate is sealed already, our catastrophe complete.

—Etty Hillesum

When I began researching resiliency, I read story after story from the Holocaust of the Second World War as well as stories about prisoners of war, decades of slavery, places of unspeakable torture and human cruelty, and sadly, more recent accounts of the aftermath of the terrorists' attacks on New York and Washington, D.C. I read the same thing over and over again. Those who went into the camps or were thrown into the chaos of September 11, 2001, with a belief in something outside or greater than themselves survived more intact. Those in the camps who had no faith or belief died, lost touch with reality, or stayed permanently scared and haunted.

Further investigation showed that faith and belief was not restricted to an ineffable power or what many call God, but included a long list of beliefs and investments greater than the victims: connectedness to family members, activism, nature, the future, mystery, and dreams, to name a few. A documentary on Anne Frank's experience in a concentration camp shed light on a little-known aspect of her death. It was well known and recorded that the light of her young life was her father. As far as Anne was concerned, the sun rose and set on him, and her feelings toward him guided her actions on a regular basis. A couple of days before Anne's death she was incorrectly told that her father had died. (She had been sleeping next to her sister, who died within the same time period.) According to this documentary, which was narrated by a woman who had been Anne's good friend through the horrors of their encampment, Anne was in decent health until hearing of her father's death. Within a couple of days of believing her father was gone, Anne died.

In my own reflection of what meaning brings to adversity, I wonder if we are not sufficient unto ourselves to go through hell. In the paradox of we are everything and we are nothing, we need to have a bigger reason, a larger endpoint to motivate and inspire us to live through horrors and rebuild our lives beyond a mere existence. There are bad things and losses we will never recover from—random events, tragedies, and chronic injustices that have no regard to fairness or reasonable expectations. And yet we are required, if we choose to live with vitality and consciousness, to relate to these events; and if we are wise we relate to them by finding meaning. A deep enough, vast enough understanding so we can rise out of the rubble and anchor ourselves in something beyond and outside of these events and injustices.

It is common, during the aftermath of momentous tragedies, to turn our eyes to the heavens, to look into the eyes of the newborn, and to find meaning in coming together and pulling extra weight to aid those in need. Most people want to live in a world with a backbone of caring and community, and sometimes horror and evil shock us into remembering our deep human need of a connection to a higher purpose beyond our narrow points of view and interest. We want to live in a world that tragedy often brings home—the awareness of how important our loved ones are in our life—what it means to hear a loved one's voice, hold a hand.

More often than not a shock of pain and terror bring the simplest of life's spiritual pleasures into bold relief. Sitting in the midst of great loss, my friend Marion described the varied colors of the autumnal apples on the hundreds of trees in the orchards, covering the ground for miles and miles, and experienced the deepest joy and awe of God's creation. How had the apples never looked as beautiful as they did in this painful moment? Adversity can bring consciousness, a deeper awareness for simple pleasures, and help us rub the sleep out of our eyes.

CHOOSING MEANING

If your soul is no stranger to you, the whole world is your home.
—KABIR

Breaking our leg, losing a temporary job, or failing an exam will probably not bring us to our knees with a plaintive cry of "Why?" but many of life's adversities and tragedies do push us to the edge of needing to understand, to see behind the veil and know the meaning of what happened. We are not born knowing patience, having depth of character, or being able to resolve conflicts. What does it mean to have to learn these qualities?

What is the meaning of the blue jay's song, a woman's muffled longing, a tear cascading over a lined and wizened cheek, loneliness, torture inflicted on our fellow human, joy in the eye as a new father watches his daughter being born? What is the meaning of a rainbow, hatred, ancestry, survival of the fittest, shades on our windows?

We are designed to grow, to absorb our families' ways, values, and traditions only to have ample time and pressure to question them and discover our own way, how to dress, how to make friends, and how to think for ourselves. But it takes conscious effort and personal responsibility to achieve personal meaning; it is a *choice*—not a given. We have to choose to contemplate infinity; it will not happen to us. And yet, to not choose can mean a shadow of a life.

People are dying here even now of a broken spirit, because they can no longer find any meaning in life, young people. The old ones are rooted in firmer soil and accept their fate with dignity and calm. You see so many different sorts of people here and so many different attitudes to the hardest, the ultimate questions. . . .

—Etty Hillesum

If we choose, we begin to discover personal values, learn particular lessons, and ask questions of ultimate values. If we choose to stay awake, sooner or later we are faced with the more fundamental value questions—questions and values that will take us out of the humdrum choices of music, food, and clothes preferences of everyday life. Sooner or later, especially when things get bad enough, we are faced with questions of good and evil and what lies behind painful difficulties and losses. Questions that challenge the status quo and wonder at the horrid spectacle of mistreatment, hate, and violence. Questions that lead us to asking why we are alive at this time. Why we are confronted with grievous tragedies, and what does life and death mean to us, personally and collectively? We are faced with directly personal questions:

- ▶ What brings meaning and purpose to my life, what gets me up in the morning, what do I live for?
- ▶ Am I dissatisfied and disgruntled because I am denying who I am?
- ▶ What does my life mean to me?
- ▶ What do I want to leave behind when I am gone?
- ▶ What might I contribute to the community?
- ▶ How do I show up in life, when am I passionate and where am I wholeheartedly committed?

We are asked to step outside and ask who we are.

If we choose, sooner or later we are pushed forward, away from unreflective beliefs toward new values, deeper understandings, and a spectrum of spiritual roots in order to enter into the search and dialogue of these questions.

Maureen came to see me during a major transition in her life. She grew up with a deep belief in a God who answered her prayers and watched over her. Having been abandoned by her mother at her birth, Maureen used this attachment to God and belief to guide herself. She was an achiever at school and had many good friends. She was raised by her grandmother, who encouraged her granddaughter's piety and praised her for her daily prayers and ever-tightening reliance on gifts from God. Maureen assumed that her success and protection from God were permanent. She decided to risk her security and choose a career path in computer technology, in which she had no training or background. After using up a year's worth of savings she found she was not learning enough or able to comprehend what was needed to put together deals. She was failing and she was shocked. She lost her usual verve, feeling not only depleted but also betrayed.

She had never failed before at anything she had put her mind and prayers toward. This experience put her faith in question. Her journey, from failure and loss of faith, took her into the pain and sorrow of her early abandonment. In some ways her faith had sheltered her from facing this early loss; with a faltering of faith she was thrust into her early years. Through tears, aching, and rage she began to reestablish her faith on more solid ground and construct ideas that gave room for negative incidents and emotions as well as open-ended questions about her realistic strengths and limitations. She reflected upon her naïve and childlike belief that she could do anything she wanted as long as she prayed hard enough and began to ponder what she called the relationship of "co-creating with God," pulling her own weight, so to speak.

Why We Need Meaning

What brings you meaning? What gets you up in the morning?

A cup of coffee with your husband, the possibilities of achieving your dream, a child's smile or giggles? And what gets you out of bed when the world is dark and bleak and you are in pain? Being a teacher to your child, being an activist for the Earth, or perhaps being a source of pure history? And where do you turn when this level of meaning no longer holds the depth and extent of your pain and fears?

I remember as a child intuiting that people who had faith or religion were in better shape than I was, longing for the capacity to rely on something or someone greater than myself. In my early years I wanted to be saved, in my young adult life I wanted blind faith so not to shoulder personal and existential angst.

In part, I intuited correctly. Deep religious faith has sustained countless people through difficult times. Whether it is believing the Buddhist doctrine of Karma, unseen lessons from a loving God who will reveal himself at a later time, or the arrival of a Messiah who will free us from suffering, people believing in something or someone outside of themselves find greater coping resources and resolve to get through traumas and personal crises as well as daily issues from child rearing to aging. Their belief offers them a solace and meaning that nonbelievers do not have. A story in the newspaper tells about a seven-year-old girl dying from polio. Her father philosophizes, "God sent her on an angel's mission: She suffered like humans so those angels would know what suffering is. She made us feel like she was an angel from birth."

In addition, statistics show that families with strong religious belief often don't add to the troubles of the world through crime and delinquency. The twelve-step programs purposefully link faith in a higher power and recovery from alcohol and drug abuse. Dr. Herbert Benson, of the Harvard Medical School, has suggested that faith—by providing meaning to one's life, hope during difficult times, and relief from existential angst—may have benefits for people's physical health, even for those with serious illnesses. Benson's belief has been corroborated by hundreds of studies establishing this link between faith and prayer and lower death rates and improved health.

And yet, at some point, many people of faith will face a dark night of the soul. As life unfolds and we are faced with difficulties or tragedies beyond our construct of meaning, we can be pulled toward even deeper reflections, having to look for new and larger patterns in the universe. From the nun who, her faith shaken by the unbearable pain of cancer, awakens to a knowing that a realized soul is more in touch with grief and pain, not less so; to the religious Jew who faltered at her father's funeral when she had to admit his seemingly useless life and chose to search Buddhism's values of reincarnation; to the person who believed that being a good person would shelter her from life's darker moments and it did not, shaking her out of long-held sentimentality; to the peace activist who found herself entertaining violent recriminations after the September 11 tragedy—these moments of truth can be pivotal. They can make us bitter and closed off or they can push us to ask more questions, seek out diverse truths, pray for further understandings; they can open us to views previously unheard of and perhaps new ways of being.

● the bigger picture

Where do you find faith? How do you examine your spiritual beliefs and deeper values?

Rabbi Hillel tells us to do unto others as you would have them do unto you. All else is commentary. In his search for meaning, the seeker and visionary Carlos Castañeda told a story of the great eagle in the sky with an open, waiting beak. All the eagles on earth gathered self-knowledge and at the time of their deaths they deposited what they had learned into the beak of the great eagle, increasing the great eagle's wisdom and understanding. Many traditions and spiritual practices are aligned with Castañeda's metaphor. We are on earth, struggling and attempting to live a conscious life so we too can add to the consciousness of God when we die and return to the collective ether.

Elizabeth Kübler-Ross passed on her conclusions after studying thousands of people at the brink of death. We are here for two reasons: to learn to love and to gain knowledge. Scholar Martin Buber reminds us that what happens to us on Earth is part of God and what we do in response to that is what is important. Dr. Bernie Siegel agrees, telling us to learn what we are here for so we will no longer be in prison. If we cannot change our life or quit what is not working, then we can change our attitude.

Carl Jung used his personal and professional experiences to convey his belief in the power of love and increasing consciousness by becoming a fully integrated human being, a being coming from the Self, which is a beacon of the Divine. By committing to increasing our consciousness and connection to the Divine over a lifetime, we would be adding health and wisdom to the consciousness of the collective, and by implication, to the universe at large.

On a lighter note, there is a story of a woman who married the love of her life late in life. She was married ten years when her husband died. Many years later the woman dies, and she says she has a bone to pick with God: Why did he wait so long to send her the love of her life?

God responded, "You first picked Bill and said you couldn't live without him. Then you got a divorce. Then you picked Jerry and felt he was the person for you. After you got a divorce from him, I sent you Frank."

"Yes," she says, "but why did you wait so long?"

God answered, "I wanted to give you your turn first."

Being in a dynamic relationship with something larger than oneself and having a larger worldview reminds us that there will be a tomorrow, there is hope; all is not lost or damaged; in fact, over time we might discover a deeper reason for the adversity and find tremendous solace in the increased consciousness. Within a larger worldview even the most mundane or traumatic events can produce meaning. Myths, history, spirituality, story, parable, and travel offer ways of broadening our view. So does reading about the saints, cultivating critical thinking about religious beliefs, studying rituals and plumbing the depths of loss and pain looking for spiritual lessons, patterns of meaning, and essential values.

There is a simple parable about three stonecutters who were building a cathedral in the fourteenth century. A passerby stopped by and asked them, "What are you doing?"

They each replied in turn:

> The first stonecutter:
> With bitterness, he says he is cutting stones into blocks a foot by a foot by three-quarters of a foot. Frustrated, he describes his life where he does this over and over and will continue until he dies.

> The second stonecutter:
> Also cutting a foot by a foot by three-quarter-foot, he says with warmth, "I am earning a living for my beloved family. Through this work my children have clothes and food to grow strong. My wife and I have a home filled with love."

> The third stonecutter:
> With a joyous voice he says, "I have the privilege of participating in the building of this great cathedral so strong it will stand as a holy lighthouse for a thousand years."

All three stonecutters are doing the same expert stonecutting. All three are doing the same repetitive physical task. The difference lies in how they approach, perceive, and view their tedious task.

FALSE PROPHETS

We are required to be authentic in our worldview and connected to its meaning. Libby hides behind the sacred. She spends her time going to spiritual retreats and devotes her energy and ideas to mastering the art of meaning and inner wisdom. And yet, people who come into contact with Libby come away with confusion and unease, stymied at the lack of connection between them. She has a sunny disposition and speaks clearly and succinctly: In response to a friend's expression of brand-new sorrow, Libby says, "You know what Thich Nhat Hanh says about peace. You can only find it within." Why should such simple wisdom and Libby's pleasant smile leave her listener feeling annoyed and puzzled? Libby has had a life filled with tragedy, from abusive alcoholic parents to an unemployed husband paralyzed by anxiety to a son who refuses to have any contact with the family. In her desire to avoid the pain, fury, and anguish she has lived with, she moves too rapidly to the larger meaning and uses spirituality as a defense against these feelings.

This is counterproductive and unfortunately all too common. Judith came into my office with several "juicy" dreams. They were dark and violent, but when I wondered out loud about the possibility of strong emotions or what might be going on her life at this time to produce these messages from the unconscious, Judith was insistent on analyzing the dreams for their archetypal and symbolic meaning. As with Libby, Judith was using her well-established love and talent for symbology and spiritual meaning to cover primal feelings and discomfort with her everyday life.

During my generation there was a mass exodus away from religious institutions. Due to hypocrisy, rituals empty of contemporary meaning, and a surge of independent thinking, thousands of people left their religious homes and looked for meaning elsewhere. It was during this time that people turned toward the East, towards the Earth, and began to look inward to find a personal connection of spirituality. In moving away from the exoteric forms of religion that held and constricted through rules and traditional rituals, people looked for meaning in the esoteric and inner forms of gnosticism, Kabbalah, and Sufism as well as homegrown rituals with personal meaning.

This exodus has had its positive points. Without this type of questioning there would be no reformation, no growing. As a result of this massive dissatisfaction, previously accepted tenets were called to the forefront and relevance was called into question. But we also need to ask a further question: Was it the faith and dreams that failed or was it we who failed? Or a combination of both?

Using our own rules, our own personally designed rituals, and our own hard-earned understanding of the deeper values of life, many of us are hiding behind the sacred. Using spirituality and meaning to rise above the muck, to run too quickly to understanding and peace without a necessary dark night of the soul. Using New Age tenets to find familiarity, security, and answers even when they too ring too hollow. Turning to gurus who guide and wisely direct, many are staying too long at the parade. Even genuine gurus cannot protect us from existential uncertainty and temporal impermanence.

We might have moved away from the constraints of an organized structure that we found empty, but many, believing in the god of security, have recreated the constraints. Instead of hiding behind the sacred, being resilient calls us to recognize and know the poignancy of impermanence, the truth in the tragic, and discover the freedom to authentically create anew and anew and anew.

MEANING IN THE WOUND

Meaning can be found in the circumstance, in the wound, in the crisis. We are called upon to open our eyes and widen our perception. The meaning of evil lies within its sound, within its horror, not in the abstract. We are called to stay awake and discover the significance of evil. Personally and collectively we are seasoned with the sting and stench of violence, hatred, and abuse.

Viktor Frankl gave the world a blessing by finding meaning within the evil of torture and blatant disregard of human dignity. While the Nazis ripped away his family, freedom, and dignity and forced him to live without sufficient food, shelter, or sustaining companionship, Frankl determined they could not have his attitude. How he saw his situation and how he responded was completely his. He turned hell into personal meaning and used his profound understanding to help others during the internment, and to this present day, his teachings help thousands of us have power over horrible circumstances. Maya Angelou, in more recent times, looked unflinchingly at her violent past and personal assaults due to racism and uses her bounding voice to stop intolerance of differences. She teaches us to speak up whenever we hear hatred, slights, and ignorance. From within the wound of tyranny and hatred she comes to the conclusion that we are all brothers and sisters.

Thich Nhat Hanh and the Dalai Lama, all too painfully wizened by oppression and hate, bring themselves and their followers to a spiritual dimension of meaning by remembering, as they suffer, that we are here to learn from suffering. Through the practice of compassion, tolerance, and love, they demonstrate a steady hand and peaceful eye even as they personally and collectively experience the injustices and evils of hate and violence. By deliberately cultivating the qualities of tolerance and love, they guide the way toward gaining perspective and staying exquisitely resilient. Within their gentle souls resides a deep knowing of timelessness that even the worst tragedies cannot erode.

TIMELESSNESS

How do we encounter timelessness? Where can we look for deeper understanding and perspective to our personal and collective traumas? Throughout time wise men and women, spiritual leaders, and sage philosophers have guided us, through myths, parables, stories, and mysticism, to the deeper archetypal regions of our psyche as well as to the universal principle of powers and creation greater than we. As we experience awe of the 2,000-year-old redwood tree, of the mysteries of lives being fashioned through important coincidences, we also can be brought to our knees with an encounter of the sacred in the unconscious.

In contrast to our Western attitude that has us evolving from the mud and slime, the Eastern consciousness has us evolving from noble ancestry: we come from the gods. With this sensibility, Eastern spirituality has guided countless numbers of people to delve deeper into themselves for successive layers of the unconscious, discovering clearer vision and sacredness emanating from the Divine within. Carl Jung, understanding this dimension, used Western language and educated us in the realms of archetypes, the universal patterns for behavior and meaning. He posited that at the core of our being resides the archetype of the Self (the Divine) that not only requires integration into our personality but also includes a deeper understanding of the numinosity or sacredness of adversity.

THE BLACK STONE AND THE WHITE PEARL

When the inconceivable happens, it is important to not only pick oneself up but also, from the still point, discover a new and embracing pattern of meaning. It is in the willingness to enter into the dialogue of continual discovering and embracing of a new pattern of meaning that the inconceivable can become the soil for transformation and triumph. When everything else fails and all that is meaningful to you is taken away, where do you turn? Where do you look for the next frontier? Committing to your own life as a spiritual pilgrimage, moving into deeper and deeper regions of the psyche and soul, can reveal omnipresent patterns and allow a kaleidoscope of meanings to shine through, changing as needed.

In Islamic study of the inner form of a person comes the story of the Black Stone and the White Pearl. I am indebted to Henry Corbin for his devotion to this body of work and to his understanding of a story that blends seamlessly into cultivating resilience in our modern world. This legend speaks to a pilgrimage accomplished throughout an entire lifetime and, according to this legend, it takes an entire lifetime to give form to the deepest spirituality that lies at the center of the human being. It takes a lifetime to unveil the hidden dimensions of our inner being, lifting the denser barriers or defenses one by one over time.

Let's begin with the secret of the Black Stone. The Stone was once an Angel among the princes of Angels before God. Because this Angel was the prince of all Angels, God chose to entrust him with all God's creatures. He had the Angel absorb or "swallow" the pact that God had set up between him and all men. The pact indicated that each man was to keep in mind who he was as well as his connection to God. Each year man was to renew their agreement to this pact and it was up to this trusted Angel to receive their promise.

It is for this reason that the Angel was present with Adam in Paradise—to remind him of his undertaking when it came time to renew his promise. When Adam departed from Paradise, he promptly forgot his promise to God. God returned to Adam and gave the Angel the appearance of a White Pearl, which he cast out of Paradise toward Adam. Adam noticed the Pearl, even became familiar with it, but did not recognize it; in fact saw it only as a stone.

In order to get his attention, the Pearl assumed the original form of the Angel. The Angel speaks to Adam, deploring his awakening and recollection. "Oh Adam! Do you recognize me? Surely Satan has triumphed within you, since he makes you forget the memory of your Lord. Where are your promise and your undertaking?" Adam awakes and weeps at his recognition of this valuable White Pearl and renews his agreement to the pact.

Then God does an interesting thing. He takes the purity and magnificence of the white pearl and gives it the appearance of a Black Stone, for this is what the white pearl looks like in a world given over to Darkness (shrouded in many, many layers of veils rendering us blind to purity and magnificence). Adam carries the stone in the form of a Black Stone, and when he tires of carrying this burden, the Angel Gabriel helps out by carrying it for a distance. According to Corbin, this sublime symbology indicates that only another Angel can momentarily relieve man of his burden of the Angel, the pact that involves his destiny with regard to the spiritual world. Adam continues his pilgrimage to Mecca renewing his mystical undertaking to this Stone, using his awareness and testimony to Paradise to advance to deeper and deeper regions of his soul.

The center or jewel that utters and remembers the divine pact within man is the pure body of light or White Pearl. It indicates an inner and esoteric authority that reigns over an outer and exoteric authority, symbolized by Satan in this text. Adam fails to recognize this authority at first though, as the pearl is veiled by the darkness of this world, by the insistent pursuit of the pleasures of this physical existence. He recognizes it when it takes its original form, when he himself, through his pilgrimage, has remembered, looked deeper inside himself, and divested it of its "garments of darkness." It is through his journey, in the company of the Angel Gabriel, that the secret of the Black Stone is revealed in this earthy dimension. Adam endures every person's journey: the process of the descent of the White Pearl into this world, where it can appear to our senses as the Black Stone and where, through our commitment to unveiling the deeper and deeper realities of our world and our psyches, we can recognize its true value. That can be our destiny (unless one chooses to live their entire life without recognizing it).

> Each son of Adam must in his turn complete the pilgrimage, . . . attain his own centre. He must rediscover the secret of the Black Stone, which is also the secret of the Angel.
>
> Then the Black Stone turns back into the White Pearl, the signature of Paradise, the Angel or Imamate within man. It depends on man whether he recovers his centre, or whether he loses it and remains forever in a state of disequilibrium. The arrival at this centre is the esoteric meaning of the rites of pilgrimage . . . because he has repossessed himself of the *potestas clavium* that offers him access to the lost spiritual world.

"It depends on man whether he recovers his centre, or whether he loses it and remains forever in a state of disequilibrium." It depends on us to advance to the deeper and deeper regions of the soul. We are painfully aware of the black stone we carry—sometimes it is a quiet nuisance and other times it brings us to our knees in desperation and prayer. Sometimes how we perceive the circumstances of the black stone is determined by how close we are to the troubles and how much distance we can accommodate while still feeling the brunt of the sword. Sometimes we learn about belief in tomorrow from an angel, especially when we are too close to the epicenter and someone else holds the larger picture. We might be aware of this angel helping us carry the stone (we can see support and friendship and even divine intervention), but how aware are we of the black stone's innermost beauty and intent? How aware are we that living from the center we are better placed to deal with life's circumstances, even the most horrific? Since we can choose to live our life without recognizing the inner white pearl, we are told not only that it exists within us but how to explore, travel, and relate to the black stone in order to discover, hidden behind the veils of defense, its true value and by living from that place of meaning transcend our difficulties.

This is a lifetime commitment, and it is a process. One does not arrive at the center, never again tested against the fates of disequilibrium. One practices devotion—the spiritual rhythm of accountability and constancy. One hones the mind and attitude, disciplining the ego's reactions and reflexes. One masters the ability of finding center, each time one loses it.

The Black Stone and White Pearl is not an isolated mythology of meaning. In exoteric and esoteric lore, in Native American and South African wisdom, in sacred texts of Hinduism and Taoism, in the stunning beauty of art and culture, in the soup kitchens and hidden caves, in the *Koran* and Brahms's *Requiem,* at the top of the mountain and the depth of the ocean, we are shown and lured to the measure of our being. The ways are diverse, the message the same. We are shown how to transcend ourselves and choose that which is noble in us.

So look to the heavens, praise the redwoods and the unending cycles of the ocean, reach out to a loved one, but above all else, advance into the deeper regions of your soul. Know your black stones, and as you renew your pact to stay awake and present to life, reflect the purity of the white pearl so that life, through its tragedies and woes, can be replenished, renewed, and resilient.

exercise

(Thanks to Angeles Arrien)

REFLECTION

Reflect on your relationship to something larger than yourself, beginning with what you were taught.

Think about this around the ages of seven, twelve, sixteen, twenty-four, your thirties, and so on.

Where did you shift philosophies, family and cultural beliefs? If you did not, what was that like for you?

Fill in the blanks in the sentences following:

▶ Thank goodness for _____ when something hard or bad happens.

▶ I could not live without _____.

What have been your wake-up calls?

Who were important strangers along your road?

pearls of great price 12

If you want to make a friend, let someone do you a favor.
—BENJAMIN FRANKLIN

I HAVE A NEIGHBOR who believes that when someone is involved in an intellectual pursuit she should not have to worry about practical matters. She feels enthusiastic about the book I am writing and wants to be part of the process in any way she can. As a result, this generous woman leaves me a plate of dinner at my doorstep whenever she cooks for her family. "I love to cook and I have to make the meals for my family anyway so it is no big deal to make a little extra and then you don't have to think about shopping or cooking, and you can use all your energy to finish your book." (She is an excellent cook, and I have become the envy of many.)

She remarks often on how grateful I am for this angelic offering. I tell her she has been an answer to my prayers. I, working overtime to complete this project while working full time in my practice, have wistfully turned to friends asking them to whisk me away for a weekend where I can write and they would cook dinner. In the midst of this request, my neighbor, not knowing of my dream, has come forward of her own accord with exactly what I have needed.

I have told this story to everyone I know, and at least half a dozen times someone has said to me, "What do you do in return; don't you feel obligated?"

Most of us grew up with the adage that it is better to give than to receive, and I suspect most of us think it is harder to give since we secretly feel a selfish desire to be given to more often than not. While we might secretly wish to be indulged and pampered, I don't believe giving is more difficult than receiving, though. It is problematic to receive because it puts us in a vulnerable position. "Here, let me help you with the dishes." "Oh, don't worry; it will only take me a second." There is more control in giving.

When we receive we feel a sense of indebtedness and a connection to the other person. Some people will go out of their way to not endure this obligation and will monitor how connected they are willing to be to another person. I heard an extreme example on the radio. A man woke up not feeling well. He drove himself to a cemetery and stayed in the car. When the staff at the cemetery noticed and checked on the car they found the man had died. His wife said she was not surprised; "He hated bothering anyone."

Many years ago a client's son was an enthusiastic member of a youth group, led by a talented young woman. This woman, with no children of her own, was tireless in her devotion to this group of adolescents. They met weekly, entered tournaments, and put on performances. The group leader was present at all events on a voluntary basis. She was not paid for these endeavors and appeared to thrive on her interactions with the kids. At a holiday performance, the parents got together and pooling money bought her roses and a gift. When a delegated mother stood to present their token of appreciation the group leader stepped back, demurred, and shyly refused to accept the flowers or the gift. She looked visibly uncomfortable, to such a degree that the mother, flowers, and gift in her hands, quietly went back to her seat. I was struck by the fact that the youth leader could not receive their gift but I was even further struck by how badly that felt to those who wanted to extend their gratitude.

By the act of taking, we make others feel needed. When we give we are in charge, not owing anyone anything. When we take, we are indebted, exposed, face to face with the awesome realization that we need, we are incomplete. If the young man's teacher could have taken and said thank you, there would have been contact among all. She would have acknowledged her need of the youth and the parents, and they would have felt wanted.

How do you feel when someone is willing to take your suggestions, your recipes, your help, your stock tips, your stories, or your gift? By the act of taking, we make others feel needed, and we thrive on being needed. In order to be needed someone has to admit to being incomplete, needing you or something you can give. We want to be asked, not taken for granted. We will not know what we can get without asking for it, and each time we give and receive, the investment between us is deepened. We know teachers who are willing to learn from their students and those who are not. We know executives who acknowledge their workers' ideas and those who claim others' ideas as their own. It has been said that in the Garden of Eden Adam was surrounded by millions of angels. And yet he was lonely because the angels did not need him. They were completely intact.

This quality is about integration, an integration of all the qualities of the resilience process. Being connected, finding greater perspectives, getting needs met, exercising the funny bone, assertive and creative. The process has

> The resilient woman is strong *and* vulnerable.

come home, spiraling back to vulnerability but in an ever-deepening, stronger fashion. Through the process, you have enlarged your sense of self and can be more comfortable in your more tender skin. And now this point of the process calls us to interdependence. To be interdependent implies equality, an *inner* equanimity of both fortitude as well as softness:

- ▶ To a marriage of strength and vulnerability
- ▶ To a union of giving and receiving
- ▶ To being independent when needed and dependent when required
- ▶ To stand firm or insistent and be open or receptive

and an *outer* equality that manifests by allowing you to be vulnerable to someone else's influence. In a trusted relationship you receive the person's feelings, quirks, love, criticisms, and even rejections.

- ▶ To be guarded in a trusted relationship or hold the stance of one-upmanship is to not risk this vulnerability.
- ▶ On the other hand, to throw in everything you have to a relationship, to require a devil-may-care physical closeness, and deposit all your longings into a relationship leaves you without the identity needed for a true encounter.

Interdependence is the establishment of a stable identity, meaning having the ability to stand alone without relying on someone else's opinion, strength, or accomplishments. It means trusting one's own judgment and instincts and then acting instead of reacting. It means withdrawing the projections that assume the other person thinks, feels, and believes the same as you do. And then, having this stable identity, recognizing your need for a helping hand and being willing to lean on others.

According to the research on this subject, resilient men and women have developed an alternative to the *extremes* of masculinity (giving) and femininity (receiving), a blending of the energetic qualities of both. This is *not* about men and women. Instead, it refers to the integration of the masculine and the feminine energetic qualities *within* all of us. The resilient are assertive and yielding, instrumental and expressive, concerned for themselves as individuals and caring in their relationships with others, depending on the appropriateness of these attributes in a particular situation. Not only the sophisticated dance of independence and reliance on others, but the internal marriage of the rest and the active, the strivings and the being, the being and the becoming, the creative and the dormant, the competency and the quietude. A jazz musician following the inner voice of improvisation is responsive to the autonomy of this talent and abandons herself to the sound and movement. She plays solo, without thought or concern of judgment or other's opinions about the music. And when the moment calls for the sound to be in concert, without reluctance she joins the symphony of sound coming from her fellow musicians. She unself-consciously follows the beat of *both*, tooting her own horn and blending in when called.

In a recent study, leading researchers in the field of resilience Emmy E. Werner and Ruth S. Smith found that their resilient subjects shared a greater interest in matters that are labeled in conventional wisdom as "feminine"; they were more appreciative, gentle, nurturing, sensitive, and more socially perceptive than the young men and women who had difficulties coping with the world around them. It is through these feminine qualities that we are more alert to the hidden treasure in troubled times, far more pliable and more in tune with the care required to traverse difficulties. It is through these feminine qualities that we can be less attached to habits, the known or familiar, with certainty we allow ourselves to meet the world freshly and adversity creatively.

It is by being appreciative and sensitive that we are prepared for chance, newness, and even adversity. We can hold ideas more loosely, having them exposed to failure and the unintended. By being socially perceptive we can appreciate the differences in people, maintaining our independence and yet remaining connected.

In a less direct fashion, other research showed similar characteristics without labeling them androgynous (at home with expressing the qualities of both masculine and feminine). Resilient traits include creativity and the ability to tolerate pain and insight into ourselves and what we are going through at any particular phase in our lives. Resilient adults show the more active traits of independence of spirit, self-respect, the ability to restore self-esteem when it is diminished or temporarily lost, and the more receptive qualities of the capacity for learning, the ability to make and keep friends, freedom to depend on others, with the skill to set proper limits on the depth of their dependency, and the ability to find personal meaning from what they experience.

From the beginning of time we humans have faced adversity. Floods, earthquakes, wars, tortures and losses of loved ones, status, careers, hope, and meaning. We all experience these losses and feel great pain. While we are vulnerable and dependent as a result, we are also resilient and instrumental because of our personal trials and tribulations. We are subjected to the change of winds in society as well as history, and we have the capacity for transformation and change; we can recognize our more destructive patterns and learn to enhance our lives as a result of societal and historical adversity.

It is through the balance of strength and vulnerability, standing still and venturing forward that we draw strength from the upheavals. It is by fostering the inner marriage of stability and change, centered and sensitive that we ready ourselves for the disorderliness of life.

In Western society, *dependency* has become a nasty word for most women. Coming from centuries-old history of forced dependency, where our mothers, grandmothers, and female ancestors were unable to fulfill their own destinies or dreams because of financial, emotional, and physical dependency on the men and society, women have embraced independence with tremendous passion. When I grew up, my choice was to become a schoolteacher or nurse, and mostly to do this until either getting married or having my first child. Today women, within glass-ceiling reason, can shoot for the moon and dream of executive positions, international diplomacy, and university presidencies. Today many women scoff at the idea of dependency and complain about "buckling under" in marriage and relish learning about finances and electric drills. They take great pleasure in eating popcorn for dinner and wearing their hair in any way they choose.

Much of childhood is geared toward autonomy—learning how to do things on our own. For many, this strong will is carried into adulthood. "I can do this myself" (in fact, in many instances I would *rather* do it myself). While many people fear dependence (including viewing connection as undesirable dependence), seeing it as weak and lacking in personal power, autonomy needs to be elastic; there are times to ignore input and there are times to reach out for support and advice. There are times for action and there are times to be still and allow for access to other ideas and opinions, to the whispers of life and/or unconscious processes to show itself.

This is a leading edge for women today. We are being initiated into knowing something, at an essential and experiential level, that knits together hundreds of years of living. We are being called to an inner marriage, a marriage of independence and dependence. An inner stance, equally at home with both identities. As the tanning of the wood and the tanning of wine issues forth a fine wine, the uniting of being and doing, of strength and vulnerability knits the resilient woman standing strong in the wind and turning to a fellow human with the outstretched hand for help. In Japanese, the word for *dependency* also means "held in high regard." It means trusting another person to take care of you. It is that level of dependency that is being talked about here.

Decades into the women's movement for equality, dozens of young women still come into my office burdened by wanting it all, by wanting to stay home with their children, by wanting to be taken care of, and by wanting the strength offered by a career or identity in the outer world. As we struggle with the pioneering of interdependence, many women fall into one camp or another.

Christine is a successful banker with a trunk full of interests and abilities. She can hold an in-depth conversation about music and the Dow. She is raising two daughters and can be the life of any party she goes to. She has traveled extensively and meets people of all cultures easily. But Christine has never done anything alone. At a wedding when her husband left the cocktail portion early to seat himself at the dinner table, Christine became agitated and off center. She berated her husband for his rudeness, telling him he had been inconsiderate. She faces the same depth of insecurities if she happens to have a different opinion than her family, friends, and even coworkers. She manages her world and activities to such a degree to not be in the position of being on her own. If and when tragedy, change, or life's difficulty shows up at her door, Christine prays she is not alone. She admits she cannot imagine how she will cope if her husband passes away before she does.

Marion, on the other hand, thrives on her independence. Having been rewarded for her quick mind, she reads voraciously and enjoys debates on many subjects. Not only does it not bother her to hold a minority position, she gets great satisfaction from pushing conversations to the point of disagreements so everyone can think deeper and learn more. She is a powerful and successful attorney, single, raising a son, and she is a superb problem solver. She thrives on people needing her and has invested hours reaching out to family, friends, and clients.

"What do you do when you need to rely on someone else? Do you go to others for help?" I asked her one rainy day. "Absolutely not," she firmly replied. I had asked her this question because both of her parents died in an automobile crash a few weeks earlier and she was in a high gear of activity to deal with her grief. She relayed a recent time that tears began to well up in her eyes when several friends approached her. They wanted to help her by taking her son to school, making some meals, and perhaps staying overnight with her a few nights. Marion involuntarily bristled, telling her friends she appreciated their willingness but she had day care and her cleaning lady could cook if she needed it. What would happen if Marion did not have the financial resources to see to her needs and was forced to rely on the kindness of her close circle?

When I reflect upon women's present status and attitude in the context of the women's movement it seems to me that we have often thrown out the baby with the bathwater. Women innately desire and need connection, the vulnerability of give and take in relationships and life. And yet, in our justified and hard-won fight toward equality we have time and time again given up tenderness. We have lost sight of the piece of information that creating partnerships and forming bonds is a sign of strength and not weakness. As we have asserted ourselves and been called disagreeable and even bitchy, we have hidden our smiles and swallowed our tears. At times we have taken self-sufficiency to absurd extremes, not daring to ask for help. The women who relish staying home with their families fight a societal pressure they feel to "make something of their lives." It is as if, somewhere along the way, we have forgotten that the women's movement was about choice—not judgment.

The trend is slowly beginning to ebb in that direction, however. As I write this, small numbers of women are exercising this choice by beginning to consciously and almost without guilt, choose to leave high-powered careers and stay home to raise their families. Today, these small groups of women and many others are riding the wave of history by fostering interdependence. After centuries of slanted dependence and decades of productive independence, they are becoming full through relationships, raising families, support groups, prayer circles, community service, and circles of friends. Quietly, in thousands of homes and buildings around the country, women are coming together to listen to each other, to help each other, to reach out to those in greater need, to pray for greater understanding and compassion, locally and globally, and to use their hard-earned wisdom in interrelated and interconnected ways. Many are using their newfound voices, rounded edges, and freedoms to raise the quality of life for themselves and others in their life.

Gracie is the first woman president of her environmental firm. She has a rational approach to life and her work world. With her to-the-point management skills and research and development abilities, she is extremely successful. Throughout school and her career she has been the only woman in her class and office and has been as effective as anyone else doing her job.

When she became president of the firm, putting her in a position of authority over a male-only staff, she instituted a new policy. Each week she takes someone out to lunch to chat and see how he is feeling about his job, his position in the firm, his coworkers, and his personal life.

This allows me to have a pulse on the people I work with. I care about each man in the office and know that if they are satisfied with their work and life we all benefit.

Of course, not everyone can be pleased, but it is amazing how much difference it makes to know that you will be asked. Asked, and know that what you think and feel matters. You don't have to be happy about coming to work but you like it when how you feel matters to someone else, especially the boss. I also make sure I send each man a birthday card; no one says anything about this in particular, but I can sense in the work environment that it is making a difference to be remembered on their special day.

Lois married David after David was successful as a chef. David was recognized for his creativity and knowledge in food and wine; one of the qualities that attracted Lois to him was his facility with his work as well as his confidence. Lois, herself a gourmet at home, soon added to David's repertoire, giving him appetizing and original ideas, feedback, and opinions. It wasn't long before David's reputation fanned out and he was being sought after on a national basis.

For many years Lois was content to be the "woman behind the man," backing him up, boosting his flagging spirits when he had traveled too often, and keeping the creative sparks alive even when David felt burned out. Over time Lois began to discover a particular flair to her ideas, certain ingredient combinations that became her signature dishes. She began collaborating with David for awhile, marrying their now distinct styles, and over time felt a strong desire to branch out on her own.

Lois opened a successful catering company where she specializes in original dishes and menus. She has also begun teaching at a local cooking school.

I love the feeling I get when I see my ideas carried out. Even if some of the unusual food combinations don't work I still have such a sense of accomplishment because I have a laboratory where I can experiment. Sometimes I lie awake at night dreaming up new concoctions and have such a great and new sense of expertise.

Karen Louise lost her mother when she was five years old. She was the youngest of seven children, and her mother's death left her father bereft and overwhelmed with his large family. He began to drink and turn to his daughters for solace and comfort. When the state discovered that he was molesting his children they were taken out of the home. The state insisted the family be split up and all the siblings go to different families and homes.

Karen Louise spent her childhood and adolescence in a state-run home for girls and, like a chapter out of Dickens, found both companionship and despair in her new "family." She missed her family terribly, yearned for her father and siblings, remembering only the good times. Even though she felt heartbroken and orphaned she formed strong bonds with many of the girls in the home. They would be at each other's throat at times but also ran and played together, whispered secret stories to each other late at night, and formed sturdy connections by the very fact that they were all in this together.

By the time she was an adult Karen Louise had learned how to fend for herself, understandably not trusting anyone else to look out for her. She carved out a life for herself, moving often but making friends wherever she lived. She turned to Sufism for understanding and perspective on her life and pain. In developing a strong belief system she tried to make sense of her early traumas. She felt a steady stream of solace in looking at all the pain she experienced as many lessons she could learn from. As a result of her dedication to healing she was a powerful presence in the world. A substantial woman, she spoke very clearly and forcefully, allowing others to experience a woman who knows who she is and what she wants.

As strong and determined as she was, she carried deep wounds and scars that affected her on a daily basis. She lived on the edge of poverty and was saddened by the fact that she was not in a relationship. She was comfortable making friends but could not allow herself to be involved romantically. She often intimidated men, scaring them off, and she was terrified of becoming vulnerable with a man. Having fended for herself throughout her childhood and having lived by herself all through her adult life, she possessed a great deal of pride in being self-sufficient and was unschooled in asking for help.

Twenty years after leaving the town she grew up in, Karen Louise felt it was time to go "home" and face her past. Not having the funds for the trip, she turned to her uncle and admitted her predicament. It was significant that she opened herself up, and her uncle immediately responded with an airline ticket. Karen Louise went home, tremendous trepidation packed in her bags along with her clothes. She had a wonderful visit with her family and set out on a pilgrimage of "yesterday." She visited her home and stood where her mother had died and sat in her bedroom where she had been molested. "It was surreal. I could remember, quite vividly, all that had happened. The good and the bad. But I felt such a distance from everything. So surreal—just surreal."

Karen Louise went to the florist shop, picked out a large bouquet of flowers, and set off for the orphanage she called home for so many years. As with her childhood home, it came as a surprise to her that it was still standing and in the exact place it was in when she left. In picturing these places in her mind for so long she was disoriented to finally see them in their full and proper dimension. She visited the home and spent time with the women who were the current caretakers. In presenting them with the flowers she extended a warm and heartfelt thank you to each woman. "I imagine the girls you spend time with now do not and cannot say thank you, but I want you to know that I appreciate what you did for me twenty years ago and these girls will also one day realize that."

Karen Louise had healed sufficiently to turn to her uncle in a time of need and allow herself to be helped by him and, through hard-earned perspective, had developed enough integrity to be able to extend her love and gratitude to the women at the girl's home.

Gracie, Lois, and Karen Louise, coming from varying directions and facing different challenges, all had to round their edges toward fuller lives of interdependence. For Gracie, bringing in a soft touch to a goal-oriented world; for Lois, striking out on her own, independent of her well-known and established husband; and Karen Louise, allowing her family back into her circle of trust as well as being willing to extend herself in gratitude (we have to be comfortable with receiving and giving when we give thanks). All three women demonstrate knowing or learning how to use their personalities to achieve a sense of dominion in their world as well as reaching out to act in concert with an extended world.

These women know that our job is to help each other and that by helping each other we can discover autonomy. Women who know genuine autonomy understand that true freedom is potted in the soil of interdependent roots. We need each other, and we need real contact between real people. We used to have customer service. A service station attendant would come to fill your car with gas and you could have a word or two to begin or end your day. Now the bank teller has moved aside for the automated machine, the grocery stores are becoming warehoused by gigantic carts and fewer human beings to check in with. The soulless malls mimic the nostalgic desire for Main Street. As we get closer and closer by telephone, fax, e-mail, and viewer telephone, we are further and further from an up close, in person, eye-to-eye human contact. Partially in response to this reality, women are coming together, in circles, to form new communities, new villages, and new ways to be connected and help each other.

When people come together for the purpose of interconnectedness, shared caring, and the uplifting of everyone present there is less room for power plays. When people are at home with contradiction, there is less lashing out of insecurity. To be resilient implies an ability and willingness to change, enter into the creative play of necessity and chance, certainty, and uncertainty. To be resilient is to develop the force of character to reinvent yourself when needed. Women are reinventing themselves and bringing breath and life to the sacred marriage of strength and vulnerability where everyone benefits, suffers together, and rejoices as one. Women who have forged a deep sense of self and are fully present and alive are forming prayer, spirit, and civic circles to further enhance their own well-being and help transform the dynamics in our present-day hierarchal culture and society. Women, in circles of all kinds, are asking the question, "What does my being in this circle bring to the world?"

This question, articulated or behind stage, finds its way into many different groups of women. Eve Ensler, founder of V-Day, an active group of women devoted to ending violence and abuse aimed at women, attended an Afghan's Women Summit. This circle of women, Afghan women who had not previously met, used their time and energy to alert the rest of the world of the universality of women's experience of violence, oppression, invisibility, and inequality.

My friend Monica is using her environmental circle to look for ways that the consumer rich Westerner can live realistically and consciously on the well-worn and overly used Earth. Knowing the connection between using plastic bags and the Afghan woman's experience of violence, the people in her circle live with the question on a daily basis, sharing practical ideas with each other. Knowing that anyone (in any aspect of life, not limited to environmental issues) who stays out of global consciousness and decision making loses any say in the decision other people make, and yet those decisions will most likely powerfully affect those of us who are involved and those of us who are not involved.

> *If ever the world sees a time when women come together purely*
> *and simply for the benefit of mankind, it will be a power such*
> *as the world has never known.*
> —MATTHEW ARNOLD, NINETEENTH-CENTURY BRITISH POET

We are all in this world, (the largest circle), in time and space, together. We affect each other everywhere and all the time. We are called upon to be resilient within the context of our own lives as well as the largest context within which we coexist. Each one of us carries within a long history, going back to the beginning of time, of successes and failures, gains and losses. We are the resilient result of an unbroken stream of lives lived and stories told in our personal ancestry. Somewhere deep inside we know the experience of forging for berries, circling and cooking around a fire, poor hygiene, the adrenal hunt for wild boar, gossiping over the back fence, war and famine, winning a medal for the best lime Jell-O, being burned at the stake, whalebone corsets, leaving the familiar in order to survive or have an adventure, and living in caves. We know the resilient response that has overcome the obstacles time and time again. We can tap into this well and we can, through courage and determination, add to its flavor and greatness.

To be living in the world today, to be resiliently responsive, to be interdependent, we are called upon to widen our circles and then widen them again and yet again. To be at home in our world, and therefore resilient ready, means including more and more as home. We live in a global community; the world has shrunk in such a way that somebody has visited and "intermarried" in every square inch of the world. Our foods come from everywhere; airborne viruses know no boundaries. We bump into each other's cultures without even traveling. What does our being home in this circle mean?

It can mean a feminine resilience (in and for men and women) that calls for the lifting up of all who desire. In contrast to hierarchal ways of making decisions, responding to hurts, injuries, and differences of opinions, a feminine resilience leaves nobody behind. In contrast to deciding our fate on external authorities, listen to an inner knowing, an inner authority that is steeped in wisdom, thoughtfulness, and imagination. In contrast to depending solely on brittle, hierarchal, black-and-white or linear ways of thinking and acting, a feminine resilience rewinds in the name of creativity, opens conversations to include many points of view, stays open to being updated, willing to change and adapt, and works toward continually fresh ideas and thinking and a truly powerful win-win. An interdependent feminine resilience means cooperation, consideration, and equality on a personal and on a global front. It means encouraging through example. In the name of cooperation, consideration, and resilience, equality can inform all of our relationships, including those with ourselves. As we take interdependence seriously and resiliently, we widen our circles of interest and cooperation. Interdependent resilience that includes:

▶ Being friendly, fluent, and sensitive with everyone's vulnerability
▶ Taking into active account everybody's realistic and reasonable needs
▶ Knowing that while everyone is equal, not everyone likes each other or can get along
▶ Not having to harm or demean the other in the name of one's insecurity or belief system

- ▶ Knowing that at times everyone or every group must stay long enough with the pain and suffering to find effective ways through the differences
- ▶ Pooling everyone's gifts and talents to make the whole stronger
- ▶ Looking for the meaning of the present day's troubles in its largest context, and
- ▶ Acting on the knowledge that we are all in this together

Life in this world is not easy, and at times it is painful and tragic. How we respond to that fact will determine our resilience. Fortunately, for all of us, it is never too late to deepen our sense of selves and strengthen our resilient response to life.

What we do in response to life's challenges makes a difference—a difference in our own life and as our present global reality aptly portrays, in the time and space of our world as well. The women throughout this book actively determining resilient responses to their difficult times have touched dozens of other people's lives as well. (And now, perhaps, have effectively touched you.)

Being more resilient in the face of life's difficulties leads to more harmony and creativity in our lives and relationships. As we increasingly develop our ability to bend with the wind and come back stronger—stronger in our connection with others, in our knowing our needs and talents, in our sense of humor, and in finding meaning to life's ordeals, we discover the harmony and creativity. Each time we consciously bounce back we can be stronger for the fall and wiser for the experience.

And since we all are in this together, we are all stronger and wiser each time one of us follows our path and creates the pearl of great price.

exercise

REFLECTION

Use a journal, artwork, and/or imagination to help you connect with your answers to the questions below (see the exercise in chapter 1 for more explanation).

Reflect upon the times you were independent in ideas, feelings, and beliefs:

- ▶ What was your comfort level?
- ▶ How did others respond to you?
- ▶ What worked and what did not work about being independent?

Reflect upon the times you were dependent (willing to rely or lean on someone else):

- ▶ What was your comfort level?
- ▶ How did others respond to you?
- ▶ What worked and what did not work about being dependent?

A PICTURE OF INTERDEPENDENCE

Create an illustration of *inter*dependence. Put on some relaxing music and close your eyes. Try not to think, plan, or control your mind—make room for the unexpected, the uncensored, the messy. Draw whatever comes.

epilogue

THERE IS A NATURAL OUTCOME to following a path—the discovery of who one is—giving back. As I work with people through many trying times of life, it is encouraging to witness a natural desire to contribute something outside of themselves as they begin to feel more whole.

There are as many ways of giving back as there are grains of sand on the shores out my window. The beautiful lines of poetry that people wrote after the terrorist attacks on New York and Washington, D.C. The volunteer work that lends a helping hand to someone in need. The wounded healer. The human rights activist, the environmentalist, the grandmother caring for her grandchildren, the philanthropy given for education, toward the end of hunger or poverty. Volunteering in the inner-city school after retiring. Bringing Christmas to a family. We bring our medical skills to countries in need. We plant gardens for others to enjoy. Caregiving for someone who is ill or dying. We run for office to bring hundreds and thousands of voices to the forefront. We raise children with love, kindness, and discipline. We teach healing arts to resident chaplains. We run our businesses with the same attitude we have for loved ones. We teach someone how to learn. We inspire by how we live our life.

We become gracious; unself-conscious, and even more resilient as we generously extend ourselves to someone or something else. We gain perspective when we see things outside of our typical viewpoint. We experience wonder at how others do things.

We give back to our family, community, and world because we know how to bounce and we want others to land on their feet.

permissions

about the author

BETH MILLER, after raising two sons, went back to graduate school to earn a Masters and Ph.D. in psychology in order to further understand the depths of the human mind. She has been studying and teaching the art of resilience for over ten years, facilitating groups, speaking, and leading seminars throughout the country. In addition, Beth has a private practice in San Francisco and teaches psychotherapy and group process at the University of California in San Francisco and the California Institute of Integral Studies.

Beth has five grandsons who know to look in her pockets for chocolate. She lives in San Francisco.